Urban Spaces in Japan

Urban Spaces in Japan explores the workings of power, money and the public interest in the planning and design of Japanese space. Through a set of vivid case studies of well-known Japanese cities including Tokyo, Kobe and Kyoto, this book examines the potential of civil society in contemporary planning debates. Further, it addresses the implications of Japan's biggest social problem – the demographic decline – for Japanese cities, and demonstrates the serious challenges and exciting possibilities that result from the impending end of Japan's urban growth.

Presenting a synthetic approach that reflects both the physical aspects and the social significance of urban spaces, this book scrutinises the precise patterns of urban expansion and shrinkage. In doing so, it also summarises current theories of public space, urban space and the body in space which are relevant to both Japan and the wider international debate.

With detailed case studies and more general reflections from a broad range of disciplines, this collection of essays demonstrates the value of cross-disciplinary cooperation. As such, it is of interest to students and scholars of geography and urban planning as well as history, anthropology and cultural studies.

Christoph Brumann is Head of Research Group at the Max Planck Institute for Social Anthropology, Halle, and Honorary Professor at Martin-Luther University Halle-Wittenberg, Germany.

Evelyn Schulz is Professor for Japanese Studies at Ludwig Maximilians University, Munich, Germany.

The Nissan Institute/Routledge Japanese studies series

Series Editors:

Roger Goodman
Nissan Professor of Modern Japanese Studies, University of Oxford, Fellow, St Antony's College

J.A.A. Stockwin
formerly Nissan Professor of Modern Japanese Studies and former Director of the Nissan Institute of Japanese Studies, University of Oxford, Emeritus Fellow, St Antony's College

Other titles in the series:

Urban Spaces in Japan

Cultural and social perspectives

**Edited by Christoph Brumann and
Evelyn Schulz**

LONDON AND NEW YORK

First published 2012
by Routledge
2 Park Square, Milton Park, Abingdon, Oxon OX14 4RN

Simultaneously published in the USA and Canada
by Routledge
711 Third Avenue, New York, NY 10017

Routledge is an imprint of the Taylor & Francis Group, an informa business

British Library Cataloguing in Publication Data
A catalogue record for this book is available from the British Library

Library of Congress Cataloging in Publication Data
Urban spaces in Japan / edited by Christoph Brumann and Evelyn Schulz.
    p. cm. – (The Nissan Institute/Routledge Japanese studies series)
    Includes bibliographical references and index.
    1. Public spaces–Japan. 2. City planning–Japan. 3. Urbanization–Japan.
    I. Brumann, Christoph. II. Schulz, Evelyn, 1963–
    HT169.J3U73 2012
    307.1'2160952–dc23   2011044609

ISBN: 978-0-415-69545-9 (hbk)
ISBN: 978-0-203-12007-1 (ebk)

Typeset in Times
by Wearset Ltd, Boldon, Tyne and Wear

Contents

Illustrations

Figures

Tables

Contributors

Christoph Brumann is Head of Research Group at the Max Planck Institute for Social Anthropology, Halle, and Honorary Professor of Anthropology at Martin Luther University Halle-Wittenberg. In addition to publications on UNESCO World Heritage, the concept of culture, Japanese gift-giving, the anthropology of globalisation and utopian communes in Japan and worldwide, he is the author of *Tradition, Democracy and the Townscape of Kyoto* (2012) and co-editor of *Making Japanese Heritage* (2010; both also published by Routledge).

Christian Dimmer is Research Associate at the University of Tokyo from which he received his PhD in urban engineering. He was a JSPS post-doctoral fellow at the Interfaculty Initiative in Information Studies of the University of Tokyo and has been an urban design consultant with architectural firms such as Arata Isozaki & Associates and property developers such as Mitsubishi Estate. He is co-founder of the Tokyo chapter of Architecture for Humanity and teaches courses on sustainable urbanism, public space, mega-cities and planning theory at Waseda University.

Winfried Flüchter is Professor Emeritus at the University of Duisburg-Essen where he was Chair of Human Geography and Foundation Director of the Institute of East Asian Studies. His research is on economic, urban and social geography (particularly demographic change and risks) with an emphasis on East Asia. Recent publications include 'Earthquake – Tsunami – Nuclear Accident: Geo-Risk-Space and Risk Society Japan in Light of the Triple Disaster 2011' (*Unikate* 40, 2011).

Carolin Funck is Associate Professor for Human Geography at the Graduate School of Integrated Arts and Sciences, Hiroshima University. Her research focuses on the development of tourism in Japan, the rejuvenation of mature tourist destinations and *machizukuri* and citizen participation. She is the author of *Tourismus und Peripherie in Japan* (1999) and co-editor of *Living Cities in Japan* (2007; also published by Routledge).

Ingrid Getreuer-Kargl is Professor for Japanese Studies at the University of Vienna. Her research focuses on past and present gender relations in Japan with particular attention to spatial behaviour and arrangements. Other research relates to early European descriptions of the Japanese and to Japanese–Austrian relations.

Tsutomu Kawada is Associate Professor of Human Geography at the Graduate School of Education, Okayama University. His research focuses on the spatial transformation of urban development areas and on regional disparities of socio-economic status in Japan. He is the author of 'Tôkyô Mitaka-shi no machizukuri ni okeru sôsharu gabanansu no shinten' (Progress of the Social Governance in Urban Planning of Mitaka City, Tokyo; *Chiri kagaku* 62, 3, 2007).

Anke Scherer is Professor for East Asian Management at Cologne Business School and the author of *Japanese Emigration to Manchuria: Local Activists and the Making of the Village Division Campaign* (2008). Her research interests are in the economy, culture and society of East Asia, particularly popular culture.

Katja Schmidtpott is Professor for Japanese History and Society at the University of Marburg. Her research focuses on the social and economic history of modern Japan with particular attention to dietary patterns, temporal behaviour, urbanisation and Japanese–German economic relations. She is the author of *Nachbarschaft und Urbanisierung in Japan, 1890—1970* (2009).

Evelyn Schulz is Professor for Japanese Studies at Ludwig Maximilians University, Munich, Germany. She has published on the novelist Nagai Kafû, discourses on Tokyo/Edo, images of the urban in Japanese literature and culture and the revitalisation of Tokyo's *roji* areas and waterways from a cultural studies point of view. Currently, she is doing research on the slow city movement in Japan.

André Sorensen is Associate Professor of Urban Geography in the Department of Geography and Programme in Planning, University of Toronto, and has published widely on Japanese urban governance, land development and planning history. His book *The Making of Urban Japan: Cities and Planning from Edo to the 21st Century* (2002; also published by Routledge) won the book prize of the International Planning History Association in 2004. Recent papers include 'Land, Property Rights and Planning in Japan: Institutional Design and Institutional Change in Land Management' (*Planning Perspectives* 25, 2010) and 'Evolving Property Rights in Japan: Patterns and Logics of Change' (*Urban Studies* 48, 2011).

Paul Waley is Senior Lecturer in Human Geography at the University of Leeds. His interests cover urban and cultural geography, both historical and contemporary, with a focus on Japan. Recent publications include 'Finding Space for Flowing Water in Japan's Densely Populated Landscapes' (with Ulrika Åberg, *Environment and Planning A* 43, 2011) and 'The Urbanization of the Japanese Landscape' (in *Routledge Handbook of Japanese Culture and Society*, edited by V.L. Bestor, T. Bestor and A. Yamagata, 2011).

Yoshimichi Yui is Professor for Urban Geography at the Graduate School of Education, Hiroshima University. His research focuses on urban housing and urban structure in Japan, Germany and India; *machizukuri* and gender in urban space are a second interest. He is the author of *Chirigaku ni okeru haujingu kenkyû* (Housing Geography in Japan, 1999) and co-editor of *Hataraku josei no toshi kûkan* (The Urban Space of Working Women, 2004).

1   Introduction

Christoph Brumann, Christian Dimmer and Evelyn Schulz

Space, very generally speaking, has been a less salient category in social theory than time. Perhaps this is related to the crystallisation of social science in a historical period obsessed with progress and development, when theories about the evolution of species, the rise and future demise of capitalism and the advance of humankind from savagery to (Western) civilisation captured scholarly and laypeople imagination. But ever since as well, we have seen recurring predictions of a growing irrelevance of space and distance, all the way from Karl Marx in *Grundrisse* – 'Capital by its nature drives beyond every spatial barrier. Thus the creation of the physical conditions of exchange – of the means of communication and transport – the annihilation of space by time – becomes an extraordinary necessity for it' (1973: 524) – to David Harvey's diagnosis of a 'time-space compression' in contemporary society (1989). And who could deny that previously insurmountable distances have shrunk in the face of jet-speed transportation and lightning-speed information flows. Yet for all the proliferation of mass media, Web 2.0, mobile phones, cheap airfares and container shipping, the insight dawns on us that for most people, their immediate surroundings in nonvirtual reality continue to be experientially important. And often enough, we find space coveted and contested, rather than stripped of its political or economic relevance.

So while an 'end of history' – viz. time – has been proclaimed, nobody has postulated an 'end of space' yet, and one instead sees claims to a 'spatial turn' (Soja 1989: 39, Jameson 1991: 154; for overviews see Bachmann-Medick 2006, Döring and Thielmann 2008, Hallet and Neumann 2009, Warf and Arias 2008) – sometimes also a 'topographical' or 'topological turn' (Weigel 2002, Hård *et al.* 2002) – across the social sciences and humanities, also in Japan (translated as *kûkanteki tenkai*). As with most other recent 'turns', there is some debate whether the magnitude of the actual reorientation justifies such a grandiose appelation, and a well-defined paradigm uniting all proponents is nowhere in sight. Geographers complain that under the buzzword, other disciplines try to reinvent theirs although they themselves may have invited such trespassing by often treating space 'as obvious, as self evident and not really in need of further examination' (Crang 2005: 199), as some from among their own ranks complain. Yet attention to space is without doubt growing, and increasingly across the social and cultural sciences it is seen from a relational perspective: space is not – or not only – simply Euclidean, an unproblematically given container in which human social and symbolic interaction unfolds; rather, it is strongly influenced by such interaction, if not produced by it in the first place. Space is not just there – to a significant extent, we ourselves make it, and social life is 'both space-forming and space-contingent; a producer and a product of spatiality' (Soja 1989: 129). The way we make space calls for scrutiny, then, and not just within the confines of a specialised discipline but in all kinds of social and cultural analysis.

In this volume, we bring such a focus to the making of space in Japan. The uses of space in that country have certainly been widely studied, and great refinement has been detected in the ways space is apportioned, utilised and put on display in traditional architecture, gardening and the visual arts. In a more metaphorical way, too, social relations have been found to be undergirded by a keen sense of situation, position and distance. Admiration for such elaboration has rarely extended to Japanese cities, however. If at all, it is the efficient exploitation of limited space – such as in the notorious capsule hotels – that arouses popular attention here. Landmark buildings are celebrated too but Japanese urban spaces more generally are not widely praised for their sensory, environmental or democratic qualities, even when – for example in the human scale and homely feel that many an inner-city neighbourhood manages to preserve – this could well be justified. Certainly, conditions for managing urban spaces have been difficult indeed: bringing close to 100 million villagers to the Japanese cities in less than a century – and one in which a war laid most of them to ashes – meant relentless, often mindless development and change beyond recognition. Where more housing units than in postwar Great Britain, France and West Germany taken together had to be built (Waswo 2002: 59), there was little room for reflection, and urban visions always lagged one step behind behind the chaotic realities of uncoordinated development. As a consequence, not only foreign observers but also the Japanese themselves often deplore the spatial degradation of their urban centres, sometimes to the point of overlooking the attractions these do hold.

The growth curve is reaching a turning point now, however, as general population figures in Japan have entered a steep and long-term decline and many cities too are verging on shrinkage. Not all of them and not all their parts will be equally affected but for many a suburb, industrial area, commuter town or provincial centre the consequences will be quite dramatic (see Chapter 2 by Flüchter). Competition for residents, visitors, employers and investors is intensifying correspondingly, bringing new demands beyond those of quantity and functionality. After two decades of economic slump, in the aftermath of the global financial crisis, and with the unprecedented destruction and human suffering caused by the earthquake, tsunami and nuclear contamination of 2011 to be dealt with, no overnight revolution can be expected, but the possibilities are certainly exciting. Japanese urbanites can finally afford to take a step back and assess the qualities of their surroundings more critically, and great change lies ahead for urban planning which – now that the pressure to provide basic infrastructure is subsiding – may finally come into its own.

Two of us – Christoph Brumann and Evelyn Schulz – thought this to be a good moment for critical reflection, taking stock of the accumulated problems, valuing the accomplishments but also looking into the future of Japanese urban space. We did so during the eighteenth annual conference of the German Association for Social Science Research on Japan (VSJF), held 18–20 November 2005 in Königswinter near Bonn. As is customary for the association's meetings, we sought an interdisciplinary and international approach, and the contributors' backgrounds ranged from geography, economy and political science over anthropology and history to literature and film studies. The lively discussions encouraged us to publish a selection of papers, including an additional chapter by Christian Dimmer who also contributed substantially to these introductory notes. In all cases, this has involved comprehensive revisions that took their time and often left little of the original presentations but produced what we hope are much richer and more comprehensive accounts.

Theorising space

Before introducing the individual chapters, let us briefly reiterate some of the main ideas behind the blossoming social scientific interest in space, in particular those of David Harvey, Henri Lefebvre and Edward Soja who are often identified as key influences. One year before Lefebvre's seminal *The production of space* (1991 [1974]), geographer David Harvey provided a theorisation of space that emphasises the difficulty of forming a proper conception of such a complex reality (1993 [1973]: 13). As his solution, he proposed a notion consisting of three somewhat overlapping but nonetheless distinct understandings.

The first and most comprehensible – also most hegemonic – of these understandings is 'absolute space'. Since Descartes's and Newton's days, we have been used to imagine space as a pre-existing, immutable and objectively mappable grid. Absolute space is seen as fully amenable to standardised measurement and calculations, and all uncertainties and ambiguities can be banished from it (Harvey 2005: 272). Second, there is a relative component to space, corresponding to the insights of Einsteinian and non-Euclidean geometry, which does not necessarily compromise our capacity for calculating and analytically controlling space. According to Harvey, the absolute view of space is too limited in that it does not account for the multiple geometries from which we can choose. The spatial frame furthermore depends 'upon what it is that is being relativised and by whom' (2005: 272). From the specific, relative perspective of the observer, distances can be represented – for example in two-dimensional maps – in terms of their absolute spatial extension. However, if one measures such distances in monetary costs, time, energy expended for transportation or topological relations, completely different representations of relative locations emerge. 'We know, given the differential frictions of distance encountered on the earth's surface, that the shortest distance between two points is not necessarily given by the way the legendary crow flies' (2005: 273). Thus, the uniqueness of location defined by bounded territories in absolute space gives way to a multiplicity of locations that are equidistant from, for example, some central city location in a relative space (2005: 272).

Third, the relational view of space suggests that in Leibniz's sense, there is 'no such thing as space or time outside of the processes that define them [...] Processes do not occur in space but define their own spatial frame' (Harvey 2005: 272). Thus, social processes and their surrounding spatial frames stand in a dialectical, mutually reflexive relationship. This means that an event at a specific point in space cannot be solely understood by virtue of what exists at that very point alone. That point is rather part of a wider continuum of varying, disparate influences and their changing and dynamic relationship in the past, present and future (2005: 274). The concept of relational space-time is especially useful for understanding abstract concepts like identity, or the political role of collective memory. Such ideas cannot be be explained with reference to absolute space or relative space alone because the memories, subjectivities and values of the people inhabiting a place or those that external observers bring to it from their own life trajectories play an important role here.

Harvey suggests that these three concepts of space shouldn't be approached independently but that it is most productive to imagine them in constant interplay and dialectical tension. An event can thus have one dimension in abstract space, one in relative space and one in relational space at the same time: '[T]here is bound to be liminality about spatiality itself because we are inexorably situated in all three frameworks simultaneously, though not necessarily equally so' (2005: 277).

Harvey's triad was not the first attempt at a more complex understanding of space. Three decades earlier, philosopher Ernst Cassirer had proposed that the 'human world of space and time' consists of three modes of spatial experience (1944: 48–61). A primitive organic spatial conception is a biological given and doesn't have to be learned through individual experience in order to be mastered. This doesn't include a mental picture or idea of space or of spatial relations yet (1944: 48–9), however, and this – perceptual space – is situated on a higher experiential level and refers to the ways our sensual spatial experience is neurologically processed and mentally registered (1944: 49). The third mode, abstract or symbolic space, which generates distinctive meanings through our readings and interpretations, is the highest level of spatial knowledge and the most difficult to understand (1944: 49–51).

Almost certainly influenced by Cassirer's ideas and overall more influential than Harvey's conception is Henri Lefebvre's *The production of space* (1991 [1974]; translated into Japanese in 2000), which shook the ground of human geography and sociology and pushed space on the agenda of cultural, literary and urban theory. For Lefebvre, space is the primary interpretative thread in order to understand the complexities of the modern world:

> space can no longer be looked upon as an 'essence', as an object distinct from the point of view of [...] 'subjects', as answering to a logic of its own. Nor can it be treated [...] as an empirically verifiable effect of a past, a

history, or a society. Is space indeed a medium? A milieu? An intermediary? It is doubtless all of these, but its role is less and less neutral, more and more active, both as instrument and as goal, as means and as end. Confining it to so narrow a category as that of 'medium' is consequently woefully inadequate.

(Lefebvre 1991 [1974]: 411)

In Soja's words, space according to Lefebvre is thus 'simultaneously objective and subjective, material and metaphorical, a medium and outcome of social life; actively both an immediate milieu and an originating presupposition' (1996: 45).

Fitting for a maverick Marxist thinker, Lefebvre's main ambition is to bring space into the production-centred framework of historical materialism. 'The "object" of interest must be expected to shift from *things in space* to the actual *production of space*', he writes (1991 [1974]: 36–7, original emphasis), calling to mind Marxian admonitions against the fetishism of viewing commodities outside their production context. Just like Cassirer and Harvey, Lefebrve proposed the application of conceptual triads for this task. The most central one of these distinguishes 'spatial practice' (*espace perçu*) from 'representations of space' (*espace conçu*) and 'space of representations' (*espace vécu*), and while this triad is on an epistemological level (how do we know about space?), it corresponds to an ontological distinction (how is space?) between physical, mental and social space. Political geographer and urban planner Edward Soja – the single author most instrumental in popularising Lefebvre – rightly points out that the components of these triads are neither externally nor internally static or fixed but simultaneously real and imagined, concrete and abstract, material and metaphorical. Furthermore, none of them is privileged over the others, and all are equally important (Soja 1996: 65).

Lefebvre is least clear about spatial practice but he ascribes it to societies, rather than individuals, and seems to see it as the particular, empirically observable behavioural routines these societies (or modes of production) impose on individuals through such means as housing, transportation, the separation of private and public life, etc. Spatial practice embraces both production and reproduction, and through performing properly within these processes, the members of a specific society acquire a certain level of spatial competence. (Clearly, we see a *Basis* here, complementing the *Überbau* of the other two ends of the triad.) Soja calls this process of producing the material form of social spatiality 'firstspace', which he sees both as medium and outcome of human activity and experience. It is a materialised, socially produced, empirical space that is 'directly sensible and open [...] to accurate measurement and description', providing 'the traditional focus of attention in all the spatial disciplines' (Soja 1996: 66).

Representations of space, the second end of the triad, are equivalent to 'conceptualized space, the space of scientists, planners, urbanists, technocractic subdividers and social engineers' (Lefebvre 1991 [1974]: 38), most often expressed through verbal or graphical means. 'This is the dominant space in any society (or mode of production)' (1991 [1974]: 38–9). These mental spaces are vital for the production of space as they impose order and design on physical space and spatial practice. According to Soja, '[s]uch order is constituted via control over knowledge, signs and codes: over the means of deciphering spatial practice and hence over the production of spatial knowledge' (1996: 67). Refering to these representations of space as 'secondspace', he agrees with Lefebvre that these are dominant in any society as they comprise the representations of power, ideology, control, discipline and surveillance.

Space of representation, the third end according to Lefebvre, is

> space as directly lived through its associated images and symbols, and hence the space of 'inhabitants' and 'users' (...). This is the dominated – and hence passively experienced – space which the imagination seeks to change and appropriate. It overlays physical space, making symbolic use of its objects.
>
> (Lefebvre 1991 [1974]: 39)

Lefebvre sees it expressed mainly through non-verbal symbols and signs. Soja calls this spatial mode 'thirdspace' and stresses Lefebvre's emphasis on unknowability, mystery, secretiveness and non-verbal sublimity of lived space in contrast to the neatly worked-out representations of space. It thus bears the potential for resistance against the dominant order, or for offering insight rather than purely scientific, positivistic views of the world (Soja 1996: 67–8).

Lefebvre, Soja and Harvey all argue for assuming a dialectic interplay between the different types of space/spatial modes they identify, and it is by concentrating on that dialectic that we can gain deeper insight into a complex urban reality. 'How space is depends on how we see (and imagine) it and vice versa' (Toyoki 2004: 382). Thus, the injection of subjectivity into the equation enables the actor to (analytically) produce space. Consequently, Lefebvre warns us that

> [k]nowledge falls into a trap when it makes representations of space the basis for the study of 'life', for in doing so it reduces lived experience. The object of knowledge is, precisely, the fragmented and uncertain connection between elaborated representations of space on the one hand and representational spaces (along with their underpinnings) on the other; and this 'object' implies (and explains) a *subject* – that subject in whom lived, perceived and conceived (known) come together within a spatial practice.
>
> (1991 [1974]: 230)

Through an oscillating motion, practice thus moves between conceived and imaginary space, between mediated reflections and lived experience, dialectically producing and reproducing identities, subjectivities and social organisation on the one hand and new spaces on the other (Toyoki 2004). According to Soja, this triad must be seen as 'both outcome/embodiment and medium/presupposition of social relations and social structure' (1989: 129).

If we drive such social constructionism to extremes and allow for no space outside human subjective experience, we will run into cognitive and pragmatic conundrums. For such reasons, there is reluctance among many to part entirely with the assumption of an objective, three-dimensional space existing outside ourselves and at least partially independent from our presence in, and observation of, it. But even such a pragmatic posture – out of sync with the theory of relativity and mathematical hyperspaces – can well be reconciled with attention not just to observable physical space but also to the uses we make of it and to the manifold ways in which space is imagined, represented, symbolically charged, ignored and denied in human societies. And it can also be reconciled with a sensibility for how this occurs not just in the dominant sectors of society and through the officially legitimised institutions, experts and discourses but also in everyday life and the semi-conscious routines of the common person.

How these different levels take shape in a given society and how they interact with one another is an empirical rather than deductive question. Methodologically, this calls for a combined strategy that requires us to consider, first, the physical spaces as such and the messages encoded in squares, buildings, etc.; second, the written or graphical representations of space (not only for what they tell us about physical space itself but also about tacit representational conventions and underlying assumptions behind architectural drafts, maps, etc.); third, the actual behavioural interaction of people with the space in question, as it is amenable to empirical observation; and fourth, people's reflections of their own and others' spatial experience as they will reveal themselves through ethnographic observation, interviews, questionnaires and the study of written texts and documents. The same four aspects would also apply in historic research about space, with the obvious proviso that we must rely entirely on documents and archeological data where we can no longer interview the studied population.

Much as Lefebvre, Soja, Harvey and others must be credited with stirring up things in geography and across the social sciences and humanities, it should be noted that such a sensibility to space and spatial experience is not entirely new to all these disciplines. Anthropology in particular has a venerable tradition of micro-observations of people's relations to space. Much of these have been concerned with natural space, such as spatial orientation and its linguistic correlates among hunter-gatherers and pastoralists (e.g. Wassmann 1994, Widlok 1997, Istomin and Dwyer 2009), or with intimate social spaces, such as the different layers of inside and outside and the cosmological messages encoded in traditional houses (e.g. Bourdieu 1979: 133–5, Descola 1994 [1986]: 108–35, Lebra 1992). But there is also a significant anthropological literature on urban spaces, such as analyses of social behaviour in public space (e.g. Jankowiak 1993: 130–63, Low 1999), people's perceptions of liveliness versus lifelessness in traditional and modern urban environments (e.g. Holston 1999, Zhang 2006: 470–2) or popular ideas about 'clean' and 'dirty' city spaces (e.g. Dürr and Jaffe 2010). We are sure that there is also much to tap into in other disciplines, such as in psychology, as also in the Japanese literature and in much work that, while failing to mention space explicitly, speaks to it nonetheless. If we don't take space simply as granted, as existing prior to social action, but as a complex, dynamically constructed concept and reality, we can begin to recognise meaningful links between seemingly unrelated empirical phenomena, research domains and academic disciplines that haven't been previously addressed, thus advancing a more comprehensive understanding of cities in Japan and elsewhere.

Introducing the chapters

Building on such a theoretical orientation, most contributions to this volume bring the concern for the social sides of Japanese urban space to the empirical level of particular case studies, both historical and contemporary ones. As a necessary background to these micro-analyses, Winfried Flüchter summarises the recent trajectories bearing upon contemporary Japanese urban spaces in the first chapter. He shows that the dominant characteristics of twentieth-century development – comprehensive urbanisation, the formation of the three metropolises of Tokyo, Nagoya and Osaka within a continuous urban band along the Pacific coast of Honshû, and the increasing concentration of all important functions in Tokyo, to the cost of Osaka and other rivals – must be supplemented by a closer look at the details. Then, it turns out that the spectacular demographic and urban expansion was selective already between 1960 and 2000 when a number of prefectures and also most cities with less than 200,000 inhabitants actually *lost* population. In the 2000s, the circle of shrinking prefectures (now a majority), cities (now also larger ones, including prefectural capitals) and commuter towns has further expanded, in line with the general decline of the Japanese population that began in 2006. The central areas of the biggest cities are still gaining rather than losing inhabitants, however, making for a substantial reurbanisation of the 'craters' caused by earlier suburbanisation. For the declining cities and urban areas, no full-fledged alternatives to the conventional planning models premised on growth have been established yet, and with diminishing economies of scale, sustaining depopulated towns will become ever more costly. Shrinkage also opens up opportunities, however, with user and cost pressure on urban spaces abating. Decision-makers, planners and ordinary inhabitants will have to actively confront these questions for which the inclusion of bottom-up processes and experimental approaches will be crucial. As Flüchter's analysis makes very clear, demographic change will be a crucial factor in the future of Japanese cities, but it will affect them and their constituent parts to very different degrees, urging us to be attentive to local variation.

Flüchter's chapter sets the stage for the following four in which Lefebvre's 'spatial practice' and 'representational space' hold prime of place, as they all deal with planned interventions in urban space and its social concomitants. Looking back in historical time, Anke Scherer alerts us to the power aspect in the design of buildings and urban spaces – their capacity to 'communicate, convince and even coerce' and finds it particularly salient in Japan's ill-fated colonial expansion to the Asian continent. Manchuria was one of the chief areas of pre-war imperialist ambitions, and from the Treaty of Portsmouth in 1905 onward, the government-controlled South Manchuria Railway Company served as a bridgehead for colonial subjugation. This culminated in the 1932 declaration of independence of the puppet state Manshûkoku, nominally ruled by the last emperor of China (from the Manchurian Qing dynasty) but in actual fact controlled by Japan. In the concession territories, major railway stations, squares, hotels and bank buildings designed after Western models transmitted a message of modernisation and development, and after 1932, the new capital Xinjing – present-day Shenyang – saw the rapid spread of awe-inspiring government and military buildings. As in other colonial territories such as the French (Rabinow 1989), the vast open spaces provided Japanese planners and architects with unprecedented opportunities and the testing ground for the creation of an 'East Asian Modern'. Curiously, the vestiges often survive today since, ideological considerations aside, the communist regime could ill afford to leave the solid structures unused.

Christoph Brumann moves us back to the present even though in his case of Kyoto, the past is never very far away. In the much glorified ancient capital of Japan, the advance of high-rise architecture into the scenic historic landscape – although much deplored – appeared unstoppable until fairly recently. The weak planning authority of Japanese municipalities, greedy developers and the sheer inertia of ordinary citizens were contributing factors. Underneath, however, lay the tacit but widely shared premise that any urban space is predominantly private, either through legal ownership or through the moral authority attributed to next-door neighbours. All the more astonishing is the speed with which the city of Kyoto adopted a new building code in 2007. The new regulations for building heights, design, signage and the protection of views are the strictest in Japan, and public discourse highlights long-term collective benefits rather than private gains and losses. Revolutionary though this move is, recognising public rights over urban space to an unprecedented degree, the established political patterns and their top-down orientation have not been overturned: the new regulations were brought about by national-level legal changes and ministry assistance, local business leaders' demands, the city administration's bureaucracy and the input of expert councils, not a broad debate with the many concerned citizens. Crucial as the critical citizens' groups impact on public opinion and key actors has been, theirs remained an indirect influence only.

Christian Dimmer continues the discussion of public space and explicitly works with the notion of its social production, taking space as not a fixed but dynamically constructed, ever-changing notion. Outlining an intellectual history of the trope of 'public space', he asks why it has been critically underplayed for so long in Japan despite its centrality as a theoretical concept in Western urban theory. The recent burgeoning of the concept in Japanese planning discourses, popular media and urban everyday life begs for explanation too, however, and the contributing actors and agencies must be identified. In pursuit of these general questions, he focuses on one specific kind of public space – the 'publicly-owned private space' or POPS. Produced through incentive planning instruments at the interface of private and public interests, POPS are freely accessible spaces that, however, are privately owned. In the course of time, these hybrids have become increasingly sophisticated. Dimmer argues that by focusing on them, it becomes possible to transcend the limitations of conventional government-centred research frameworks and encompass the values and meanings attributed to public space by market and civil-society actors. By comparing the progressive, local government-initiated planning approach of Yokohama City with that of Tokyo's Ôtemachi, Marunouchi and Yûrakuchô district where the resident business community has been the chief player in providing widenend, shop-lined sidewalks and indoor plazas, he is able to demonstrate the complex forces informing the social production of the notion of public space in contemporary urban Japan.

Carolin Funck, Tsutomu Kawada and Yoshimichi Yui critically assess several recent attempts to involve ordinary citizens in urban planning processes, comparing a number of prominent Japanese and German cases. This is an inquiry into the everyday functioning of civil society in two economically similar states with different planning regimes and traditions. The authors find that in Nishisuma and Higashi-Nada in Kobe, resident-based activities still tend to fill the gaps left by a retreating state, and the NPO organisations founded there have trouble securing continuous funding. More public attention has been directed to the protest activities and organisations against a new road plan for the historic harbour town of Tomonoura in Hiroshima prefecture. Germany, through the legal form of the *Verein* (voluntary association), offers better legal conditions for civil-society initiatives than Japan, but in the conversion of former military buildings in Freiburg into a model district, not all bottom-up proposals were realised, and the NPO itself ended up bankrupt. The so-called district management experiment in Berlin went furthest in empowering citizens, all the way to budgetary decision-making, but here again, the phasing out of public funding made itself felt. The authors reveal a number of common problems but also a growth and diversification of participation forms, and they find that the channels of communication between citizens and local governments are improving in both countries.

A second group of chapters is concerned with what is 'space of representations' in Lefebvre's scheme, that is the lived space of human social interaction that may, or may not, stand in a harmonious relationship with planned space. Here again, we have a historical opener in which Katja Schmidtpott focuses on an ubiquitous element in the social appropriation of urban spaces, the neighbourhood associations that despite their weak legal status exist in all Japanese cities large and small. Widely studied throughout the social sciences, they are often looked up to as a possible answer to social issues such as aging populations and shrinking households. Common lay and academic stereotype sees this bottom-up form of social organisation as a remnant of village society in urban contexts. Actual historical studies, however, paint a more differentiated picture, and Schmidtpott herself turns to early twentieth-century Tokyo, that is the formative period of present-day neighbourhood associations. She finds little continuity with pre-Meiji urban communities, and initial moves came from landed elites eager to provide basic services demanded by local governments rather than from a general craving for local community. Neighbourhood associations with roughly similar infrastructural and social roles as today did not become a general phenomenon before the 1920s, and here again, vested interests – such as in voter support for local elections – were the driving forces. It was mainly financial pressure that brought neighbourhood associations to finally raise membership fees, open up to all residents of their territory and invoke community and family ideals for neighbourly life. Predictably, this didn't convince everyone, and a steady stream of new residents and diverging class interests led to widespread abstention, particularly by those (e.g. factory workers) who had alternative ways to organise. Projecting the purposely inclusive and largely recreational neighbourhood associations of today into the past, this means, amounts to writing historical fiction.

Paul Waley follows up with modern-day civil society activities in Tokyo and addresses the continuing struggle between advancing global modernity and the wish to retain the existing, historically grown urban landscape with all its identity values. Diagnosing an absence of state engagement in urban conservation, he explores a number of urban sites in Tokyo's Taitô ward. Stasis and neglect are dominant for Ueno Hill with its famous museums and historic sites and for the Sensôji temple area, with official policies silencing the underprivileged minorities resident in the area. The Yanaka district, a well-preserved historical area, is the field of activity for a number of non-confrontational groups and initiatives, with all their typical limitations. In contrast, Shinobazu Pond below Ueno Hill did see more confrontation, and plans to build a garage underneath it had to be shelved in 1997 on account of citizen protest. This frustrated the hopes of the local shopkeepers' association but fulfilled those of a coalition of local residents, university professors and environmentalists who had opposed the facility. Waley concludes that civil-society groups face difficulties in effective place-making, as long as the state does not get involved more substantially and provide a more supportive legal and administrative framework for their bottom-up activities.

Narrowing down the focus even further, the next two chapters focus on the individual experience of urban space. Ingrid Getreuer-Kargl brings a concern for social hierarchy to the micro-level of individual persons who, by inhabiting urban spaces and moving through them, appropriate them in more or less conscious ways. She starts out from theoretical considerations about the social construction of space and how these reflect power and gender relations, and building on the concept of 'spacing' as introduced by sociologist Martina Löw and on Pierre Bourdieu's idea of 'bodily hexis', she explores the gendered appropriation of space in a suburban train station in the Tokyo area. Her close-up empirical observations reveal that gender differentiation in bodily comportment is least pronounced in the access area where instrumental tasks – buying tickets, getting through the control gates, hurrying for the train – occupy the commuters' minds. But when waiting on the platform and when sitting or standing in the often crowded trains, the attention to one's body posture increases. Gendered expectations of good manners take over then so that men sit, stand and move in more relaxed and also spatially more expansive ways than women who are careful to present an upright posture, keep legs and knees together and draw in elbows.

Interesting also, when forming groups, women's bodies invariably face each other in a circle whereas men appear to feel less of a need to demonstrate their togetherness in physical ways. As Getreuer-Kargl clearly demonstrates, social hierarchies inform even the most mundane levels of appropriating urban space, and for the time being, they are still premised on a male 'right of place' in many walks of life.

Evelyn Schulz turns to the Benjaminian figure of the *flâneur*, the urban stroller, and his/her presence in literary writings on Tokyo in modern and pre-modern times. Many a guidebook, for instance, is conceived as a series of strolls through Tokyo, and the reader-stroller then becomes the 'diachronic *flâneur*' in Benjamin's sense who is sensitive to his own memories and the traces of others in the places s/he walks. The celebrated master of the *flâneur* literature is novel-ist Nagai Kafû who, in describing his own extensive walks through the city, jux-taposed modern Tokyo with premodern Edo, lamenting the gradual loss of the latter's glory. Other authors such as Kimura Shôhachi and Kobayashi Nobuhiko followed in his footsteps, and so does a contemporary genre of guidebooks that lead the reader to the *roji* (alleyways), celebrating them as spaces of everyday life and intimacy. Such books are of crucial importance for the mediation and representation of urban spaces, which can be regarded as containers of living patterns that existed long before Tokyo became the centre of the Japanese economy with all its negative side effects such as rising property prices, environ-mental pollution, traffic congestion, sprawl, enormous growth in population and industries as well as isolation and anonymity in this densely populated mega-city. What is nascent here is a counter-discourse to urban modernism, and Schulz sees great potential for the figure of the *flâneur* in future reconceptions of Japa-nese cities.

In a concluding chapter that opens up our vision to the future of urban spaces, André Sorensen muses about the consequences of Japan's 'grand social experi-ment in population decline' for urban spaces, predicting a profound, often prob-lematic, but potentially also beneficial impact. He is convinced that with their tradition of mixed usage, many inner-city neighbourhoods in Japan could be among the most liveable urban areas anywhere in the world. But to succeed in this respect, they have to prevail in the ever more intense contest for retaining and attracting population. Otherwise, the decay of inner-city buildings and areas, urban fringes with uncoordinated development aborted halfway, and entire ghost towns in the place of former industrial and regional cities appear possible. The question of liveability becomes increasingly central in public discourse and urban planning which in itself is a major change. There is still the danger, however, that any successes in one place will be to the cost of others in what is a zero-sum game for the ever fewer remaining Japanese.

As the above chapters indicate, this is without doubt a lively time for Japanese cities and the spaces they comprise, with uncharted trajectories lying ahead. We are convinced that many of the dimensions we address in this volume – power versus participation, public versus private, memory versus amnesia – will remain central to their understanding. We hope to demonstrate that an open-minded, multi-disciplinary approach giving equal attention to the physical aspects of urban spaces and to their social significance has much to contribute to the study of contemporary cities.

Technical note: For the Romanisation of Japanese terms, we use the modified Hepburn system. Long vowels are indicated by a circumflex except in the city names Tôkyô, Ôsaka, Kôbe and Kyôto where we henceforth omit them. Rendering consonants as in English, vowels as in Spanish or Italian, and double vowels as distinct sounds brings you reasonably close to the Japanese pronunciation. Japanese family names precede given names.

Acknowledgements: We are grateful to Alison Elks, Leanne Hinves, Hannah Mack, Ed Needle, Stephanie Rogers, Claire Toal, Allie Waite and the series editors for their dedicated work on this book.

References

Bachmann-Medick, D. (2006). 'Spatial turn', in D. Bachmann-Medick (ed.) *Cultural Turns: Neuorientierungen in den Kulturwissenschaften*, Reinbek: Rowohlt.

Bourdieu, Pierre (1979) *Algeria 1960: The disenchantment of the world; The sense of honour; The Kabyle house or the world reversed: Essays*, Cambridge: Cambridge University Press.

Cassirer, E. (1944) *An essay on man*, New Haven: Yale University Press.

Crang, M. (2005) 'Time: space', in P. Cloke and R. Johnston (eds) *Spaces of geographical thought: Deconstructing human geography's binaries*, London: Sage.

Descola, P. (1994 [1986]) *In the society of nature: A native ecology in Amazonia*, Cambridge: Cambridge University Press.

Döring, J. and Thielmann, T. (eds) (2008) *Spatial Turn: Das Raumparadigma in den Kultur- und Sozialwissenschaften*, Bielefeld: Transcript.

Dürr, E. and Jaffe, R. (eds) (2010) *Urban pollution: Cultural meanings, social practices*, New York: Berghahn Books.

Hallet, W. and Neumann, B. (eds) (2009) *Raum und Bewegung in der Literatur: Die Literaturwissenschaften und der Spatial Turn*, Bielefeld: Transcript.

Hård, M., Lösch, A. and Verdicchio, D. (eds) (2002) *Transforming spaces: The topological turn in technology studies*, published online at www.ifs.tu-darmstadt.de/fileadmin/gradkoll//Publikationen/transformingspaces.html.

Harvey, D. (1993 [1973]) *Social justice and the city*, Athens, GA: University of Georgia Press.

Harvey, D. (1989) *The condition of postmodernity: An enquiry into the origins of cultural change*, Oxford: Blackwell.

Harvey, D. (2005) 'Space as a keyword', in N. Castree and D. Gregory (eds) *David Harvey: A critical reader*, Oxford: Wiley-Blackwell.

Holston, J. (1999) 'The modernist city and the death of the street', in S.M. Low (ed.) *Theorizing the city: The new urban anthropology reader*, New Brunswick, NJ: Rutgers University Press.

Istomin, K.V. and Dwyer, M.J. (2009) 'Finding the way: A critical discussion of anthropological theories of human spatial orientation with reference to reindeer herders of Northeastern Europe and Western Siberia', *Current Anthropology*, 50: 29–49.

Jameson, F. (1991) *Postmodernism, or, the cultural logic of late capitalism*, Durham, NC: Duke University Press.

Jankowiak, W.R. (1993) *Sex, death, and hierarchy in a Chinese city: An anthropological account*, New York: Columbia University Press.

Lebra, T.S. (1992) 'The spatial layout of hierarchy: Residential style of the modern Japanese nobility', in T.S. Lebra (ed.) *Japanese social organization*, Honolulu: University of Hawaii Press.

Lefebvre, H. (1991 [1974]) *The production of space*, Oxford: Blackwell.

Low, S.M. (1999) 'Spatializing culture: The social production and social construction of public space in Costa Rica', in S.M. Low (ed.) *Theorizing the city: The new urban anthropology reader*, New Brunswick, NJ: Rutgers University Press.

Marx, K. (1973) *Grundrisse: Foundations of the Critique of Political Economy*, London: Penguin.

Rabinow, P. (1989) *French modern: Norms and forms of the social environment*, Cambridge, MA: MIT Press.

Soja, E.W. (1989) *Postmodern geographies: The reassertion of space in critical social theory*, London: Verso.

Soja, E.W. (1996). *Thirdspace: Journeys to Los Angeles and other real-and-imagined places*, Oxford: Blackwell.

Toyoki, S. (2004) 'Constructive spatial criticism on critical spatial construction', *Ephemera: Theory & Politics in Organization*, 4: 376–84.

Warf, B. and Arias, S. (eds) (2008) *The spatial turn: Interdisciplinary perspectives*, London: Routledge.

Wassmann, J. (1994) 'The Yupno as post-Newtonian scientists: The question of what is 'natural' in spatial description', *Man*, 29: 645–66.

Waswo, A. (2002) *Housing in postwar Japan: A social history*, London: RoutledgeCurzon.

Weigel, S. (2002) 'Zum "topographical turn": Kartographie, Topographie und Raumkonzepte in den Kulturwissenschaften', *KulturPoetik*, 2(2): 151–65.

Widlok, T. (1997) 'Orientation in the wild: The shared cognition of Hai‖om Bushpeople', *The Journal of the Royal Anthropological Institute*, 3: 317–32.

Zhang, L. (2006) 'Contesting spatial modernity in China', *Current Anthropology*, 47: 461–84.

2 Urbanisation, city and city system in Japan between development and shrinking

Coping with shrinking cities in times of demographic change

Winfried Flüchter

The city, urbanisation and the city system are essential elements for understanding the spatial structure and the economic development of a country. A well-organised urban structure is regarded as a basis, and a precondition for economic success. As for Japan, among the many determining factors of her impressive economic development, this point has been regularly underestimated, if not completely neglected. However, what is the meaning of 'city', what is the essence of 'urban'? How has urbanisation, the city and the city system changed in modern Japan? For what reasons? Through what effects, and with what problems?

This chapter outlines and examines three key concepts. First, the concept of the city, the degree of urbanisation and the stages of the macro-scale city development and city system of Japan from the post-war era up to the present. Second, against the background of a rapid demographic change, emphasis is placed on the city of present-day Japan between 'development' (growth) and 'shrinking' (decline); the spatial juxtaposition – the dichotomy between areas of increase and decrease – must be carefully differentiated. Finally, the problems and challenges of 'shrinking' and of coping with 'shrinking cities' in times of demographic change are analysed at the local level.

Introduction

The urbanisation in Japan, as elsewhere, was primarily a consequence of industrialisation. An excess of workers in small-farm agriculture motivated the flight from the countryside that began at the turn of the twentieth century, and initially it had many positive effects. The personnel reductions in traditional family operations provided impetus for agriculture to improve efficiency and labour productivity and at the same time provided a welcome source of labour for industry. The result was an urbanisation that was already very impressive during the inter-war period, and reached its peak around 1940.

The urban system in Japan saw its framework nearly completed around 1920. Both Tokyo and Osaka had developed as the top centres of the national urban system, which was characterised by a bipolar structure. Tokyo had emerged as the dominant city of central and northeast Japan, Osaka had become the most important city of west Japan. In the hierarchy below these leading cities were Kyoto, Nagoya, Yokohama and Kôbe. Though hierarchisation, the interdependence of the leading cities was not yet very much developed (Murayama 2000: 263). During the pre-war period Nagoya showed signs of rising to number three in the national urban system.

Post-war urbanisation: city expansion, metropolisation, megalopolisation

Urbanisation and the concept of the city

According to the Japanese community ordinance (*Stadt- und Gemeindeordnung*) enacted as early as 1889, the bestowing of the status of a 'city' (*shi*) was dependent on a minimum population of 30,000 inhabitants (Narita *et al.* 1989: 89). From a statistical point of view, a *shi* in modern Japan included any municipality that exceeded a threshold value of 30,000 inhabitants. Meanwhile, this value, which had varied during the last decades between 30,000 and 50,000 persons, has now been officially fixed at 50,000.

Whatever the threshold value of a city may have been, the share of population living in settlements labelled 'cities' increased impressively from 18.0 per cent as early as the pre-war period (1920) to 37.7 per cent (1940) when it reached its first climax (Figure 2.1). At the end of the war in 1945 it decreased sharply to 27.8 per cent, particularly in the largest metropolitan regions, which witnessed an evacuation of more than half of their population to rural areas. After the Second World War the share of urban population grew correspondingly fast to 37.3 per cent (1950) as a lot of former metropolitan people remigrated. Afterwards, the percentage of the population living in 'cities' rose dramatically, first to 56.1 per cent (1955), then to 75.9 (1975), 78.7 (2000) and finally 86.3 per cent (2005).

Since the national population was generally growing from 56.0 million (1920) to 127.8 million (2005), the total 'city' population also rose over the 85-year period by 100.3 million, particularly during the phase of high economic growth between the late 1950s and the mid 1970s. According to Harris (1982: 56, cited in Sorensen 2002: 172), 'among major countries, Japan has had the highest, sustained, long-range average rate of urban increase'. Sorensen is right in arguing that, albeit the scale and duration of urbanisation has been enormous, it is important to qualify this impression somewhat. The sharp increase in the urban population during 1950–1955 and 2000–2005 is partly due to amalgamations of villages (*son, mura*) and towns (*chô, machi*) into larger administrative units to achieve economies of scale in service provision. The incorporation of many rural communities into 'cities' (*shi*) inflated the urban population artificially (Sorensen 2002: 172). Another reason for the inflation of the urban population is the fact, that a lot of so-called cities do not reach the minimum size of a *shi* any longer (neither 50,000 nor 30,000), due to a heavy *loss* of inhabitants over the last years and decades.

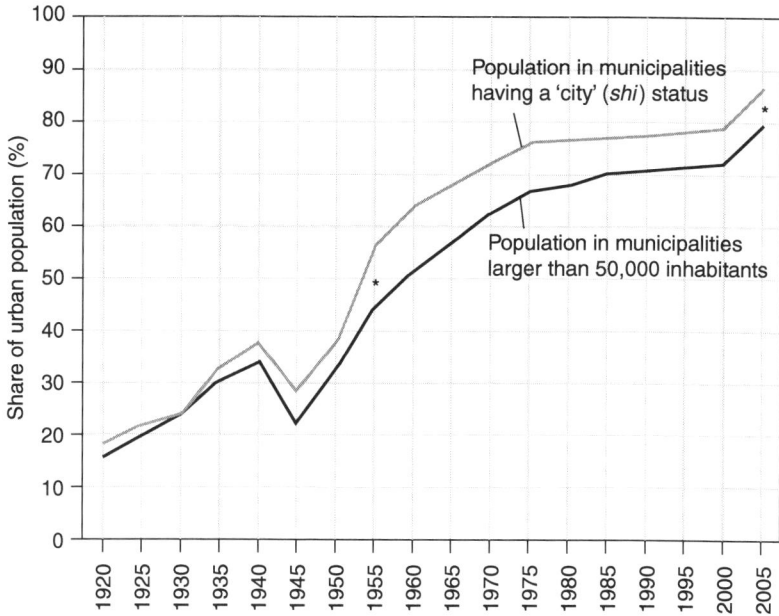

Figure 2.1 Urbanisation in Japan in 1920–2005, according to different measuring of urban population (source: Population Census of Japan 1920–2005; editing: W. Flüchter/H. Krähe).

Note
* Significant increase of the number of local governments officially recognised as 'city' (*shi*), due to amalgamations of local governments during the previous five-year period.

Therefore, it makes sense to define 'city' more precisely, e.g. every community over 50,000 inhabitants, regardless of whether it is labelled a 'city'. Then, the degree of urbanisation appears less dramatic but nevertheless impressive, i.e. an increase in the growth rate from 16 per cent in 1920 to 79.4 per cent in 2005 (Figure 2.1). If we ignore the interruption of the war, the urban population increased from 1920 until the mid 1970s (65 per cent) sharply and steadily by 0.9 per cent per year, grew then only a little until 2000 (72 per cent) by 0.3 per cent per year, and finally increased relatively strongly by 1.5 per cent per year until 2005, the latter mainly due to amalgamations of communities. Taken together, the fact that about four-fifths of the Japanese population live in cities of over 50,000 inhabitants gives evidence of the high degree of urbanisation in Japan. In the international context this is an extremely big share, considering that the minimum threshold of 50,000 in Japan is very high compared with other industrialised countries.

However, do those statistics really reflect the level of urbanisation? What is the essence of 'urban'? Where does the city begin, where does it end? In a highly urbanised country like Japan there is no longer either physically or socially a

simple, clear-cut division of town and countryside rather than a rural–urban continuum, the city between urbanity and rurality, i.e. 'rurbanity', 'Zwischenstadt' or
'desa-kota' (from the Malay Indonesian desa = village and kota = city). For overcoming the weakness of the 'city' definition, the Population Census of Japan introduced the new term 'densely inhabited district' (DID) in 1960 for delineating the
contours of urbanisation (Flüchter 1998: 46). The DID is intended to correspond to
the urban built-up area and is defined as groups of contiguous enumeration districts
each of which has a population density of 4,000 inhabitants or more per square kilometre, and whose total population is 5,000 or more. In 1960, 43.7 per cent of
Japan's population lived in DIDs on just 1.03 per cent of the national territory. By
2005, it had increased to 66.0 per cent of the population on 3.32 per cent (2005) of
the total area, with an average population density in the DIDs decreasing from
10,563 (1960) to 6,714 inhabitants per square kilometre (2005). By comparison,
Berlin (892 square kilometres) had 3,818 inhabitants per square kilometre (2006).

From metropolisation to megalopolisation

As industrialisation increased during the post-war period, the motivations and
effects of domestic migration changed. The more the economic upswing influenced
urbanisation processes and the attractiveness of cities, the more clearly it changed
from a *push* effect of the rural area to a *pull* effect of the city. The concentration of
population and the overdevelopment of agglomeration areas went hand in hand with
thinning and underdevelopment in the rural and peripheral regions. This trend,
which was particularly strong during the phase of greatest economic growth
between 1955 and 1973, has clearly weakened since the mid-1970s, but it has
nevertheless continued to worsen the imbalance in regional population distribution.

Figure 2.2 focuses on cities only over 100,000 inhabitants shows the remarkable urbanisation process in 1965 during the first stage of high economic growth.
When compared with the situation in 1940 three phenomena are striking. First,
on the *top local* level, the further population increase of Tokyo (city 8.9 million)
and Nagoya (city 1.9 million) compared with a population stagnation in Osaka
(city 3.2 million). Yokohama (1.8 million) ranks fourth followed by Kyoto (1.4
million), Kobe (1.2 million) and Kitakyûshû (1.04 million), which in 1963
became a city of a million due to the amalgamation of five communities.[1]
Second, on the *metropolitan* level, the enormous increase of cities around the
three metropolises, particularly Tokyo and Osaka, which reflects the suburbanisation of the population since the early 1960s and as a whole contributed to a
remarkable *metropolisation* of each the three metropolises. Third, on the *supra-
regional* level, an extreme form of urbanisation far beyond metropolisation, i.e.
a *megalopolisation* delineated as one large regional belt of cities between the
Tokyo and Osaka metropolitan region, i.e. the Tôkaidô Megalopolis, extending
further west to northern Kyûshû (Kitakyûshû, Fukuoka), including the inland sea
coastal belt. This buildup is particularly strong in the Tokyo Metropolitan
Region, whose share of the Japanese population increased from 16.7 per cent
(1960) to 27.0 per cent (2005).

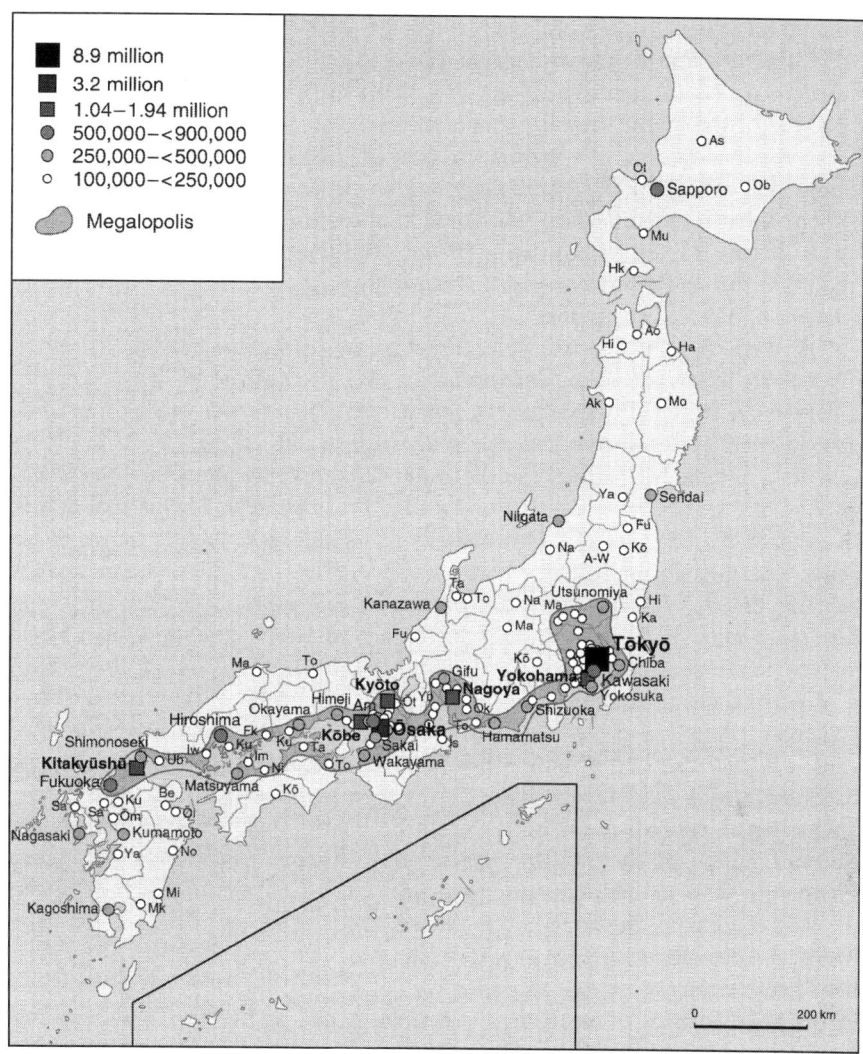

Figure 2.2 Japanese cities over 100,000 inhabitants and the Japanese megalopolis, 1965 (source: P. Schöller 1969; editing: W. Flüchter, with adaptations; cartography: H. Krähe).

The national city system: from a bi-polar to a one-polar structure

The population exodus from the rural areas toward the major cities had a tremendous impact on the national urban system (Glickman 1979). Tokyo, Osaka and Nagoya developed into the 'three major metropolitan areas'. Among these cores of the 'Tôkaidô megalopolis', the capital city of Tokyo recorded dramatic dynamics and grew into a major node not only within the national but also within the international urban system, becoming a world city in the same league as London and New York. Companies relocated their headquarters out of Osaka and elsewhere into Tokyo, which appeared to be 'sucking' core management functions out of its main rival Osaka and other areas (Murayama 2000: 264).

The attraction of the capital became so strong that since the 1990s the talk has been of a 'one-point concentration on Tokyo' (*Tôkyô ikkyoku shûchû*), i.e. the domination of the Tokyo Metropolitan Region not just in terms of the sheer size of population or manufacturing distribution but in the geography of the service sector of the Japanese economy, particularly top-ranking service functions important for decision making and controlling, such as company headquarters, financial and producer services.

The development to a one-polar structure of the Japanese urban system is particularly the result of the post-war period, but also of history. The strong centralisation of the country by the shogunate government in Edo during the Tokugawa period (1600–1868) and the relocation of the capital from Kyoto to Edo-Tokyo in the Meiji restoration of 1868 were important preconditions for the moving of the regional centre of gravity from the core area of Japan in the West (Kansai) to the East (Kantô). However, as far as merely economic functions are concerned, this shifting did not start until the 1930s. Until then Osaka was the leading centre of Japan in terms of economics. However, since then Tokyo has developed into the dominating metropolis in Japan, downgrading Osaka by far and in every respect now.

Four reasons have contributed to the outstanding role of the capital Tokyo (Flüchter 1997: 4f.): First, the plan or state control economy (*kyôsei keizai*) caused by the war and effective since 1937 initiated the trend of moving the headquarters of leading companies to Tokyo, against the background of a strengthened centralisation of government control over private companies. Second, in the early post-war period the Supreme Commander of Allied Powers (SCAP), as the command and control centre of the occupation power, the USA, tied on this and strengthened the Tokyo-oriented development. Third, the decision to let the Olympic games of 1964 take place in Tokyo and hence the priority to expand important infrastructural facilities in favour of the capital (e.g. opening of the Tôkaidô Shinkansen and part of the Tômei expressway) triggered strong thrusts, especially in the phase of extremely high economic growth. Forth, the globalisation of the Japanese economy particularly since the Plaza Agreement of 1985 provided the internationally greatest incentive of a further concentration of highest central functions in the capital Tokyo as a 'global city'.

Outside of the megalopolises Tokyo, Osaka and Nagoya, the next most important cities in the hierarchy of the Japanese urban system are the regional core cities Sapporo, Sendai, Hiroshima and Fukuoka. Particularly Sapporo and Fukuoka succeeded in expanding their respective hinterland, to a degree that the talk has been, too, of a 'one-point concentration on Sapporo' and of a 'one-point concentration on Fukuoka', respectively, i.e. the domination of regionally top-ranking service functions related to their *hinterland*.

The modern Japanese city between development and shrinking, 1960–2000 and 2000–2005

Mapping the results of the Japanese Population Census (taken every five years) from the period of high economic growth until 2005 gives instructive information about the development of the cities in modern Japan. The following analysis of the increase and decrease of the population is differentiated according to:

* the size of the city: from less than 50,000 to several million inhabitants;
* the location of the city: metropolises versus periphery, nuclei of metropolises versus fringes of the metropolises, nuclei of the periphery versus rest of the periphery;
* the period of time: the period 1960–2000 compared with 2000–2005.

City development 1960–2000

A comparison of population developments of prefectures and cities with more than 200,000 inhabitants between 1960 (when the phase of very high economic growth began) and 2000 (the last but one population census) provides essential insights into regional and urban development in Japan. Whereas the overall population has grown considerably from 94.3 million to 126.9 million, or by 34.6 per cent, during those 40 years, 12 of 47 prefectures suffered absolute losses, three of them in the greater Tôhoku region and nine in southwest Japan. Another 22 prefectures increased in absolute terms but remained below the national average. This applies to large areas of central Japan outside the metropolises, parts of Kyûshû and the peripheral northeast.

As far as the large(r) cities of *more* than 200,000 inhabitants are concerned, their share of the overall population increased from 33.1 per cent in 1960 to 47.8 per cent in 2000. Nearly all these 107 cities were able to increase their population considerably (Figure 2.3a). Among the few exceptions are on the one hand the two former marine harbours and sites of shipyard industry Sasebo and Kure, both of which experienced a painful process of deindustrialization, and on the other hand the two metropolises Tokyo and Osaka, which show a drop of population too, if only in their core (*ku*-area) (Figure 2.3b). In contrast, most of the larger cities in the suburbanisation belt of these metropolises grew considerably in population, particularly in Greater Tokyo.

However, if only cities with less than 200,000 inhabitants are considered, two findings are instructive. These cities – relatively small ones from a Japanese point of view – show on the one hand an enormously strong growth of population in the suburbanisation belt surrounding the three metropolises Tokyo, Osaka and Nagoya as well as the regional core cities Sapporo and Fukuoka (an increase by some 100 per cent within 40 years, i.e. by a two-digit percentage per year). On the other hand, however, the large majority of these smaller cities recorded a drop of population, both absolutely and compared with the average values for these cities in Japan. On the local level, drops of population can be extreme,

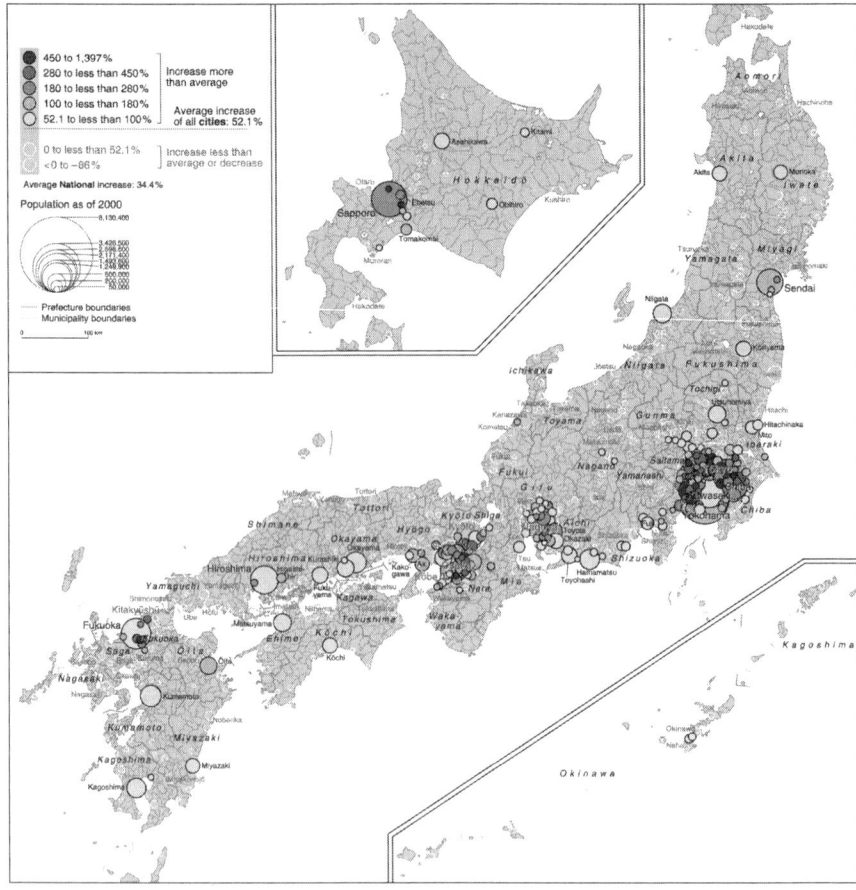

Figure 2.3a Cities with above-average growth, 1960–2000 (editing: W. Flüchter, with adaptations; cartography: H. Krähe; source: Sômushô tôkei-kyoku (Population Census of Japan), different years.).

particularly in 'company towns' like Hitachi or Muroran, which depend exclusively on one great company. In cases where such a company closes its factory, the lost jobs cannot be compensated in the community and young workers in particular leave the place in order to look for a new job elsewhere. Consequently, deindustrialisation is closely linked with population decrease and aging. This process is most dramatic in former coal mining areas such as Sorachi (Central Hokkaidô) and Chikuho (North Kyûshû). The former coal mining region Sorachi became important around 1900 when Hokkaidô was being developed, reached the height of its economic development in the 1960s, and has since undergone a catastrophic decline. In this economically blighted area, in between the agglomerations Sapporo and Asahikawa, the very existence of six cities is at risk as a

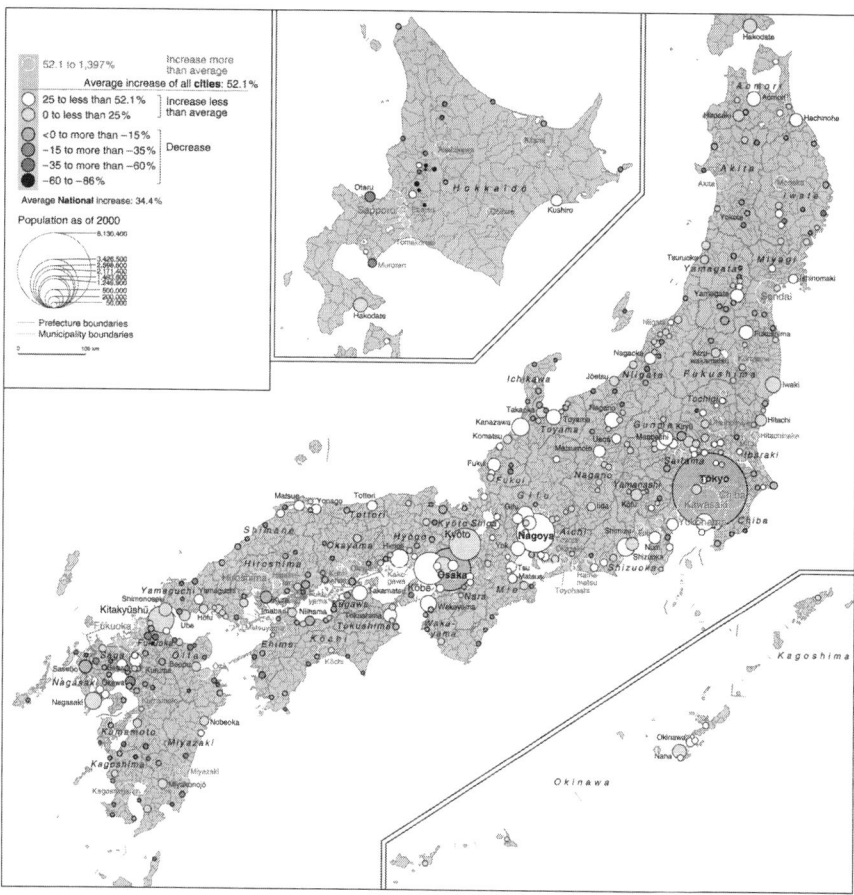

Figure 2.3b Cities with below-average growth, 1960–2000 (editing: W. Flüchter, with adaptations; cartography: H. Krähe; source: Sômushô tôkei-kyoku (Population Census of Japan), different years.).

result of disastrous population declines: Yûbari (–86.3 per cent), Utashinai (–84.4 per cent), Mikasa (–75.9 per cent), Akabira (–71.2 per cent), Ashibetsu (–68.7 per cent) and Bibai (–64.3 per cent). These sad negative figures represent records for Japan as a whole. They count as 'cities' (*shi*) only in a formal sense; statistically (to say nothing of functionally) they really have no right to be counted as such. All of them are well below the threshold of 50,000 inhabitants that growing communities now need to exceed to be counted as cities. Five of these six cities no longer even qualify under the older *shi* criterion of a minimum of 30,000 residents. Utashinai is the most extreme case, with only 6,000 inhabitants (compared to 38,000 in 1960). It is strange that the former mining communities have nonetheless retained the rank of 'city' in the statistics, though it is understandable from the perspective of political correctness: regions that have been exploited economically and ecologically should not have to suffer a degradation in status as well.

Nonetheless, the general results of the decades between 1960 and 2000, show that there can be no talk of 'shrinking cities', neither with regard to the larger cities of more than 200,000 inhabitants, nor in the case of the metropolises Tokyo, Osaka and Nagoya, provided these are understood as metropolitan *regions*, in the context of their spacial and functional interrelations with their *umland*. In contrast to these larger dynamic cities the mass of smaller cities situated outside the metropolitan regions and greater regional centres suffers severe losses of population.

City development in 2000–2005

Again, we start by comparing the population development of the prefectures. Whereas the overall population has grown slightly from 126.9 million to 127.8 million, or 0.7 per cent, over these five years, 31 of 47 prefectures have suffered absolute losses, i.e. the entire northeast of Japan except Miyagi (with the regional core city Sendai) and all of southwest Japan except Fukuoka (with the regional core city Fukuoka). Another six prefectures have increased in absolute terms but have remained below the national average, among them the prefectures Osaka and Kyoto.

Compared with the period of relatively high economic growth, 1960–2000, two findings for city development are striking in the period 2000–2005, namely the much larger number of shrinking cities (Figure 2.4b) and the impressive growth of population in the core areas of the metropolises (Figure 2.4a).[2]

First, with regard to *shrinking* cities, it is obvious that particularly the small(er) ones in peripheral areas are suffering losses, in continuation of the process from 1960–2000. Again, the developments have been most dramatic in the above-mentioned coal mining area Sorachi (Hokkaidô), first of all in Yûbari, a very large community at 763 square kilometres (equivalent to 87 per cent of the area of the state of Berlin!). This 'city' recorded 117,000 residents in the early 1960s and dropped to 11,439 persons in 2009, i.e. by 90.1 per cent in less than 50 years or by 1.9 per cent per year. Its share of people older than 64 years is nearly twice as high as the national average of 23.1 per cent (2010). Jobs have been scarce since the closure of the last pit in 1990. Municipal efforts to revitalise the local economy by shifting from *tankô* (mining) to *kankô* (tourism) failed to stop socio-economic decline: In 2006, Yûbari went bankrupt and has become dependent on a drip feed of financial support from the central government (Flüchter 2008, Seaton 2010).

However, apart from these small(er) cities in peripheral areas, bigger industrial cities are also affected, such as the former 'million city' Kitakyûshû (993,000, –1.8 per cent in five years) and many others with a population of more than 200,000, like Sasebo (248,000, –1.2 per cent), Kure (251,000, –3.2 per cent), Shimonoseki (291,000, –3.5 per cent), Shimizu[3] (230,000, –2.9 per cent),

Amagasaki (462,000, –0.8 per cent) and Hakodate (294,000, –3.6 per cent). Additionally, an astonishing number of prefectural capitals record a drop of population. As regional centres of administration, economy and culture, they usually showed positive population results in the past, mainly due to intra-regional migration. However, this long-term trend seems for many of them to be broken. Particularly the smaller prefectural capitals (200,000 to 455,000 inhabitants) in peripheral areas record an absolute decrease of population.[4] But also larger prefectural capitals at the fringe of the metropolises show a drop in population.[5] Some further prefectural capitals have slightly grown in absolute terms but have remained below the national average of 1.0 per cent (of all cities in this period).[6] Considering all these cities, one could assume that their negative population developments are due to suburbanisation processes, i.e. to a growth of population in communities in their *umland*. This, however, only applies to exceptions. The weak performance of all mentioned cities mirrors the reality.

Second, the enormous *growth* of the population in the core of the metropolises (except Kyoto) is astonishing. This is related to new tendencies of metropolitan development, i.e. *reurbanisation* (Matsumoto 2004, Okata and Murayama 2011), which was in the offing as early as the late 1990s. During the decades before, from the 1960s onwards, it had been *suburbanisation*, which had been typical for the metropolises. These processes had resulted in a substantial increase in population in the outskirts, population decline in the city centres of metropolises, and extremely long and costly commutes (Flüchter 1997). This trend has begun to reverse in the 1995–2000 period already, particularly in Tokyo, where the 23 wards (Tôkyô-ku in 2005: 8.5 million people) increased in numbers by a total of 163,000 inhabitants, or 2 per cent. This growth has been widely surpassed in 2000–2005 by a total of 348,000 people, or 4.3 per cent. This positive result is particularly strong in the three central wards Chûô, Minato and Chiyoda, i.e. in the formerly deepest places of the 'housing crater'. This new development of reurbanisation was accompanied by merely a slight increase or even decrease in the population of cities situated at the fringe of the metropolises.

The trend towards *reurbanisation* has a number of causes: first, a drop in real estate prices (as a consequence of a long-term recession) that is nationwide but particularly strong in metropolitan core areas; second, state, prefecture and municipality measures to increase the supply of housing in city centres (motivated by the model of the vertical, compact, multifunctional city); third, the demand from a varied clientele (singles, working couples and wealthy older people) for urban housing close to the city centre as an alternative to suburbia (Hohn 2002); fourth, a law passed in 2002, limited to a period of ten years, with 'special measures for the urban revitalisation of metropolitan regions'.

Closely connected with 'development' and 'shrinking' is the phenomenon of vacancy (*Leerstand*). Despite a long recession, office buildings in Tokyo have continued to be built since the 1990s at such a rate that a concentration of office space in the central municipal districts Chiyoda, Chûô, Minato, Shibuya and Shinjuku is found as nowhere else in the world. This has led to intense discussions of the so-called Tokyo 2003 problem: a glut of office space in 2003.

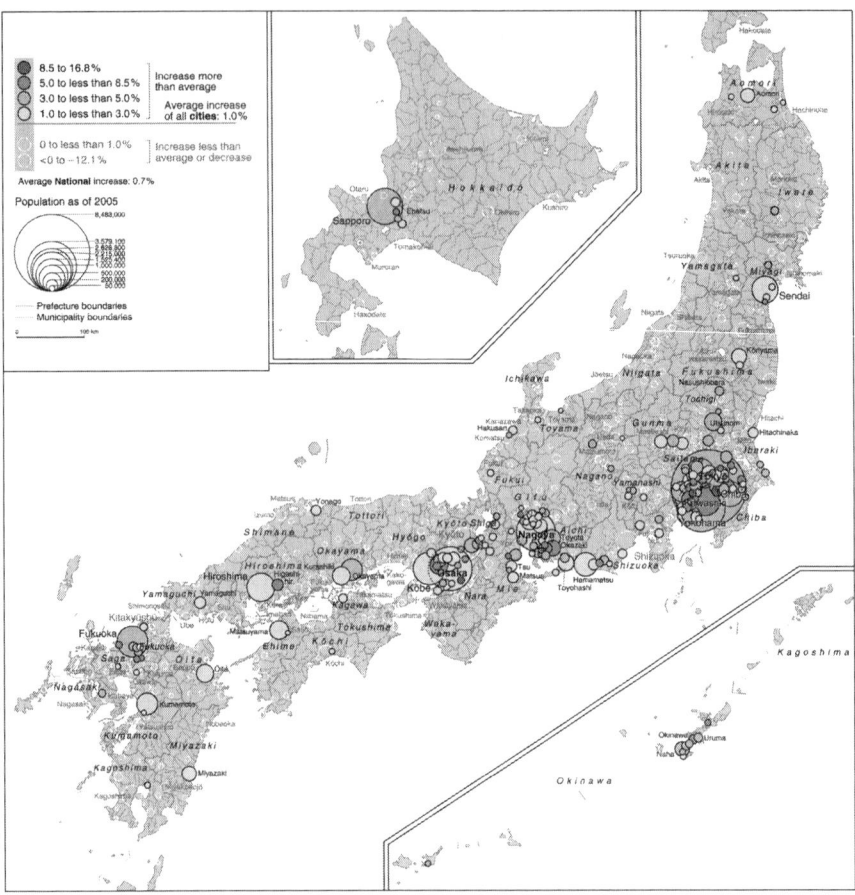

Figure 2.4a Cities with above-average growth, 2000–2005 (editing: W. Flüchter, with adaptations; cartography: H. Krähe; source: Sômushô tôkei-kyoku (Population Census of Japan), different years.).

It remains to be seen whether the vacancy rate for office space, 8 per cent in 2003, 9 per cent in 2010, represents a normal level for long-term planning for the future or is a cause for panic. To answer that question it is necessary to distinguish among office types. Experts presume that the so-called 'A areas', comprising 13 per cent of the total office space and distinguished by location convenient to public transportation, modern infrastructure and new, earthquake-safe buildings, will be in sufficient demand. So-called 'B areas', by contrast, which are (relatively) less central, completed before 1981 and less earthquake-safe, are generally expected to be more difficult to rent in the future as demand becomes increasingly selective. It is very likely that the 'sword of Damocles' of high vacancy rates is hanging over this type of building.

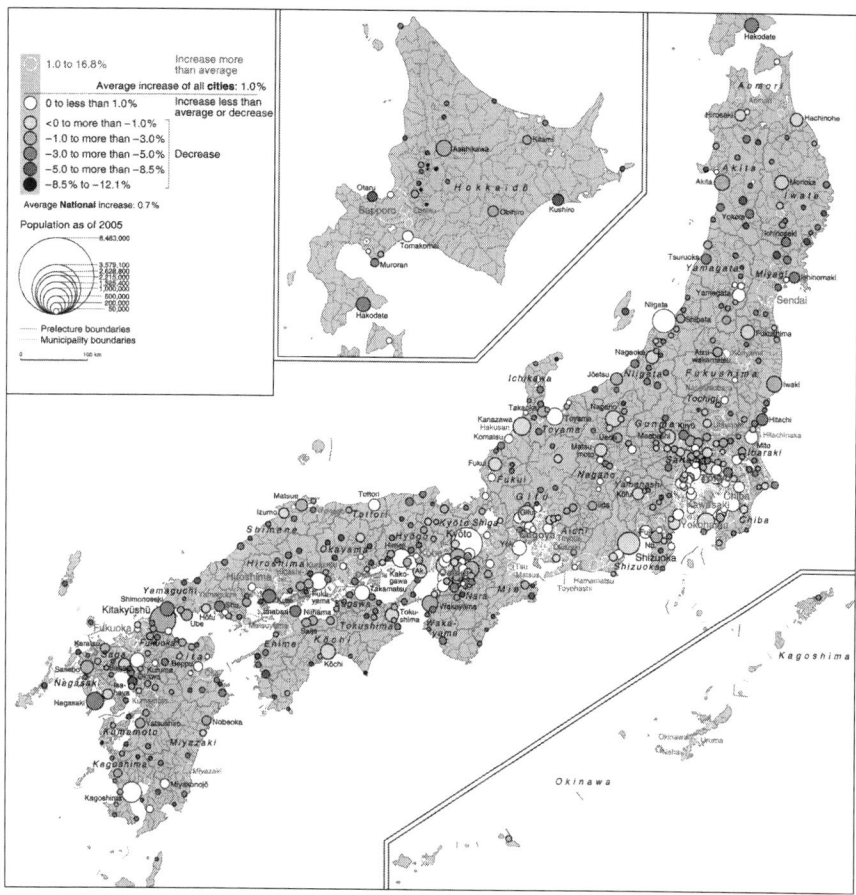

Figure 2.4b Cities with below-average growth, 2000–2005 (editing: W. Flüchter, with adaptations; cartography: H. Krähe; source: Sômushô tôkei-kyoku (Population Census of Japan), different years.).

The question remains whether the trend to reurbanisation of housing means that the phenomena of vacancy will be a problem for suburbia as well. There is no doubt that the demand for housing on the edge of metropolitan regions is decreasing. The 'new towns' of the 1960s and 1970s (now jestingly called 'old towns') are stagnating; many have already seen a clear drop in population. Thus far, however, vacancy problems have only affected residences with poor transportation connections, especially those remote from train stations. The fact that the population in many new towns is decreasing is not in itself a reason to speak of vacancy problems, much less of shrinking cities, in urban peripheral areas. In general, the decline can be explained by generational change: the arrival of young families 40 years ago, the departure of the children who have now matured, with the parents remaining behind, but with more living space (Flüchter 2005).

Shrinking as a challenge: coping with shrinking cities in times of demographic change

Japanese society is essentially a vital urban society in which it is hardly possible to envisage the problem of 'shrinking cities'. Even during Japan's long recession, from which the country has only slowly recovered, the cities seem too dynamic for that. Despite the fact that the economic situation has been precarious for so long, the construction boom has continued unabated not only in the rural peripheries but in the large cities themselves. Today's Japan gives the impression that its planning for urban and regional development, energy and transport is still based on predictions of growth.

Problems and challenges

It is indisputable, however, that, following decades of continuous increase, Japan's population has peaked at 127.7 million inhabitants (2006) and that, after a period of stagnation, it will decline to about 95 million inhabitants by 2050, a decrease of 25.6 per cent (data based on the middle series of the population projection made in December 2006). The total fertility rate, for which a value of *c.* 2.1 is necessary to ensure population stability, has fallen from 2.23 (1967) to 1.2 (2010), one of the globally lowest. Unlike Western Europe, the population losses in Japan cannot currently be mitigated by immigration. Japan's self-image as an ethnically and socially homogeneous country and the psychological barriers to foreign infiltration are very high, so that its immigration laws are correspondingly restrictive.

The problems are made worse by the fact that Japanese society is aging more rapidly than that of any other country in the world. In 2010, life expectancy is 82.2 years, 85.7 for women and 78.9 for men. In 2010, the percentage of people over 64 is 23.1 per cent; the figure predicted for 2050 is 39.6 per cent. 'Shrinking and aging' of the population is a topical theme in Japan (Ômura and Arita 2005). In the peripheral rural sections the problems that will face the whole country in the long term are already reality: dramatic declines in population, extreme aging of society and problems of maintaining a sustainable infrastructure. A big challenge is the financial crisis of the municipalities, given their increasing expenditures for maintaining a basic local infrastructure. In urban studies, governance research is helpful to understand the slow and often conflict-ridden interplay of actors in the process of urban shrinking and ageing.

For coping with the challenges of and answers to issues of shrinking and ageing, comparative international research is thought-provoking. Demographic ageing and shrinking is widespread not only in Japan. Comparing the situation between Japan and Germany is particular interesting because of the extreme demographic challenges to which both countries have to respond. The degree of shrinking and ageing in a short period of time seems to be the most striking problem in the economically blighted areas of both countries. In East Germany, large regions suffer from an abrupt collaps, shocking both economically and socially. These problems can be compared with those in relatively small-scale deficit areas of 'sunset industries' in Japan. However, in large parts of Japan outside of the metropolitan regions, there is a slow, creeping process of decline, hardly felt as fatal. This can also be observed in declining industrial areas of West Germany. Here the drop of population is less drastic because of the influx of foreign immigrants who fill housing gaps but contribute to migrant problems in certain urban districts.

'Shrinking and ageing' is often associated with vacancy rates. Compared with East Germany where high vacancy rates in the housing market are widespread and extremely challenging, in Japan the surplus of empty dwellings even in the problem areas appears less serious because of the regular scrap and build of traditional residential buildings every 27 years (!) on average (Sawada *et al.* 2004: 190ff.), a habit which can be seen as ecologically harmful but efficient for reducing the problem of vacancy rates. Mining settlements built for the long term, like the 'colonies' of the Ruhr Valley in Germany, simply do not exist. Rather, miners in Japan, even in Hokkaidô, which has very cold winters, lodged in simple wooden houses that fall quickly into ruin once mining is abandoned – the word 'vacant' is misleading in this context. However, with regard to traditional Japanese shopping streets of local and regional cities, there is a widespread surplus of empty or closed shops, problems that are described as shutter-dôri, i.e. shuttered down shopping arcades. They can be explained by the overlapping of different facts, particularly the increase in new shopping centres outside the old city centre (although the city's population as a whole may drop tremendously), the high age of many shopkeepers and their limited financial resources for renovating their shops.

Options for actions

The challenges associated with shrinking processes are enormous. Hitherto the catchword 'shrinking' or even 'change without growth' was nearly unthinkable for decision makers, politically and practically not acceptable, its connotation exclusively negative, theoretically discernible only in first signs of approaches (Kabisch 2006). In the industrialised countries the 'Fordistic' development model was dominant for a long time: availibility of work in principle, full employment, industrial mass production, growth of prosperity, etc. With regard to urban development this means: continous population growth, increase of jobs, necessity of permanent new housing. This model is going to be replaced by a 'post-Fordistic' one, the contures of which are not yet really clear. Table 2.1 may show perspectives for coping with 'shrinking'.

As for 'shrinking', both Germany and Japan show symptoms of a turn in governance. This, however, appears to be more realistic in Germany where 'shrinking' is going to be realised as something that has to be dealt with actively by

Table 2.1 Polarisation of urban planning culture: a turn in governance?

	'Fordistic'	'Post-Fordistic'
Leitbild/Norm	Orientation on business: Growth	Orientation on society: Sustainablity (economic, ecologic, societal)
Priority of urban planning	Urban development: Distribution of quantitative gains (inhabitants, jobs)	Downsizing, Stadtumbau, Stadtrückbau: Stabilisation, revitalisation, qualitative development (housing milieu, infrastructure_traffic)
Management of space	Development of new areas and of infrastructure facilities as a preliminary work and incentive for investments	Re-use of a space and buildings, selective downsizing, adjustment of infrastructure facilities to new needs
Zoning	Separation of basic functions (living, working, etc.) à la Charta of Athens 1933/1934	Small scaled mix of basic functions
Political organisation	'Urban government'	'Urban governance'
Decision structure	'Top down', 'efficient', time-saving: intransparent, prone to corruption	'Bottom up', 'inefficient', time-consuming: more transparent, less corruption
Citizens' participation	Not appropriate, however civil-societal responsibility welcome	Participative, more decision competence desired, organisation in NPOs
Network	Neocorporatistic, exclusive	Nonuniform, open, diffuse
Ground/Terrain: Ownership	Property conception of 'Dominium': neoliberal interpretation of property as sacrosanct: municipalities do not have a possibility of intervention	Property conception of 'Patrimonium': traditional separation of property rights and usufruct (use rights): offers chances for flexible urban planning → long-term lease, nonprofit foundations, neighborhood cooperatives, taxation of disused property
Inter-municipal relationship	Competition (for getting inhabitants, factories), sectoral incentives	Cooperation, balance-oriented rules, multi-scale cooperation

Column headers (italic subtitles under main heading):
- 'Fordistic': Classical planning based on growth
- 'Post-Fordistic': Sustainable planning based on stabilisation_

Notes
Partly adapted from Müller 2003: 38, own design.

making use of 'post-Fordistic' schemes like urban *governance* (instead of urban *government*), i.e. flexible urban management forms, in order to alleviate the increasing problems. In Germany, 'growth' is no longer regarded as a paradigm of urban development. In Japan, however, 'growth' still dominates urban development. The consciousness of the necessity of action for overcoming the spatial problems of 'shrinking' seems to be relatively low in Japan – curiously, given the even more dramatic demographic change when compared with Germany.

Shrinking and the problem of 'cost remanence'

Closely connected with 'shrinking' is the problem of 'cost remanence' (Figure 2.5). A decreasing population has to be sufficiently supplied with urban infrastructure facilities such as sewage, water, electricity (heating/airconditioning), schools, hospitals, snow removal, etc. On the one hand, total expenditures decrease as a result of decreasing population. On the other hand, however, and most important, expenditures *per head* increase dramatically the more severe the population drop is. Consequently, cost remanence is very important for understanding different solutions of handling the housing vacancy problem.

Compared with Germany, in Japan the surplus of empty dwellings seems to be less serious as a result of the regular scrap and build of traditional Japanese houses within a time of only one generation. Traditional Japanese house building is characterised by a relatively 'light' or 'easy' type of construction, which usually consists of one- or two-storeyed houses in timber construction built without cellar/basement. Another factor closely connected with relatively flexible house building is the less developed 'hard' infrastructure such as sewerage, which until recently lacked or still is lacking high standards. Considering Japan is a wealthy country, households are provided with electricity received via cables running above ground rather than underground, appearing ephemeral rather than long-termed. Contrary to these sociocultural and technical peculiarities, which make scrap and build easier and hence can be regarded as a potential for reducing the problem of vacancy rates, geographical characteristics like heavy snowfall lead to relatively high remanence costs in affected regions. This is specifically true for Japan's 'snow country' (*yukiguni*), a region on the Japan seaside hit by heavy snowfall and a dramatic drop and ageing of population. Here the remanence cost per person for the removing of snow becomes so expensive, that the affected municipalities have to think about giving up snow removal in remote districts (cf. the case of Yûbari in Flüchter 2008: 82).

Shrinking as an opportunity

'Shrinking' is not evil per se but also offers opportunities, especially for countries and regions that are extremely densely inhabited and until recently have shown an immense increase in population. Both densely populated Germany and much more densely populated Japan can make use of the opportunities of shrinking, such as relief of the real estate market, less congestion and fewer traffic jams, more urban living and increases in housing quality produced by newly free space, ecological potentials for improving the environment, commercial advantages through offering space in industrial estates for low rents and taking into account 'cycle economies' (*Kreislaufwirtschaft*) centred on local needs.

In the post-war period national and local governments in Germany and Japan have made their spatial planning policies by assuming ever-growing socio-economic conditions. However, in the coming era of rapid demographic shrinking and ageing, issues of vitality loss in communities become prominent. Shrinking and ageing are phenomena that in the near future will be significantly intensified in both countries. Thus, policy makers need to tackle the problems of the demographic shift actively, develop creative strategies for shaping and managing 'shrinking' and find courage for unconventional experiments (see Table 2.1), for example by: promoting bottom-up involvement and citizen participation in policy shaping and implementation instead of traditional top-down conventions in infrastructural planning policy domains; organising inter-municipal networks for the purpose of cooperation instead of competition; ensuring that residents are sufficiently informed and provided with satisfactory infrastructural facilities in an affordable manner. For organising the problems of demographic

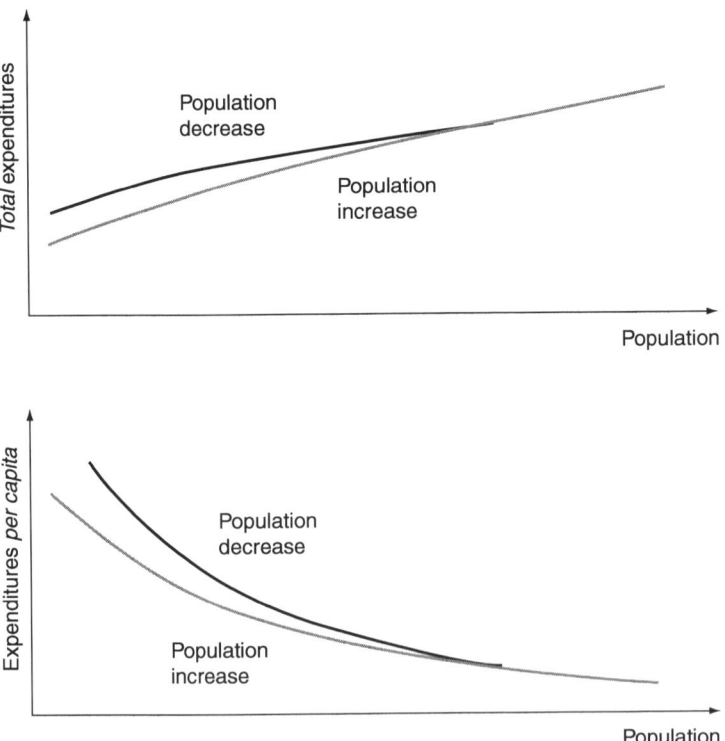

Figure 2.5 The problem of cost remanence related to urban infrastructure (source: Killisch and Siedhoff 2005: 61).

change sustainably, a consequent paradigm shift in planning and development 'from growth to shrinking' is necessary. In this context, urban landscape design including the planning of housing and public spaces, contraction of urban spaces and revitalisation of urban centres are research fields that deserve special attention.

Conclusion

The role of history has been an important factor in the entire evolution of a city-oriented culture in Japan. Significant foundations for Japan's urbanisation were already laid in the Tokugawa period, then in the following Meiji and pre-war periods. However, the most dramatic phase and change in Japan's urbanisation occurred from the post-war era to the present, and is characterised by the following findings:

The 'city' (shi) *as the essence of 'urban'?* The statistical distinction between a 'city' (*shi*), a 'town' (*machi, chô*) and a 'village' (*mura, son*) no longer provides a clear scale for urbanisation. In reality, the threshold values for *shi* (currently 50,000 inhabitants) do not necessarily say very much about the urban character, due to an artificial inflation of urban population caused first, by amalgamations of communities into larger administrative units, and second, by a heavy loss of inhabitants in communities labelled cities that now fall shy of the minimum size of a *shi*.

Impressively high degree of urbanisation: Given a minimum threshold of 50,000 inhabitants per community as a criterion for 'urban', about four-fifths of the Japanese population can be regarded as representative of urbanisation. The Japanese population is a society of large cities; as much as 22 per cent of the population lives in cities with more than one million inhabitants, and 51 per cent in cities with more than 200,000 inhabitants (2005).

Strong hierarchic national city system headed by Tokyo: Post-war urbanisation, characterised by city expansion, metropolisation and megalopolisation, resulted in a national city system which changed from a bipolar structure (Tokyo and Osaka) to a 'one-point concentration on Tokyo' (*Tôkyô ikkyoku shûchû*). This was due to governmental and entrepreneurial decisions to make full use of agglomeration economies, enabling Tokyo to compete internationally with other top-ranking global cities like London and New York.

The Japanese city between 'development' and 'shrinking': From the 1950s until the late 1990s, the large majority of cities showed an impressive increase in population. In reference to these decades of high economic growth, there can be no talk of 'shrinking cities' except in smaller peripheral cities in depressed areas, like mining. However, since the late 1990s, in contrast to the core areas of the metropolises and the dynamic regional core cities, nearly all cities in the rest of Japan suffered loss of population due to deindustrialisation, the ageing of society and the reurbanisation processes typical of the metropolises. The situation is especially severe in areas based on declining ('sunset') industries. What is true for these areas today can be seen as an early warning sign for larger parts of

Japan in the future, because independent of deindustrialisation, the entirety of the Japanese population is decreasing (since 2005) and ageing – dramatically in the remote areas.

Suburbanisation versus reurbanisation: Suburbanisation, typical of Japanese metropolises (particularly Tokyo) since the 1960s, caused a considerable drop in population in core urban areas and strong growth at the outskirts of the metropolises. However, it did not really contribute to a shrinking of the metropolises, provided these are understood as regions including their umland. Astonishingly, since the late 1990s, suburbanisation has begun to reverse dramatically in favour of reurbanisation, benefiting the city centres formerly seen as 'housing craters'. The new trend towards reurbanisation means that 'shrinking' will, in the long term, become a problem for suburbia as well.

'Shrinking' as a challenge: Urbanism and vitality are typical of large Japanese cities. New challenges such as recession, population decline and an aging society have not been enough to cause the Japanese to question their preference for urbanism, and particularly for those cities on top of the Japanese city system. However, there is hardly any public discussion of 'shrinking cities' – an increasingly threatening phenomenon – which, especially set in the context of an 'aging society', will dramatically challenge the majority of Japan's cities and demands for intelligent urban governance.

Coping with 'shrinking cities' in times of demographic change: 'Shrinking' is not evil per se. It also offers opportunities, especially for a country like Japan, which is extremely densely packed and has until recently shown immense increase in population. Japan can make use of the opportunities of shrinking, in particular falling land prices, relief to the real estate market, less congestion and fewer traffic jams and the increased urban living and housing-quality produced by newly free space. Policy makers need to develop creative strategies for actively shaping and managing 'shrinking' with urgency. Unconventional experiments related to the contraction of urban spaces and to urban landscape design may lead to a turn in governance and urban planning culture; a shift from the 'Fordistic' model (classical planning based on growth) to the 'post-Fordistic' one (sustainable planning based on stabilisation) could be on the horizon. However, the necessary precondition for this turn requires a paradigm shift in planning and development 'from growth to shrinking'.

Notes

1 Kokura-shi, Moji-shi, Tobata-shi, Wakamatsu-shi and Yawata-shi.
2 Particularly in Tôkyô-ku (wards, 8.48 million people, +4.3 per cent) including her quasi-satellites Kawasaki (1.33 million, +6.2 per cent), Yokohama (3.58 million, +4.4 per cent), Chiba (924,000, +4,2 per cent), in addition Nagoya (2.22 million, +2.0 per cent), Ôsaka-shi (2.63 million, +1.3 per cent), Kobe (1.53 million, +2.1 per cent), in contrast stagnant population in Kyôto-shi (1.47 million, +0.0 per cent) as well as in most of the cities situated at the fringe of the metropolises.
3 According to the Population Census 2005, Shimizu is no longer an independent city, due to its amalgamation into Shizuoka (2005: 701,000 inhabitants) of which it has become a ward (Shimizu-ku).

4 In 2005 values and from northeast to southwest, these are Aomori (311,000, −2.3 per cent), Morioka (287,000, −0.6 per cent), Akita (333,000, −1.1 per cent), Fukushima (292,000, −0.1 per cent), Kôfu (194,000, −1.0 per cent), Kanazawa (455,000, −0.4 per cent), Nagano (378,000, −0.1 per cent), Matsue (197,000, −1.3 per cent), Tokushima (268,000, −0.1 per cent), Kôchi (334,000, −0.1 per cent), Saga (207,000, −0.9 per cent), Nagasaki (443,000, −3.2 per cent).
5 Such as Maebashi (319,000, −0,6 per cent) in Kantô, Gifu (400,000, −0.7 per cent) in Greater Nagoya, Nara (371,999, −1.3 per cent) and, particularly striking, Wakayama (376,000, −2.8 per cent) in Greater Osaka.
6 Such as Yamagata (256,000, +0.2 per cent), Toyama (421,000, +0.1 per cent), Tottori (202,000, +0.5 per cent) and Takamatsu (338,000, +0.4 per cent), but also much more important ones like Niigata (785,000, +0.7 per cent) and Kagoshima (604,000, +0.4 per cent).

References

Flüchter, Winfried (1997): Tôkyô quo vadis? Chancen und Grenzen (?) metropolitanen Wachstums. In: Apel, Ulrich, Holzapfel, Josef and Pörtner, Peter (eds): Beiträge zum 8. Deutschsprachigen Japanologentag München 1996, München: Japan-Zentrum der Ludwigs-Maximilians-Universität, CD ROM: 522–548. = Duisburger Arbeitspapiere Ostasienwissenschaften, Heft 15.

Flüchter, Winfried (1998): Japan: Geographische Fragestellungen, Strukturen, Probleme. In: Mayer, Hans Jürgen and Pohl, Manfred (eds): *Länderbericht Japan*. Bonn: Bundeszentrale für politische Bildung, 14–49.

Flüchter, Winfried (2005): Japan: Shrinking Cities between Megalopolises and Rural Peripheries. In: Oswalt, Philipp (ed.): *Shrinking Cities*. Vol. 1, International Research. Ostfildern-Ruit: Hatje Cantz Verlag: 83–92.

Flüchter, Winfried (2008): Schrumpfende Städte als Herausforderung: Japan, Hokkaidô und der Fall der Stadt Yûbari. In: Elis, Volker and Lützeler, Ralph (eds): *Zwischen Wachstum und Schrumpfung – Neue Tendenzen der Regionalentwicklung in Japan.* Japanstudien: Jahrbuch des Deutschen Instituts für Japanstudien Band 20. München: Iudicium, 69–102.

Glickman, Norman J. (1979): *The Growth and Management of the Japanese Urban System*, New York: Academic Press.

Hohn, Uta (2002): Ökonomischer und stadtstruktureller Wandel in Tokyo. In: *Zeitschrift für Wirtschaftsgeographie*, 46. Jahrgang, Heft 3/4: 228–245.

Kabisch, Sigrun (2006): Stadtumbau Ost und West: Chancen und Grenzen von Schrumpfung. In: Kulke, E., Monheim, H. and Wittmann, P. (eds): *Grenzwerte, Tagungsbericht und wissenschaftliche Abhandlungen des 55. Deutschen Geographentages Trier 2005*. Berlin, Leipzig, Trier 2006, 257–265.

Killisch, Winfried and Mathias Siedhoff (2005): Probleme schrumpfender Städte. In: *Geographische Rundschau* 57, 2005, Heft 10, 60–67.

Matsumoto, Yasushi (2004): From Suburbanization to Reurbanization: Demographic Issues of Tokyo. In: *Comprehensive Urban Studies*, Vol. 83, March: 82–105.

Müller, Bernhard (2003): Regionalentwicklung unter Schrumpfungsbedingungen. Herausforderungen für die Raumplanung in Deutschland. In: *Raumforschung und Raumordnung* 1–2, S. 28–42.

Murayama, Yuji (2000): *Japanese Urban System*. Dordrecht, London: Kluwer Academic = *The GeoJournal Library* 56.

Narita, Ryûichi, Kinichi Ogura and Akio Yoshie (1989): Japan. In: Engeli, Christian and

Matzerath, Horst (eds) *Modern Urban History in Europe, USA, and Japan: A Handbook*, Oxford: Berg.

Okata, Junichiro and Akito Murayama (2011): Tokyo's Urban Growth, Urban Form and Sustainability. In: Sorensen, André and Okata, Junichiro (eds): *Megacities. Urban Form, Governance, and Sustaibability*. Tokyo et al.: Springer, 15–43. = *Library for Sustainable Urban Regeneration* Vol. 10.

Ômura, Kenjirô and Tomokazu Arita (2005): A Research on the Urban Regeneration Policies in an Age of Shrinking Cities in Japan. Paper presented at the 11th International Conference of the EAJS (European Association for Japanese Studies), September 1, 2005, University of Vienna, Austria.

Sawada, Seiji, Tomiyasu, Hideo and Masamitsu Nozawa (eds) (2004): Sanierung und Erneuerung von Großwohnsiedlungen. Lösungsansatz Offenes Bauen/Refurbishment and Renovation of Large Housing Estates. The Open Building Solution. A Report from a Study Group in Tôkyô. Tokyo: Marumo Publishing.

Seaton, Philip (2010): Depopulation and Bankruptcy in Yubari: Market Forces, Administrative Folly, or a Warning to Others? In: *Social Science Japan Journal* (published online January 2010).

Schöller, Peter (1969): Ein Jahrhundert Stadtentwicklung in Japan. In: *Colloquium Geographicum* 10, Bonn: 13–57.

Schöller, Peter (1978): Japan. In: Schöller, Peter, Dürr, Heiner and Dege, Eckart: *Ostasien*. Frankfurt: Fischer Taschenbuch Verlag, 325–440.

Sômushô tôkei-kyoku (Ministry of Internal Affairs and Communications Japan, Statistics Bureau) (2006): Heisei jûnen kokusei chôsa zenkoku todôfuken shikuchôson-betsu jinkô, yôkeihyô ni yoru jinkô (2005 Population Census of Japan, Preliminary Counts of the Population on the Basis of Summary Sheets). Tokyo: Nihon tôkei kyôkai (Japan Statistical Association).

Sorensen, André (2002): *The Making of Urban Japan*. London, New York: Routledge Curzon.

3 The colonial appropriation of public space

Architecture and city planning in Japanese-dominated Manchuria

Anke Scherer

Introduction

Besides their many architectural and aesthetic aspects, city planning and the construction of public buildings also have a political dimension. The traditional layout of Chinese capital cities, for instance, later adopted for the construction of Japanese capital cities in the sixth and seventh century, corresponds to cosmological principles and is therefore a symbol of social and political stability (Wheatley and See 1978). Haussmann's well-known city planning projects, like the creation of big boulevards and many representative public buildings in Paris in the nineteenth century, are usually associated with the modernisation of the city, especially since these projects have equipped the city with modern drinking water provisions and a working sewage system. On the other hand the new layout of the city was also a demonstration of the power of Napoleon III. Wide boulevards and marching grounds for soldiers could also be used for parades and other demonstrations of military power (Jordan 1996). An infamous example for the use of city planning and the design of public buildings as a display of power are the projects of Albert Speer, who planned and, in 1939, finished the New Reich Chancellery (Neue Reichskanzlei) for Adolf Hitler in Berlin and who would have redesigned the centre of Berlin into the ultimate demonstration of Nazi power if he had had the time to implement his plans for the new capital Germania (Schönberger 1981, Reichardt and Schäche 2005).

Impressive public buildings and city layouts were also used by colonial administrations worldwide to demonstrate their power and to impress the locals. Japanese bureaucrats were no exception to this rule. In many parts of East Asia, which had been dominated by Japan in the first half of the twentieth century – the colonies Taiwan and Korea as well as other occupied or dominated territories like the puppet state of Manshûkoku – the Japanese had a significant influence on the layout and design of big cities. Colonial governments in Taiwan and in Korea for example constructed massive buildings for the Japanese governors in the centre of the capital cities to remind the populace of the distribution of power in the country. The people in the colonies associated these symbols of power with the Japanese repression and, as in the extreme case of the headquarters of the Japanese colonial regime in Seoul, even geared their frustration with the colonial situation against the actual building long after the end of the colonial rule when they demolished the edifice in 1996 (Lankov 2005). Besides the erection of dominant buildings for the Japanese administration, there were many other Japanese interferences in the public space. This chapter examines the modelling of urban space by Japanese city planners in Manchuria. Urbanisation and the use of public space is taken as an example to analyse the ideas and concepts behind the Japanese creation of what they called an East Asian Modern in northeast China in the first half of the twentieth century.

In his study *Architecture and Authority in Japan*, William Coaldrake has shown how architecture in Japan has been a manifestation of authority throughout the ages. Buildings communicate, convince and even coerce, and thus it is essential for the understanding of what Coaldrake calls the vocabulary of authority to decipher the code with which urban structures communicate (Coaldrake 1996). City planning and urbanisation during the phase of Japanese domination in Manchuria is an excellent example that can be used for an analysis of the contents as well as the outcome of this form of communication, not the least because the region was usually perceived as a *hakushi*, a white page, and a laboratory or testing ground for projects that could not be realised within Japan proper. David Tucker discusses large-scale plans for agricultural settlements in the rural regions of Manchuria as a prime example of utopian ideas that were developed to appropriate space for a new, modern East Asia under Japanese guidance (Tucker 2005). These settlements were so utterly utopian and unrealistic that they were never built, but the sheer scope of the plan as well as its rigid rationality is evidence for the intended show of strength and the megalomania of the Japanese authorities in Manchuria. Prasenjit Duara quotes the large-scale projects in infrastructure and in the urban sector in Manchuria as a part of the modernity project whose purpose was to develop Manshûkoku as a nation-state that was internationally recognised as the avant-garde of the Northeast Asian Modern (Duara 2003).

In order to show the connection between the Japanese will to dominate Manchuria and turn it into a showcase of a specifically East Asian modernity, the creation of urban infrastructure will be analysed by first explaining the power structure in the region in the first half of the twentieth century. Then the physical take-over of the territory with infrastructure projects and the creation of a new power centre will be examined. To assess the effects of these efforts, reactions to the results of Japanese planning will be looked at. Urban planning and infrastructure projects are thus analysed as potent tools for social engineering in the process of the attempted creation of a Japanese-led East Asian modernity in Manchuria.

Manchuria and Manshûkoku

Manchuria was never a Japanese colony like Taiwan and Korea, but nevertheless some Japanese authors call the state of Manshûkoku, which existed there from 1 March 1932 until 20 August 1945 a *shokuminchi* (colony). The usual appellation in Chinese literature as well as in some Japanese and Western studies for this short-lived entity is 'puppet state'. The term 'puppet' is used to describe the claim of the Japanese government and, more specifically, parts of the Japanese Army to control the state of Manshûkoku. This control was exercised through members of the Kantô Army, which was created in 1919 to guard and administer Japanese concession territories in northeast China. The concession territory was called Guandong in Chinese, and thus its Japanese pronunciation Kantô gave the name to the army in charge. The Kantô Army subsequently became the main power in the region, initiated the founding of the state of Manshûkoku and made sure that every Chinese-Manchurian government official had a Japanese deputy as 'counsel' (Coox 1989).

According to a definition by Max Weber, power 'is the probability that one actor within a social relationship will be in a position to carry out his own will despite resistance, regardless of the basis on which this probability rests' (Weber 1947: 152). Thus regardless of Manshûkoku's official status of independence from Japan, power was exercised by Japanese military men and bureaucrats forcing their will on Chinese-Manchurian government officials who acted as their 'puppets'. Since Japanese bureaucrats and planners in Manchuria thus acted in a colonial manner, this article analyses their city planning activities within the framework of colonial appropriation of public space. The creation of urban infrastructure was an activity of the Japanese authorities, an expression of the Japanese desire to dominate and shape the region.

The South Manchurian Railway Company

Whereas in the Japanese colonies of Taiwan and Korea the capital cities had been existent and functioning as real cities before the advent of Japanese forces, first the mostly empty concession territories in Manchuria and later the decision to build a new capital city for the state of Manshûkoku offered rather unlimited possibilities for city planning and monumental architecture. These activities were carried out by the second important actor of Japanese domination in Manchuria besides the Kantô Army: the South Manchurian Railway Company (Minami Manshû tetsudô kabushiki gaisha), usually called by the abbreviation of its Japanese name: Mantetsu.

The Mantetsu was an important tool for the Japanese penetration of northeast China. It was founded 26 November 1906 with an initial capital of 200 million yen to play a role for the Japanese interests in the region similar to the one the East India Company had played for the British Empire in India and was therefore placed under strict government supervision. Its president was appointed by the Japanese government and received his orders from the Prime Minister. Half of its initial capital was the tracks, facilities and rolling stock of the former Russian-owned Chinese Eastern Railway that the Treaty of Portsmouth, which ended the Russo-Japanese War of 1904/05, had assigned to Japan. The other capital came from the sale of shares to the public as well as from bank loans (Beasley 1987: 135–136). By the 1920s, the Mantetsu had developed into an industrial venture with a wide range of subsidiaries in mining, manufacturing and trade. Moreover, it had become an important agent in the administration of Japanese concession territory in Manchuria, the so-called Railway Zone comprising station towns and mining districts along the railroad between Dalian and Changchun, which had also been given to Japan in the Treaty of Portsmouth. Besides railway stations the Mantetsu created all kinds of public buildings and infrastructure and thus shaped the outlook of all major cities in the region (Matsusaka 1996: 98–99).

When the Mantetsu was awarded the railroads and facilities of the former Chinese Eastern Railway Company in 1906, Changchun, the northern end of this railroad, consisted of some Chinese dwellings and a few narrow roads. At that time it was the place where the Japanese sphere of influence in Manchuria met with the Russian sphere of influence, which also meant that the different track widths of the former Chinese Eastern Railway and the Russian railroad confronted each other. Thus cargo had to be reloaded from one type of freight car onto another, and passengers had to disembark and change trains. When the Mantetsu took over the concession territory south of Changchun station, it started with the construction of a new station building with a round square in front of it. Two similar squares were created in the west and in the east of the concession territory and connected with broad roads. The whole territory was then covered with streets arranged regularly as on a chessboard. In this grid the Mantetsu erected several new buildings, including a school, a hospital, office buildings and apartments for its employees (Nishizawa 1996a: 103–104).

One of the first projects tackled by Mantetsu on the new concession territory in Changchun, however, was the construction of a big Western-style hotel opposite the station in the summer of 1907. This hotel, which was originally geared towards Western diplomats, journalists and businessmen, became the first of the so-called Yamato Hotels, a chain of hotels constructed and managed by Mantetsu at every major stop of its railroad. The hotel in Changchun was first conceptualised as the counterpart of the Modern Hotel in Harbin. This spacious art nouveau hotel in the centre of Harbin had been opened in 1906 by a Russian Jew. At the beginning of the twentieth century Harbin was one of the centres of art nouveau architecture only matched by Nancy and Brussels; its culture was highly influenced by the large community of Russian emigrants living there (Bakich 2001; Clausen and Thögersen 1995). The Modern Hotel in Harbin was state-of-the-art at that time. The Yamato Hotel chain consisted mostly of newly constructed or, as in the case of Dalian, totally refurbished impressive Western-style buildings with art nouveau decorated banquet halls, marble floors and elevators. Leaving out the typical features of high-class Japanese *ryokan* (traditional Japanese hotels) like spacious public baths and *tatami* (rice straw mat) banquet rooms, the hotels offered only Western-style rooms, all with private bathrooms. The message for the visitor was that the Japanese influence in Manchuria brought modern Western standards to the region by offering a first-class hotel at major railway stations, as would be expected in European cities as well. With these hotels and the equally impressive station buildings Mantetsu appropriated the public space connected to travelling and signalled to visitors and the city population alike that it was in charge of creating a modern infrastructure (Nishizawa 1996a). The creation of urban facilities that provided modern (Western) standards for international travellers legitimised the presence of the Mantetsu and thus justified its claim to the territory.

City planning

Another example of appropriation of public space is the enlargement or the construction of the major cities in Manchuria in general. Cities like Dalian and Fengtian (nowadays called Shenyang), which had already existed as cities before the arrival of the Japanese, were enlarged massively by the creation of new roads, places and public buildings on the Japanese concession territory around the railway stations. This development can best be observed in Fengtian by comparing city maps from 1908 through to 1937 (Figure 3.1).

Starting from the railway station a regular grid of roads was laid out with boulevards leading diagonally to a central square. Over the years the space, first only marked by roads, boulevards and squares, was filled with houses, public buildings and shops, thus turning into urban space. These grids, also used in Dalian, Changchun and other Manchurian cities, were imported by Mantetsu architects and city planners who had been trained in the West. Gotô Shinpei, a politician and well-known social reformer was the first president of Mantetsu. When the construction section of his new company was faced with the task to design the layout of the concession territories around the railway stations, he sent one of his architects, Katô Yoshikichi, who was in charge of designing the concession area around the Changchun railway station, on a study tour to Europe. Katô came back to Manchuria deeply impressed by the boulevards of Paris and the place de L'Arc de Triomph as well as the Baroque layout of the inner city of Mannheim with its streets in a chessboard-like grid (Nishizawa 1996a: 105). The influence of these ideas can be also seen in the above-mentioned city maps of the new part of Fengtian.

Fengtian used to be the capital of the Manchu rulers in the seventeenth century before they toppled the Chinese Ming Dynasty in 1644 and moved to Beijing to rule all of China as emperors of the Qing Dynasty. The city has an imperial palace; the two founding fathers of the Qing Dynasty are buried in large tombs outside the city. Thus the spatial take-over of the ancient Manchu capital was something of a challenge for the Mantetsu. It solved the problem by constructing a new modern city adjacent to the old Fengtian. Even today the city has two city centres, one with old city walls and the palace museum, i.e. the traditional Chinese city, and another one with the railway station on the concession territory urbanised by the Mantetsu (Nishizawa 2000: 78–79).

The creation of a new capital

Its long history, however, and its historical buildings made Fengtian unfit to serve as the capital of the newly founded state of Manshûkoku. This state –

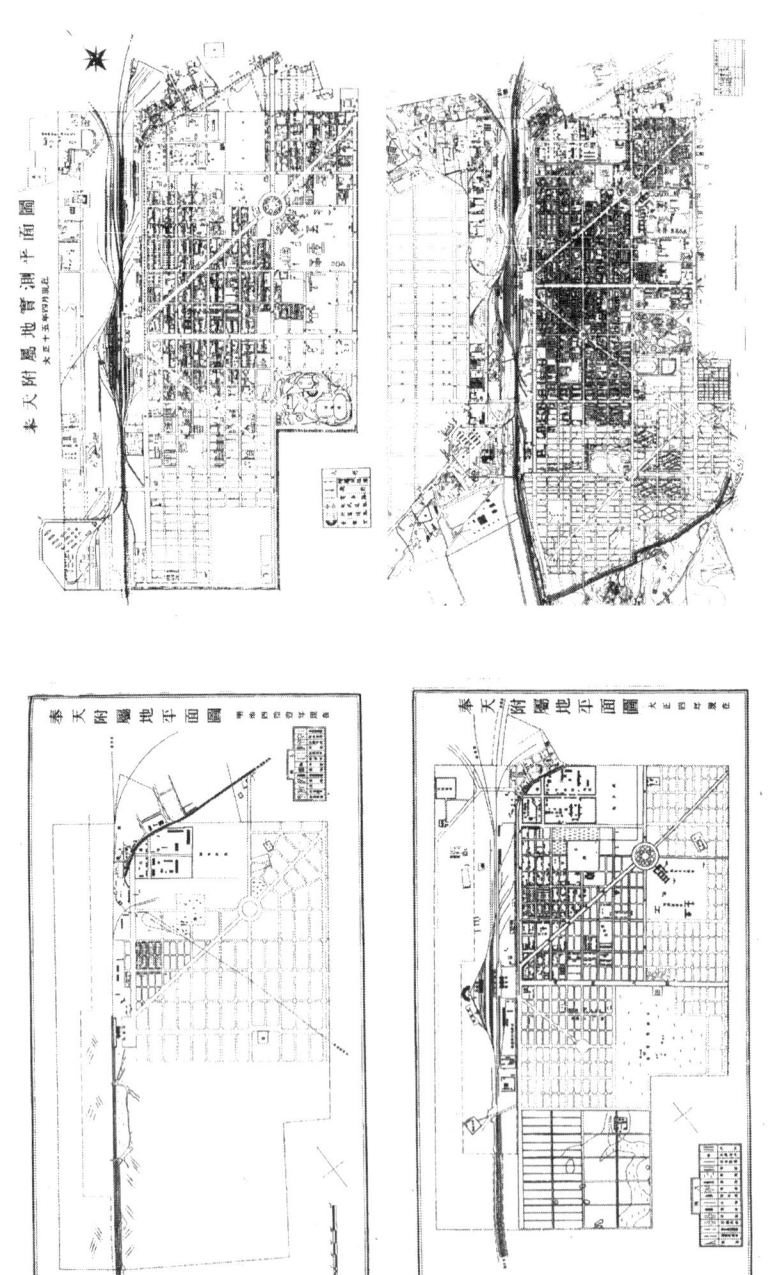

Figure 3.1 Development of the Japanese concession territory around Fengtian station: 1908 (upper left), 1915 (lower left), 1925 (upper right) and 1937 (lower right) (reprinted with permission from Kawade shobō shinsha) (Nishizawa 1996a: 86–87, reproduced with permission).

internationally only recognised by a few other states like Nazi Germany, Fascist Italy and the Vatican – was founded on 1 March 1932 as a puppet state of the Japanese Kantô Army. The last emperor of the Qing Dynasty, who had abdicated as a child in 1912, was first made the president of this new state and on 1 March 1934 he was crowned emperor of the now constitutional monarchy in Manshûkoku. Changchun, the hamlet without a history, which had been turned into something of a town by the construction work of Mantetsu's architects and city planners, was made the capital of Manshûkoku on 10 March 1932 and renamed Xinjing (Japanese: Shinkyô), which means 'New Capital' (Koshizawa 1988: 90, 94).

The declaration of Changchun, now called Xinjing/Shinkyô, as the capital of the new state started a wholly new phase in the appropriation of public space in Manchuria. In the first 25 years of Japanese activities in the region it was mostly Mantetsu activities changing the public space. Its main focus was on the creation of modern infrastructure, like hotels, hospitals and apartment buildings. Although civil in nature these projects had already staked the Japanese claim in Manchuria, just like the branch office of the Yokohama Species Bank in Dalian (Figure 3.2).

This bank, founded in 1880 with generous government assistance, was in charge of fostering Japanese economic activities abroad and it was the main supporter of Japanese businesses in Manchuria. This agent of Japanese influence in Manchuria naturally also claimed a prominent public space in the new city centre of Dalian, directly opposite the Yamato Hotel. When Xinjing became the capital,

Figure 3.2 The former Yokohama Species Bank in Dalian (photographed by the author in 2002).

however, it needed more than travel and business infrastructure. A political centre had to be created. Since Xinjing nee Changchun had no history of being a centre of administration – the capital of the region was actually neighbouring Jilin – there were hardly any administration buildings. Thus the new government of Manshûkoku had to erect buildings as fast as possible. Sôga Kensuke, originally from the construction section of Mantetsu, was made head of the newly created architecture section in the department for capital construction. As early as 6 May 1932 he received the order to construct two new government buildings. The construction site was situated literally in the middle of nowhere at the outskirts of town. Guests attending the cornerstone ceremony for the first building had to be driven to the site in cars along the unpaved roads and stood around wearing rubber boots. The construction site was so far out of town that it even had to be guarded against guerrilla attacks (Koshizawa 1988: 182–187).

The architects were under great pressure to finish the new government buildings as soon as possible; construction plans were just dragged to the construction sites and adapted to local conditions and developments on the spot. Consequently the first two government buildings were completed in 1935, in the next year the Legislative Yuan, the parliament of Manshûkoku, could move into its new building. Only a few years after the formal takeover of the Japanese puppet state in Manchuria a whole new architecture of power had been created in the city of Xinjing. The most interesting feature of the new capital is not so much the rapid construction of ministries and other government buildings; it is the location of the centre of real power within the topography of the city.

The architecture of power

As already mentioned, Pu Yi, the last Qing emperor was first made head of the state and then emperor of Manshûkoku. Thus he needed an imperial palace in the capital of his new state. Traditionally the imperial palace in a Chinese capital has to be situated centrally in the northern part of the city. This corresponds to the Confucian notion that the emperor is like the polestar, shining brightly and fixed in the northern hemisphere. Consequently the Japanese city planners in Xinjing met with fierce resistance of the Chinese bureaucrats of the new regime, when they first relegated the construction site of a new palace for Pu Yi to the south of the city. A compromise could be reached by building the new palace in the northeast of the city, which was still better than a southern location. The north of the city was already occupied by the pre-1932 symbols of Japanese influence: the Mantetsu railway station, the Yamato Hotel and last but not least a Japanese post office which just like the Yokohama Species Bank was an important piece of Japanese state sponsored and controlled infrastructure. Just south of these facilities, however, lay the real centre of power of Manshûkoku. Situated on a hillock at the intersection of the north–south and the east–west axis of the city was the headquarters of the Kantô Army (Nishizawa 1996a: 107–110). Whereas the newly created government buildings in Xinjing are usually more Western than anything else in outward appearance, the Kantô Army's headquarters is crowned by a tower that strongly resembles the fortified castles of the Warring States and Tokugawa Period (Figure 3.3).

This mixture of a Western body and a castle-like top was actually rather popular in the Japanese sphere of influence in Asia in the 1920s and 1930s, especially with army buildings (Itani *et al.* 2000: 155). In the case of Xinjing the headquarters' tower nicely dominates the city centre and the new government quarter at its south. The location has not lost its fascination: today the building houses the provincial centre of the Chinese Communist Party.

The office building of the Taiwan Governor's Office has an equally impressive outlook. When Taiwan became a Japanese colony after the Treaty of Shimonoseki, which ended the Sino-Japanese war in 1895, the first governors used an old Qing Dynasty building for the administration. Gotô Shinpei, however, the island's chief civil administrator until he became the first president of the Mantetsu in 1906, argued that a modern office building should replace the old leftover from the previous regime. The construction of the new office building was finally started in 1912 and was completed in 1919. The Taiwan Governor's office building is constructed of red brick and looks more European than Asian. At the time of its construction it was the largest building in East Asia, sporting a

Figure 3.3 Former headquarters of the Kantô Army in Changchun (photographed by the author in 2002).

tower in its centre that was originally planned to be six stories high but ended up having eleven floors. It was clearly laid out as a symbol of Japanese power and is used today as the Office of the Taiwanese President (Jin 2001).

The office of the Japanese Governor General in Seoul was also meant to be an impressive proof of Japanese power in the country. In 1911, one year after Korea was finally annexed by Japan, it was decided to construct a new building for the colonial headquarters. Just like its counterpart in Taibei, the building looks rather Western at first in its neo-classic style, but when viewed from above it has the shape of the character *nichi*, the first part of the Japanese country name Nihon. Its construction began in 1916 and, interestingly, was overseen by the German architect Georg de Lalande. It was finished in 1926 and was built to deliberately block the public's view of Gyeongbok Palace, the ancient residence of Korea's kings. Since its dome was designed to symbolize a Japanese crown, the dome was torn down first in 1995 amidst great nationalistic pomp when Korea celebrated the 50th anniversary of the country's liberation from Japanese colonial rule, before the whole building was demolished in the following year (Lankov 2004). This late but forceful reaction to a piece of architecture proves not only that the respective building had communicated the authority and represented the domination by colonial administration. It also directs the focus to the image that architecture conveys to the observer.

Contemporary comments

As it is argued that these administration buildings as well as the new infrastructure were to serve as an embodiment of the Japanese claim for power as well as symbols of the modernisation brought to the region by the Japanese rule, it is necessary to check how these efforts were received in the West. To propagate its civilising mission, the Mantetsu published a booklet in 1933 containing *Tales of three cities in Manchuria* (Dalian, Fengtian and Shinkyô/Xinjing). The Japanese author reminds the reader that the Japanese Government, through the South Manchurian Railway Company, 'takes the responsibility upon itself to function as a civilizing force'. He compares the warlord family of Zhang Zoulin and his son Zhang Xueliang who ruled parts of Manchuria before the founding of Manshûkoku and who squeezed 'the life blood of the Manchurian peasant farmers to the last drop by the bitter and heartless taxation' to the evidence of 'the Japanese aspiration to serve the public welfare' by building infrastructure, schools and hospitals in Manchuria. For him the Yamato Hotels are 'the last word in accommodation, and one bound to make Americans think of home and home comforts. For there is nothing in all the Far East that is quite so American in every detail as this newly built hotel in the very heart of the New State of Manchukuo.' A new airport soon to be completed in the vicinity of Shinkyô would turn 'this new capital of the new State soon into the air travel centre of the North Eastern Asia.' (Adachi 1933: 12–16, 21).

It is easy to discard these impressions as mere Japanese propaganda; however, they clearly show the intended audience for which the construction of the new civilisation in Manchuria took place, namely the West. And observers from Western countries often responded in the form desired. Many visitors from Western countries like the US, Switzerland, Germany etc. painted a very positive picture of Japanese influence on urban development in Manchuria. They all agree that Japan brought progress, orderliness and cleanliness to the region. The contrast used by many authors is with 'old' Harbin, dominated by Russian emigrants, run down, poor and dirty (Cordes 1936: 54). An American named James Scherer visited Fengtian in 1933 because he had spent some time there as an English teacher 10 years before. He praised the total modernisation of public infrastructure in the city, especially the new hospital and the new medical college built by Mantetsu. To him, Mantetsu was the harbinger of progress in the region which had already turned Dalian into a modern, i.e. European city: 'Indeed, this famous city is more European than Asiatic' (Scherer 1933: 43).

Japanese architects and the East Asian modern

These impressions Western observers had from Japanese facilities and architecture were clearly intended by those who commissioned the city planning and architecture. On the one hand big administrative buildings in Xinjing, Seoul and Taibei were thought to intimidate the locals and show them where the real power lay in their countries. On the other hand these buildings were certainly also addressed to the Western countries to prove that Japan was bringing modernity and progress to the otherwise backward Asian countries. Japanese architecture and city planning were meant to bring modern infrastructure to urban spaces and convince the Western world that Japan was on a civilising mission in Asia. In his analysis of 'Manchukuo and the East Asian Modern', the subtitle of his book *Sovereignty and Authenticity*, Prasenjit Duara argues that the powers in charge of Manshûkoku tried very hard to construct a national identity in a state that could not be built upon a common ethnic identity with its diverse inhabitants. Thus these state-builders based their claim for power upon their creation of an 'East Asian Modern'. One effect of the efforts to construct this East Asian model of a modern state was that Manshûkoku was used as an experimental field for the implementation of ideas that could not be realised within Japan itself (Duara 2003: 247–251).

For architects and city planners the various infrastructural projects and especially the rare chance to construct a country capital from scratch offered the unique possibility to tackle projects on a scope that crowded urban spaces in Japan did not provide. Many of the Japanese city planners and architects commissioned to design public buildings in the colonies and Manchuria perceived their workplaces not as foreign countries, but just as the Japanese periphery (Nishizawa 1996b: 252–253). They worked in this periphery because the colonial setting offered them a unique chance to realise big projects that they probably would have never to do in Japan. Many of the architects who worked for the Mantetsu in Manshûkoku were young and would have had to wait for years for their first proper assignment in Japan. Most of them had some international

Figure 3.4 The Legislative Yuan, the Parliament of Manshûkoku in Changchun (photographed by the author in 2002).

experience; some of them had been students of famous architects like Frank Lloyd Wright or Le Corbusier. So they saw themselves as bringing the newest international standard to the public space in the Japanese dominated sphere. The modern government buildings in Taibei, Seoul and Xinjing were standing for the alleged modernity of the Japanese politics exercised in these settings. The building which housed the Legislative Yuan, i.e. the parliament of Manshûkoku, in Xinjing looks strikingly similar to the Parliament Building in Tokyo, both of them demonstrating to the outside world that a modern government was working inside those walls (Figure 3.4).

Touring the Manchuria project

It is highly questionable whether these efforts succeeded in convincing Western countries of Japan's positive influence in the region. Travelogues acknowledging Japanese progressive influence on Manshûkoku usually date from the first half of the 1930s, i.e. from the time before the outbreak of the Sino-Japanese War in 1937. When the contradiction inherent in the construction of Manshûkoku as a military dominated puppet state and its civilian infrastructural projects became increasingly obvious in the course of the war, the Japanese claim to create a model for an Asian modern lost its credibility at least for those countries that had no political alliance with Japan (Duara 2003: 247–248). The modern travel infrastructure with Western style hotels was not so much used by foreign travellers admiring the new modern state, but was mostly frequented by Japanese tourists in Manshûkoku. As early as 1914, just two years after its founding in Japan, the Japan Tourist Bureau (JTB) had opened a branch office in Dalian. In the 1920s and 1930s a rising number of better-off Japanese tourists picked Manchuria as their destination for a holiday. Young people accounted for a major part of Japanese tourists in Manchuria, since students of Japan's elite universities often received travel arrangements in Manchuria as graduation presents and student groups were granted discounts on all kinds of expenses through subsidies by the Ministry of Education (Young 1998: 259–268). JTB opened branch offices in all major cities in Manchuria and offered an 'East Asia Pass' that entitled its holder to fare reductions for many train and ship tickets. The Mantetsu operated a high-speed train called Asia-Express, which needed a mere eight hours for the 700 kilometres from Dalian to Xinjing and reached a maximum speed of 120 kilometres per hour (Nishizawa 2000: 29).

The modern travel infrastructure created by the Mantetsu as well as some other suppliers provided the basis for a travel boom of Japanese tourists in Manchuria. At the end of the 1930s a statistic published by JTB lists nearly three million overnight stays of Japanese travellers in hotels of major Manchurian cities (Japan tsûrisuto byûrô 1941: 293–295). An array of Japanese travel handbooks for Manchuria provided those travellers with information, writers published their travel accounts and inspired further people to go to Manchuria and have a look at this wonder of modernity themselves. From 1934 JTB even started the publication of a magazine that specialised in 'Manchuria Travel' (Manshû ryokô) (Young 1998: 259–268).

Conclusion

The appropriation of public space in Manchuria took place in several stages. Before the founding of the puppet state of Manshûkoku, it was mainly the civil agent of Japanese dominance in the region, the Mantetsu, which structured the public urban space with all kinds of infrastructure projects executed by its construction section. Its activities were first restricted to its so-called concession territories adjacent to its railroads. Since these areas were mostly empty or scarcely developed spaces, the city planners and architects of the Mantetsu had the unique chance to build urban structures from scratch. They employed concepts which they often imported for instance from Europe because they deemed them modern.

The Japanese dominance in Manchuria reached a new stage with the founding of the puppet state of Manshûkoku. This new state did not only need a civil infrastructure of railway stations, hotels, hospitals and school buildings, it also needed a new administrative infrastructure now. One of the basic requirements of a country is a capital with buildings housing the different institutions connected with the government. The Japanese dominated government used this occasion to conceptualise a new regional centre with the new capital city of Xinjing/Shinkyô. This was a deliberate move away from Fengtian, the former regional centre of culture and administration. The new centre was conceptualised along a clear symbolic layout of power distribution with the headquarters of the Kantô Army at the apex and the palace of the nominal head of state in a compromised location.

In many respects Manshûkoku was used by its Japanese 'handlers' to create a new type of modernity, an East Asian Modern. Young Japanese architects and city planners were given the chance to realise their ideas of state of the art architecture in Manchuria. The result of their shaping the public space was also a manifestation of Japan's claim to lead the former backward area of Northeast China into modernity. The specific form of urbanisation and city planning administered by Japanese authorities was meant to be the evidence that Japan had mastered Western civilisation and could thus lead the region into a material modernity. In the beginning, i.e. before the outbreak of the Second World War, this effort was acknowledged by Western observers. After the beginning of the Sino-Japanese War in 1937, however, the focus of the attention shifted from the infrastructural achievements of the Mantetsu and the government of Manshûkoku to Japanese aggression on the Asian continent. The myth of the new Asian modernity in Manchuria was only taken seriously by the Japanese public. Japanese tourists travelled to Manshûkoku even in the late 1930s in large numbers to tour the Manchurian project and experience the 'Japanese achievements' there first hand.

For the non-Japanese inhabitants of Manshûkoku these 'Japanese achievements' were a constant reminder of their oppression. However, the Japanese city planning and architecture had shaped the urban spaces in Manchuria on such a massive scale that it could not be eradicated after the end of the Japanese domination. The only symbols of Japanese oppression which were more or less fully demolished were the Shintô shrines that had been constructed all over the country. They were seen as a pure embodiment of the Japanese emperor system and the foreign culture that was forced upon the non-Japanese people in Manchuria and were torn down as soon as possible. Only in rare cases were the buildings refurbished and put to another use (Nishikawa 1996b: 258–259). The administrative infrastructure as well as other civil infrastructure like stations and hospitals, however, had to be used out of necessity even after the end of the civil war between Chinese Nationalists and Chinese Communists and the founding of the People's Republic of China (PRC) in 1949, since there were no other buildings to accommodate the new institutions of the PRC and no money to construct new buildings. Thus although the contents and the function of the buildings which had housed the former agents who had tried to create the new East Asian Modern changed, the architectural hardware of the Japanese appropriation of public space in Manchuria has largely survived until today.

References

Adachi Kinnosuke (1933): *Tales of Three Cities in Manchuria.* Tokyo: South Manchuria Railway Company.

Bakich, Olga (2001): 'Émigré Identity: The Case of Harbin.' In: Lahusen, Thomas (ed.) *Harbin and Manchuria: Place, Space, and Identity.* Special Issue of the South Atlantic Quarterly, 99 (1), 51–73.

Beasley, William G. (1987): *Japanese Imperialism, 1894–1945.* Oxford: Clarendon Press; New York: Oxford University Press.

Clausen, Sören; Thögersen, Stig (1995): *The Making of a Chinese City: History and Historiography in Harbin.* Armonk/N.Y. and London: M.E. Sharpe.

Coaldrake, William H. (1996): *Architecture and Authority in Japan.* London and New York: Routledge.

Coox, Alvin D. (1989): 'The Kwantung Army Dimension.' In: Duus, Peter, Myers, Ramon H. and Peattie, Mark R. (eds) *The Japanese Informal Empire in China, 1895–1937.* Princeton: Princeton University Press, 395–428.

Cordes, Ernst (1936): *Das jüngste Kaiserreich. Schlafendes/wachendes Mandschukuo [The youngest empire: Sleeping/waking Manchukuo].* Frankfurt/Main: Societäts-Verlag.

Duara, Prasenjit (2003): *Sovereignty and Authenticity. Manchukuo and the East Asian Modern.* Oxford *et al.*: Rowman & Littlefield Publishers, Inc.

Itani Hiroshi; Koshino Takeshi and Kado Yukihiro (2000): 'Building Construction in Southern Sakhalin During the Japanese Colonial Period (1905–1945): Buildings, Architects, Contractors and Construction Sections of Government Offices' in: *Acta Slavica Iaponica,* 17: 130–160.

Japan tsûrisuto byûrô (ed.) (1941): *Manshû ryokô nenkan: Shôwa 16 nen [Yearbook of Manchuria Travel: 1941].* Tokyo: Hakubunkan.

Jin Yang (2001): 'The Head Office.' In: *Taipei Review,* January 2001: 30–31.

Jordan, David (1996): *Die Neuerschaffung von Paris: Baron Haussmann und seine Stadt [The recreation of Paris: Baron Haussmann and his city].* Frankfurt/Main: S. Fischer.

Koshizawa Akira (1988): *Manshûkoku no shuto keikaku [The planning of a capital city for Manshûkoku].* Tokyo: Nihon keizai hyôronsha.

Lankov, Andrei (2004) 'The Seoul Capitol Building' In: *The Korea Times,* 4 August 2004 (online edition: http://search.hankooki.com/times/times_view.php?term=lankov++&path=hankooki3/times/lpage/opinion/200408/kt2004080418425354130.htm&media=kt).

Lankov, Andrei (2005) 'Going Down in History' In: *The Korea Times,* 24 February 2005 (online edition: http://search.hankooki.com/times/times_view.php?term=lankov++&path=hankooki3/times/lpage/opinion/200502/kt2005022419245054130.htm&media=kt).

Matsusaka, Tak Y. (1996): 'Managing Occupied Manchuria, 1931–1934.' In: Duus, Peter, Myers, Ramon H. and Peattie, Mark (eds) *The Japanese Wartime Empire, 1931–1945.* Princeton: Princeton University Press, 97–135.

Nishizawa Yasuhiko (1996a) *'Manshû' toshi monogatari: Harubin, Dairen, Shinyô, Chôshun [City tales from Manchuria: Harbin, Dalian, Shenyang, Changchun].* Tokyo: Kawade shobô shinsha.

Nishizawa Yasuhiko (1996b) *Umi o watatta Nihonjin kenchikuka – 20 seiki zenpan no Chûgoku tôhoku chihô ni okeru kenchiku katsudô [Japanese architects who went overseas: The activities of architects in the northeastern region of China in the first half of the 20th century].* Tokyo: Shôkokusha.

Nishizawa Yasuhiko (2000) *Mantetsu: 'Manshû' no kyojin [The South Manchurian Railway Company: The Manchurian giant].* Tokyo: Kawade shobô shinsha.

Reichardt, Hans J. and Schäche, Wolfgang (2005): *Von Berlin nach Germania [From Berlin to Germania]*. Berlin: Transit Verlag.

Scherer, James A.B. (1933) *Manchukuo: A Bird's Eye View*. Tokyo: The Hokuseido Press.

Schönberger, Angela (1981) *Die neue Reichskanzlei in Berlin von Albert Speer: zum Zusammenhang von nationalsozialistischer Ideologie und Architektur [The New Reich Chancellery in Berlin by Albert Speer: The relation of National Socialist ideology and architecture]*. Berlin: Mann.

Tucker, David (2005): 'City Planning without Cities. Order and Chaos in Utopian Manchukuo.' In: Tamanoi, Mariko Asano (ed.) *Crossed Histories: Manchuria in the Age of Empire*. Honolulu: University of Hawai'i Press, 53–81.

Weber, Max (1947): *The Theory of Social and Economic Organization*. Glencoe: Free Press. Translation by Talcott Parsons of volume 1, part one of 'Wirtschaft und Gesellschaft' first published in 1922.

Wheatley, Paul; see, Thomas (1978): *From Court to Capital: A Tentative Interpretation of the Origins of the Japanese Urban Tradition*. Chicago and London: The University of Chicago Press.

Young, Louise (1998): *Japan's Total Empire: Manchuria and the Culture of Wartime Imperialism*. Berkeley; Los Angeles; London: University of California Press.

4 Re-uniting a divided city

High-rises, conflict and urban space in central Kyoto

Christoph Brumann

Introduction

As anyone who ever felt disturbed by traffic congestion, construction noise or littered sidewalks can confirm, urban spaces are contested. One person's use of such spaces affects that of other persons, and while the effect may sometimes be welcome – such as when a vibrant street life is seen as attractive – it is not always so, with people's judgements of what constitutes a positive addition to their perceptual environment varying widely on top. Nuisances may have the emphemerality of a cigarette butt on the pavement but can also be more permanent, such as when formerly public spaces are fenced in or when new buildings change accustomed views. Very few such interventions will be seen as negative by everyone; usually, some people benefit, often very considerably. The question, then, is how to reconcile these benefits with the losses of others, particularly when the latter derive from the development of privately owned real estate. Who has the right to decide over the city, particularly its publicly accessible parts, and what benefits are offered in compensation when these public parts are negatively affected? These are perennial concerns in cities the world over.

In Japan, Kyoto has been at the forefront of this debate for a long time. For the longest part, this was a highly fractioned debate, with many little localised battles fought independently, often under the shared assumption that they deal with essentially private matters. Within just a few years in the 2000s, however, this assessment has been completely reversed. Not only is Kyoto urban space a matter of legitimate public concern now, but the city also has installed the most stringent building control measures of any Japanese city and is regarded as a model for similar ambitions across the nation. What the future of Japanese urban space may hold in store may possibly be anticipated here, and the purpose of this chapter therefore is to give an analytic account of the previous situation in Kyoto, the great change and the contributing social forces. In the Lefebvrian categories sketched in the introduction, it is also an enquiry of how *espace perçu* (the given physical realities of the city and people's set routines in dealing with them) and *espace conçu* (the city as envisioned by planning regulations and initiatives) do not just provide the pre-existing framework for *espace vécu* (the appropriations of space in people's social activities) but can also be lastingly influenced by the latter, particularly when these activities become more organised.

Kyoto's townscape troubles

In a country that counts among the leaders of global modernity, Kyoto is known as the haven of tradition. It was the capital and emperor's seat between 794 and 1868 and one of the leading urban centres throughout Japanese history. Today, the city is overshadowed by the modern capital and global city Tokyo and by the regional competitors Osaka and Kobe, but it continues to be a stronghold for all kinds of traditional pursuits and institutions. Most sects of Japanese Buddhism and many traditional arts and crafts, including the influential schools of tea ceremony, have their national headquarters here and are serviced by large numbers of traditional artisans. For kimono production and trade, too, Kyoto is central, and the geisha districts of the city (cf. Dalby 1983) rank among the most renowned and mystified (e.g., Golden 1997 and the eponymous feature film). Above all else, the around 50 million visitors annually come for the city's unmatched architectural heritage of Buddhist temples, Shintoist shrines, imperial palaces and gardens, including 14 UNESCO World Heritage sites. The visitors search for ancient Japan and its refined aesthetics in what is often called *Nihon no kokoro no furusato* ('home of the Japanese heart/mind'). Heritage has tangible benefits for the city: not only tourism but also other local industries and the large number of educational institutions partake of its high-brow, elegant reputation.

Kyoto is widely considered a scenic city. Not only are there more historic buildings to be relished than in any other Japanese city of comparable size, the medium-sized mountain ranges surrounding the city and the river spaces traversing it provide for beautiful vistas. But in present-day Kyoto and particularly in the centre of town, there are also streets and quarters that offer little in terms of visual appeal and do not look much different from any other Japanese city. And often enough, modern high-rise architecture blocks the view of the surrounding mountains. Kyoto's residents have not been complacent about this, and new construction has ignited public controversy so often that the special term *keikan ronsô* ('townscape disputes') has been coined for these quarrels. Landmark cases were the debates about the 131-metre tall Kyoto Tower in 1964 and about the new station building and the new Kyoto Hotel (both 60 metres) around 1990. In these three cases, the protests did not prevent the completion of the buildings as planned but in 1998 the mayor withdrew his proposal to build a copy of a Parisian footbridge in the centre of town, which had met vociferous opposition. Citizen protests were also successful against a number of other planned developments such as dams and golf courses in or near the foothills in the 1980s and 1990s, and since then these areas where most of the famous historic sites are concentrated have been comparatively well protected by the city's building codes.

What continued to proceed unabated until very recently, however, was the *manshon rasshu* ('*manshon* rush') in the centre of town. This area where hardly a building stood taller than three storeys in the 1960s is nowadays dotted with high-rises, and most of these are so-called *manshon* (from English 'mansion'), that is, condominiums with sometimes more than a hundred apartment units. The general appeal of Kyoto and the closeness to subway lines to Osaka and Kobe and to a large array of shopping, medical, educational and cultural facilities have nurtured a 'city-centre return boom' (*toshin kaiki*), comparable to what other Japanese cities now experience. Commuters to the larger cities, post-parenthood couples returning from the suburbs, the rising number of permanent singles and families attracted by the top-level schools and cram schools (*juku*) in the area sustain a lively demand for affordable living space. The *manshon rasshu* is often associated with the 'Bubble' period of unrestrained land speculation of the late 1980s and early 1990s but in actual fact, most *manshon* in Kyoto are younger, and the tallest were built only in the last couple of years. Almost anyone in Kyoto I asked dislikes *manshon* and denies that high-rise development proceeds in an ideal manner, and almost any new condominium provokes anything from silent grumbling to organised resistance in the immediate neighbourhood.

Therefore, one should expect citizen protests to be as widespread as in the above-mentioned controversies. Contrary to cases such as the French footbridge, however, the *manshon* issue has had difficulty in becoming a truly public concern, and little restrained the high-rise advance for a long time. This requires an explanation. But so also does the sudden turnaround in 2007 when Kyoto City adopted a building code that brought the *manshon* frenzy to what appears to be a complete stop. Relying on ethnographic fieldwork in 1998/99 (17 months), 2001 (two months) and 2007 (one month),[1] I will attempt to provide one in the following which will lead us into the deep structures of the social production of Japanese urban space, in a case whose most recent evolution could become a model for the future development of cities all over the country.

Legal and economic background

High-rises in central Kyoto were built from the 1980s into the mid-2000s, first of all, because they could be built: almost all of them observed existing building regulations painstakingly. The current building height regime in Kyoto goes back to the building code of 1973 which itself responded to a series of national-level legal amendments in the mid and late 1960s (Hohn 2000: 77, 80–81, Sorensen 2002: 213–214). This major overhaul established the 'floor-area ratio' (FAR; *yôsekiritsu*) as the central measure for urban development. Rather than limiting the absolute height, this variable (the total floor area of all stories divided by the lot area, expressed in per cent) controls the bulk of buildings, allowing the developers greater freedom to expand either horizontally or vertically. In contrast to other cities, Kyoto City's officials – who had just experienced the Kyoto Tower dispute – managed to retain absolute height limits. In the core area of the Tanoji district, however, these were set at 31 metres (corresponding to 10 or 11 stories) for the narrow back streets and 45 metres (14 or 15 stories) for the main avenues, combined with FARs of 400 and 700 per cent respectively. The area was also zoned as a 'Commercial District' (*shôgyô chiiki*) rather than a residential one. This means that slant-line (*dôro shasen*) regulations are eased and a neighbour's 'right to sunshine' (*nisshôken*) may be ignored so that new buildings can quite literally come within arm's reach of the houses next door. In actual fact, almost the entire area was still residential, and many back streets remain so today. The existing traditional town houses (*machiya*) did not rise higher than 8 metres, with an FAR of rarely more than 160 per cent. Therefore, the building code of 1973, although stricter than those of other large cities, was a blueprint for redevelopment even when some time had to pass before its potential began to be exploited in earnest.

In the late 1980s, however, high-rise development took off, and what little discretion Kyoto City still had under the highly centralised Japanese planning system was used to ease rather than hinder the trend. In 1988, for example, the city assembly passed an ordinance introducing the national-level 'comprehensive planning system' (*sôgô sekkei seido*) as a municipal planning tool. This provision allows for additional height beyond the applicable limits if part of the plot is left unbuilt and made accessible to the public, and while it was passed to allow rebuilding Kyoto Hotel at 60 metres' height, numerous high-rise condominiums also made use of it in subsequent years. In 1994, the *manshon* received a further boost by a national law allowing for discounting all jointly used space (halls, walkways, garages etc.) from their FAR, resulting in a bulk bonus of around 20 per cent. Also, street access for fire engines was no longer prescribed as long as fire hoses could reach the building from a more remotely placed engine. This means that large plots of land surrounded by narrow, often crooked alleys or lying in the centre rather than on the edges of a street block – not at all rare in Kyoto – have become potential *manshon* space too.

Promoting the *manshon* industry was an express goal of the latter amendments, given that corporate and public construction slumped in the recession of the 1990s and early 2000s. And indeed, condominium construction went up rather than down in that period: the steeply dropping land prices and fierce competition in the construction business made the apartments increasingly affordable. Also, the land supply in central Kyoto was steadily refilled by the many bankruptcies particularly in the kimono wholesale business that brought comparatively large and centrally located lots on a market where *manshon* developers were often the only buyers. For all these reasons, the cost of a *manshon* apartment of 80 square metres in central Kyoto had fallen to the thirties of million Yen in 2001 whereas it would have been double or even three times as much a decade earlier. By 2001, the *manshon* market had already retreated from the back streets into the zones along the main roads with their more tolerant construction limits: anything below 11 storeys was no longer profitable, and such heights could only be realised in the 45-metre zone. But there, the *manshon rasshu* continued in full swing: while there were only a handful of high-rises with more than 11 storeys in 2001, their number had increased to at least 40 by 2007, with the skyline of central Kyoto becoming ever more jagged.

In almost all cases, the new *manshon* are of the *bunjo* type, meaning that the apartment units are sold to individual owners rather than rented, preferably already before the house is completed. This brings the developers maximum short-term profits but, rather predictably, has not always worked in favour of construction quality. Press articles and hundreds of internet homepages complain about 'faulty *manshon*' (*kekkan manshon*), sloppily built condominiums in which, for instance, the water pipes start to break after a mere ten years. *Manshon* apartments could lose as much as half of their value within the first few years, with their resale price sometimes dropping below the remaining installments of the housing loan, a 'negative equity trap' (Waswo 2002: 109). So far, however, such perils have not deterred potential buyers. This is mainly because other than in the Bubble period, *manshon* apartments are not sought for their asset value but for using them up, so to speak, in a housing market where the choice of rental apartments especially for families continues to be highly limited (Waswo 2002: 59). Young families often aspire to move on to a single-family home in the suburbs at a later stage, and elderly couples with their children safely established also care little about the future resale potential. Buyers and developers thus come to collude in what can be called a culture of throwaway housing: poorly executed as many Japanese condominiums are by international standards, large-scale refashioning or a total rebuild may become imperative after only 30 years, as is currently happening with the first generation of suburban *manshon*. Yet such measures require a consensus among the many dozens of apartment owners that, given the diversity of their financial resources and time perspectives, is difficult to achieve. In the suburbs, *manshon* rebuilds are financed by adding floors, with the proceeds from selling the extra apartments paying the investment for the initial owners. Yet the *manshon* in the central Kyoto of the 2000s already exhausted the height and FAR limits fully, raising the question what their future would be.

Developers, neighbours and local government

There are a number of reasons for the *manshon*'s lack of popularity among those who do not inhabit them. To start with, most Kyotoites agree that the high-rises do not only block precious vistas, they are also considered rather unsightly themselves. A survey in which I had 170 informants living and/or working in Kyoto sort a pack of building photos according to their personal preferences revealed that *manshon* are the least liked building type for almost everyone, regardless of age, gender, education or origin. I heard complaints about another high-rise going up and disfiguring Kyoto's built environment all the time whereas positive comments were extremely rare.

The closer one actually gets to a *manshon*, however, the more other than visual concerns move to the forefront. Demolition of the old structure and construction of the new one can take a year or more, filled with noise, dust and the danger of accidents affecting the neighbours. When the new structure is completed, its physical presence makes itself felt. Depending on the direction, neighbours may be cast into perpetual shadow, having to live with the lights switched on all day, and they also face increased heating costs, blocked air circulation, drainage problems when huge walls cast back the rain onto their plot, gardens ruined by lack of sunshine, and the absence of visual privacy. Also, the ground may shift under the weight of the massive structure next door, warping the framework particularly of the foundation-less traditional houses so that their windows, doors and sliding partitions no longer function properly. *Manshon* companies are liable for obvious damages, and the condition of neighbouring houses is usually documented previous to construction. Many neighbours lack the expertise to make such documentation watertight, however, and it falls on them to prove that the structure next door did in fact cause whatever damage occurred.

In addition to its physical presence, a *manshon* brings in dozens of new households and the corresponding pedestrian and vehicle traffic. While this may help to reinvigorate neighbourhood associations and local festivals, not everyone will appreciate the new liveliness, and long-lasting social ties that have bound the old-time neighbours for generations are challenged or even disrupted by the influx of scores of newcomers who often are not interested in contributing their own share to neighbourhood life. The attending benefits tend to concentrate on particular people, such as shop owners, or they spread far beyond the immediate neighbourhood, such as increases in the city's tax revenues or refilled classes in the nearest school. In contrast, many neighbours have little to look forward to when another *manshon* goes up.

Therefore, neighbours often do not resign themselves to the inevitable and join forces for *manshon hantai* (*manshon* protests) instead. In doing so, however, they often face an uphill battle. To begin with, they receive little advance information. Typically, neighbours only learn about a high-rise project when the plot is being cleared and the prescribed signboard with the construction details goes up. At that stage, however, a building permit often has been already applied for – or even issued by – the municipal authorities so that the developers have a head start. Almost all *manshon* plans follow the building rules, so bringing legal charges will only delay but not prevent the project. *Manshon* companies are not immune to other sorts of pressure, however, so that houses adorned with banners, streamers and posters protesting about a nearby construction project are a common sight in central Kyoto. As potential buyers will not only visit the model apartments set up elsewhere but also walk to the construction site, they thus learn of the conflict, and informants assured me that at least some of them reconsider their buying interest.

Manshon developers therefore try to avoid such open protests. Their first step is to offer so-called 'solution money' (*kaiketsu-kin*); routinely, about 5 per cent of the total cost is set aside for such compensations. The developers also often propose minor size amendments, for example reducing the height by one floor or two, although it is often difficult to tell whether these are premeditated. If neighbours do not comply, many developers will then try to drive wedges into the neighbours' solidarity, for instance by going from door to door and spreading bad rumours about protest leaders or secretly buying the cooperation of key individuals. Tales of protest leaders who themselves ended up in the best apartments are part of *manshon hantai* lore. Another strategy is suing the neighbours for damages, and while this is usually without substance, it stills manages to scare off many people. When neighbours still don't give in, threats of physical violence or actual exposure to it have also been reported. I myself witnessed no such instance but in one conflict I followed closely, underworld-looking men were overheard loudly discussing the dangers of *manshon* protests in a nearby café.

In all this, developers have an edge over the protesting neighbours since they are big corporations with nationwide experience in applying such measures whereas most neighbours are beginners. Also in many cases, the developers do not officially figure themselves and instead leave the shadier business to subcontractors or even the subcontractors of subcontractors so that their own corporate image remains clean. The subcontractors most often pose as construction or demolition firms but 'neighbourhood measures' (*kinrin taisaku*) are their real specialisation, and some of them make no attempt at looking respectable.

An aspect that often complicates matters is the unresolved issue of the *burakumin* or, as they are most commonly called in Kyoto, *dôwa*. About 10 per cent of the city's population are believed to belong to this discriminated minority. As is well known, it encompasses the practitioners of various polluting or despised professions and their descendants but otherwise is culturally indistinct from majority Japanese so that someone's place of birth in a *tokushû buraku* (literally 'special settlement') is the only hint to a *dôwa* identity. In the post-war period, discrimination has become illegal, and Kyoto City has spearheaded affirmative action policies of all sorts, often reacting to public protest by *dôwa* representatives. These policies are officially abolished today but continue in a sort of clandestine way. A major scandal exposed in 2003, for instance, involved the payment of public subsidies to several *dôwa* organisations in Kyoto. Tellingly, the bureaucrats in charge said that they had seen through the inflated bills and fictitious services but had not wanted to expose them for fear of damaging mutual relations between *dôwa* and non-*dôwa*. The standard line about the importance of 'human rights' (*jinken*) on almost every brochure and publication by Kyoto City tells it all: citizens are reminded that *dôwa* continue to be entitled to redress for past injuries, but at the same time, the issue is not to be named openly. Many Kyotoites behave accordingly: even university professors would commence any more detailed intimations to me with '*jitsu wa hanashite wa ikenai kedo* ... (I really shouldn't tell you but...)', and even otherwise courageous citizen activists would remind one another of speaking softly so that passers-by could not overhear them.

The subcontractors entrusted with intimidating the neighbours often parade their – real or fictitious – *dôwa* origins since they know that most majority Japanese in Kyoto will become apprehensive. 'When it is *yakuza* [i.e. the Japanese mafia], you can at least call the police, but against *dôwa*, they won't do anything', one activist's wife told me, and other informants said that the situation in Kyoto has developed into 'counter-discrimination' (*gyaku-sabetsu*). I cannot tell whether this is an exaggerated perception but it appears to be widespread. Also, the real *dôwa* in the subconctractors' ranks are most likely to know who is a fellow *dôwa*, even among those who have successfully moved out of *dôwa* areas and live inconspicuously in the midst of majority neighbours. I was told of one case where this threat of exposure was believed to be the reason behind the sudden withdrawal of an initially courageous neighbour from *manshon hantai*.

Through a combination of these measures and by simply pushing through, *manshon* companies manage to realise their plans with only minimal modifications. They hold the prescribed information meetings for the neighbours that, as I witnessed, can develop into rather angry exchanges, good opportunities to have one's illusions about harmony-loving Japanese set straight. But there, the neighbours will meet only junior staff or the subcontractor's representatives, and they often consider the fact that the companies refuse to even speak to them in person as specially frustrating. Incidentally, one also never sees representatives of the *manshon* firms in public discussions of town planning. These corporations avoid having a public face as much as possible and do get away with it.

When all these tactics achieve their goals, neighbourhood solidarity often ends up seriously damaged, with social wounds that may go deeper than those produced by the physical building. Not all developers behave the same, but the fact that some do is common knowledge, and even the less ruthless companies will no doubt profit from the apprehension their peers inspire among many ordinary citizens.

What do public authorities do about these conflicts? Fairly little, most *manshon* opponents would have responded until recently. City government officials claim that their hands are tied, given that they must observe the legal framework and issue a building permit; and in fact, the city was sentenced to paying damages in a prominent case where it had tried to delay it. Still, even though many bureaucrats personally and sometimes also publicly deplore the current development, I never heard of their passing secret warnings to the neighbours once a large plot of land changes hands. Throughout the 1990s and early 2000s, there have been repeated discussions of downzoning (i.e. the establishment of stricter height limits) in the city government's bureaus and the several advisory councils (*shingikai*) it set up for discussing the future of the city centre. These never led to substantive action, however, not least so because quite a few well-meaning bureaucrats argued against coercion and instead sought progress through *machizukuri*, i.e. consciousness-raising and (in this case guided) grassroots activism on a neighbourhood level. Many *manshon* opponents tend to see such activities as a mere diversion, however, and see undue closeness between the current conservative, LDP-supported city government and the real estate and construction industry, sometimes even identifying particular bureaucrats whom they suspect of corruption. I must emphasise that most bureaucrats I spoke to gave little reason for such suspicions and many showed genuine concern, but this found no reflection in the city's official policies, much as these are usually based on the bureaucrats' drafts and not on the elected assemblypeople's input.

Remaining passive also made good economic sense for the city. Municipalities in Japan have little fiscal autonomy, similar to Germany but very different from, for example, the United States. Around two-thirds of a city's budget are handed down from the national ministries, but these monies usually come with narrow directives and often have to be laboriously applied for. Therefore, the locally raised taxes – 36 per cent of Kyoto City's total revenue in 2002 – are particularly desirable. And almost half of these are made up by the fixed assets tax (*kotei shisan-zei*) and the town planning tax (*toshi keikaku-zei*) raised on land and buildings. New and large buildings are most valuable and are taxed at the highest rates, and so also are those plots of land that have the loosest restrictions and thereby the highest building potential. Given that Kyoto City's finances are at a historical level of depletion, it is therefore understandable that the city hasn't become too active about downzoning, and since the city's bureaucrats had to endure repeated salary cuts in recent years, they too will not mind attempts to secure the tax base.

It thus paid for the city to celebrate the historical architecture and the revitalised traditional town houses and model future visions of the city on them while at the same time refraining from imposing limitations that would really prevent *manshon* from being built. In addition, there are also other advantages: the two central wards Nakagyô and Shimogyô that since the 1960s had lost nearly half of their populations have begun to grow again, and without the *manshon* dwellers, shrinkage would continue apace, as in other parts of town. Such growth, of course, is good for local businesses and schools and makes the centre livelier, and in an ironic twist, it also brings patrons to the restaurants and shops opened in renovated historical buildings and *machiya*. Debate about the question whether the advantages of *manshon* development outweigh the townscape damage and the direct neighbours' plight would therefore be not at all unreasonable. Not much of such general discussion was taking place until recently, however, and even when the *manshon* firms confronted angry neighbours, cost pressure and the legality of their projects were usually the only arguments they brought forth.

Privatising public space

This brings me to what I see as the root of the problem: *manshon* trouble continued for such a long time because there was a tacit agreement that the high-rise condominiums are a matter between the developers and the immediate neighbours of the building site, that is the people whose private property is most affected. It is obvious that the *manshon* companies want it that way, thus minimising the number of opponents, but so do the neighbours at a gut level, often against their own best intentions.

One revealing case concerned the working meeting of one *manshon hantai* group. It had formed to oppose a structure that in addition to its height of 45 metres (15 floors) and width of 86 metres was planned with an unattractive façade with open walkways to a major avenue that had just been expensively refashioned into Kyoto's 'symbol road'. In the meeting, the activists discussed their plan to form a citizens' group to debate the future of that road, in an attempt to engage citizens beyond the immediate neighbourhood. All the more surprisingly, the activists quickly agreed that there should be two different membership fees for that new group, a higher one for immediate neighbours and a lower one for all others. When I asked if this didn't contradict their very intention of making the 'symbol road' a public cause, they objected at first, but a bit later they dropped the idea of different fees. I assume that this meant I had a point but it is significant that the divide between neighbours and non-neighbours is such a deeply ingrained impulse. And reflecting the same attitude, in the further activities of that group, two direct neighbours of the planned *manshon* were made the official spokespeople of the protest. Much more than they, the leaders of a successful neighbourhood revitalization initiative were the driving forces but since these lived further away – even if only a couple of steps – it was understood that placing them in the forefront would have undermined the protest's credibility. Such tacit privileging of the immediate neighbours crops up all the time in Kyoto, and countless other instances observed during fieldwork could be cited.

The result of this attitude is a private battle between just two parties, a corporate giant and a small group of often inexperienced neighbours. The city government is accused of passivity by the neighbours but usually because it refuses to side with their specific plight rather than because of its general planning policy. And largely left out too are the buyers of the *manshon* apartments. Several times I heard *manshon* opponents say that the buyers cannot be blamed for the developers' sins. Any indirect responsibility of those who through their demand sustain such sharp practices, however, was not addressed.

Of course, the direct neighbours are hit hardest by a high-rise, so privileging their concerns is understandable. But doing so means that all those who are more tangentially affected – such as the tens or even hundreds of thousands of residents and visitors who will lay eyes on a building at some point during its existence – have no place in the conflicts. As a consequence, the public interest in a visually attractive city went largely unrepresented even when in the aggregate, the combined weak interests of ordinary 'city users' may be weightier than the strong interests of just a handful of direct neighbours.

In the past, this privatisation of public scape was quite effective for building control. In the Tokugawa period, the neighbourhoods of Kyoto, the so-called *chô* or *(o-)chônai* reaching from one street corner to the next, were tiny republics onto themselves, free to regulate their own affairs as long as they didn't cause trouble for their samurai overlords. Neighbourhoods gave themselves written regulations, the so-called *chôshikimoku* or *chôsadame*, and in Kyoto a considerable portion of these were building regulations. Most dealt with fire prevention but the appearance of houses was included too (Itô 1993). Neighbours today retain their right to make their own rules: in the Building Standards Law (*Kenchiku kijun-hô*), there is a provision for *kenchiku kyôtei* (building covenants). Owners of contiguous plots of land may set up mutually binding restrictions on buildings and their uses, usually for periods of five or ten years but freely renewable. This legal instrument is extensively used in newly built suburban areas of Kyoto. In the central city, however, the concluded *kenchiku kyôtei* could until recently be counted on the fingers of two hands. Moreover, almost all of them were adopted in defense against a concrete *manshon* threat and not out of an unprovoked, preemptive concern for the future of one's living environment.

Well into the twentieth century, neighbours depended on one another and could not easily ignore each other's concerns. Households expected to remain within the neighbourhood or nearby where their reputation would travel with them even in future generations, and they often relied on family businesses servicing local customers, so they had an incentive to conform to social expectations. In the age of education-based careers and job mobility, however, such restraining concerns are often gone. It pays to move out and sell choice real estate, and those who come in the old residents' stead – the *manshon* companies – have no time horizons at all, as their ambition is to sell all apartments and thereby sever the connection with their product as soon as possible. Since the developers service a nationwide market, they also have little to fear from ruining their local reputation; their commercials on national television easily make up for the damage. Time horizons are short too also for the many buyers that are interested mainly in living space for the immediate future, not in a lasting asset for subsequent generations. Given all these difficulties, it is understandable that neighbours often join undeclared non-aggression pacts and will not mobilise for building covenants: even two of the major activists against the French bridge project – people not accustomed to give in lightly – told me that they had remained silent when their neighbours had rebuilt at undesirable heights. They described this as typical for Kyoto and explained that thereby, they had at least kept their moral right to do what they please with their own property in the future.

The new building code of 2007 and the contributing forces

Anyone familiar with the situation heretofore described can only be surprised about what happened in 2007. In spring, the city assembly adopted the *keikan jôrei* ('townscape ordinance'), actually a set of amendments to six existing municipal ordinances.[2] These expand the protected areas around a number of famous historic sites and traditional neighbourhoods and along the rivers, and almost the entire historic core of Kyoto (as of the late nineteenth century) is now an 'Aesthetic Area' (*bikan chiku*). In all cases, this means that building regulations have become stricter, clearer and more locally specific. The new rules are modeled on the historic architecture and ask for traditional features or visually similar solutions whereas other options such as certain non-traditional colours for walls and roofs have been banned. Even in the core area, new structures in the back streets now have to feature gabled roofs at traditional angles (*kôhai yane*) covered with clay roof tiles (*kawara*) or copper sheets, separate roofs (*hisashi*) over the ground floor, a setback of the façade from the fourth floor upwards (i.e. everything exceeding traditional building heights), and enclosures of free spaces and parking lots by traditional-looking earthen walls (*hei*) and gates (*mon*). In a particularly bold step for an East Asian city, rooftop billboards and all blinking neon signs have been banned in the entire city. The permissible sizes for shop signs and billboards have been greatly reduced, and those that do not conform must be removed within the next seven years.

The new rules also include special provisions for a number of famous vistas, introducing the concept of *chôbo keikan* ('vista landscape'). The views offering themselves from 38 specific vantage points may no longer be affected by new construction. Some of these vantage points are located within the World Heritage temples, shrines, and gardens and the imperial palace (*gosho*) and detached palaces (*rikyû*) and are meant to ensure that any new construction in the vicinity remains invisible from inside the precincts. Other vantage points more actively protect what can in fact be seen, including several celebrated views from the city into the hills, from famous lookout points such as the Daimonjiyama mountain or the wooden verandah of the Kiyomizudera temple onto the city, and along particular rivers. Not only do these rules prohibit new buildings from blocking the view, they also impose particular roof shapes and colours on those that stand within 500 metres' distance. Here again, the specific rules are detailedly adapted to the respective locality, in remarkable contrast to the old rules that only set very general limitations.

The most momentous measure, however, is the reduction of permissible building heights. Instead of the previous five height zones (10, 15, 20, 31 and 45 metres) there now are six (10, 12, 15, 20, 25 and 31 metres), and on more than 30 per cent of the city's area – including almost the entire historic centre and hillside area – heights have been decreased. In most cases, this means reduction to the next-lower step on the rung, which along the main streets in the city centre already replaces the former limit of 45 metres with 31 metres. In the back streets of the centre, however, limits drop by no less than three steps, from 31 to 15 metres.

It is estimated that more than 1,800 buildings – many of them *manshon* – violate the new restrictions so that a six-digit number of Kyotoites now live or work in technically illegal structures. Of course, the new rules cannot be applied retrospectively, and in contrast to signage, no transition periods can be imposed on those already existing buildings that do not conform to the new demands. The life span of most modern-day construction in Japan, however, is rather limited. The prefabricated structures (*purehabu*) that are by far the most common single-family homes cannot be repaired and become ramshackle in a mere 30 years or so, and as already outlined, ordinary *manshon* do also require at least a major overhaul after such a time period. Reconstruction at the same height and with the current design features, however, will be impossible now. So if the new rules remain in place for the next half-century or so, only a few buildings violating the height restrictions will remain, and the desired historicising design features will have spread widely. This is a bold move, and it is all the more astonishing as other big cities go exactly the opposite way: in Tokyo or Osaka, the highest *tawâ manshon* (tower *manshon*) are approaching 200 metres, and local governments actively court the developers for the tax income these structures bring.

During my field stay of 2001, such a turn of events was still nothing short of unthinkable: the privatisation of public space described above was the expected state of affairs, and most *manshon* opponents were pessimistic about the future. One new condominium, however, had just made waves: this 10-storied, 31 metres tall structure had just been set into the core of one of the large rectangular street blocks in the centre, and while it was hardly visible from the nearest streets and therefore not primarily a townscape problem, it came as close as one or two metres to the rear of some of the old, two-storied houses fronting the streets. Therefore, Kyoto City's standing Construction Commission (Kenchiku Shinsa-kai) – a body largely nominated by the mayor and therefore usually docile – complained that while the building observed construction rules, it violated all the city's planning goals and *machizukuri* efforts. Reacting to this unprecedented step, the mayor summoned another advisory council composed of university professors, lawyers, business representatives, other experts and the standard two ordinary citizens (one male, one female) meant to bring in the people's voice. Following its recommendation, a number of new slant-line regulations for the centre's back streets were adopted in 2003. Except on very large lots, this made the full exploitation of the height limits impossible. *Manshon* activity had retreated to the main-street areas by that time, however, and there, everything was left unchanged.

Very likely, this would have been the limit of what Kyoto could have achieved on its own, but more was to follow. Field research in 2007 suggests that this was due to a fortuitous combination of a number of forces, including national ministries, Kyoto's business leaders, a municipal administration that could not ignore their demands and citizens' groups that managed to sustain a sense of urgency among all these actors.

The local government's critics emphasize the importance of the national level, and had Kyoto City had any intention of issuing the strict rules of 2007, there would have been little sense in adopting the half-hearted ones of 2003 in the first place. The turning point in this narrative was the 'Landscape Laws' (*Keikan-hô*) passed by the Diet in 2004. Three separate laws defined landscapes and townscapes as 'common property of the people' (*kokumin kyôtsû no shisan*) and introduced new types of 'landscape areas' (*keikan chiku*) allowing more detailed prescriptions for buildings sizes, forms, colours and materials than those offered by the previous legal instruments. They also permitted the introduction of subsidies and tax incentives, and all these measures can be applied for not just by public agencies but also by NGOs or the concerned property owners. As the most important change, however, the new laws delegate planning authority to the prefectural and municipal government level rather than imposing detailed national rules. This step at long last empowers local administrations, which heretofore had only been able to use non-binding 'administrative guidance' (*gyôsei shidô*) for any town-planning measures that exceeded the scope of national laws.

This national-level legal initiative did not come out of thin air but in itself reacted to several preceding *manshon* conflicts. The most prominent of these was the legal battle about a 44-metres tall *manshon* development in Kunitachi near Tokyo that had been completed in 2001. In the opponents' eyes, the new buildings endangered the charms of the Daigaku-dôri, a well-known street lined by cherry trees that cuts through the campus of Hitotsubashi University. In 2000, the Tokyo District Court (Tôkyô chisai) ruled that these high-rises had 'impaired the townscape benefit to an unbearable degree' (*keikan rieki o jûnin gendo o koete shingai suru*) for their neighbours and ordered the removal of all building parts above 20 metres' height which practically would have meant the demolition of the entire buildings. Several appeals brought the case up to the Supreme Court (Saikô saiban-sho), which finally repealed the decision in 2006. Still, one of the usually conservative law courts had formulated a 'right to the townscape', and this increased the pressure on the national government to give this right a formal framework and pass the Landscape Laws.

In addition to this legal instrument, Kyoto City also received personal support from officials of the Ministry for Land, Infrastructure and Transport (MLIT) which absorbed the former Ministry for Construction in 2001. The temporary dispatch (*shukkô*) of ministry officials to prefectural and municipal governments for periods of three or five years is common practice in Japan and widely regarded as an important – although because of its clientelistic character also controversial – tool to cultivate relations between different government levels and to disseminate advanced expertise (Akizuki 2002, Inoki 2002). Often, these personnel dispatches are only for temporary projects but sometimes they also become routine procedure, with specific posts reserved for national dispatchees. One of the three vice-mayor posts of Kyoto is such a dispatchee position, and from 2004 to 2007 it was held by Môri Shinji, a MLIT town-planning expert who had previously been involved in drafting the Landscape Law. Informants unanimously described him as the energetic leader in the formulating Kyoto's new rules. Also, another more junior ministry official involved in drafting the national law had herself just returned from a previous stint in Kyoto. This means that the national law was formulated with Kyoto in mind, and the city then became a test case for applying the new public powers. Importantly, however, the national influence did not meet resistance among local bureaucrats. Especially among the junior ranks, informants said, many had been waiting for their chance to end the state of powerlessness, and they worked enthusiastically, even on weekends or all night long if need be.

Importantly also, the elected head of the administration, mayor Masumoto Yorikane, steadfastly defended the plans when they met public criticism in the final stage. This is the result of a major conversion since earlier, he had been more active in proposing French bridge copies than protecting Kyoto's townscape. Crucial here was the unanimous support by Kyoto's business leaders – the mayor's major political allies – for the new measures. Kyoto's business world had not always involved itself with townscape matters, particularly not in a public way. Real-estate and construction companies are part of the city's business associations, and townscape protests especially against the more prominent projects were often led by left-leaning, union-supported political forces with which Kyoto's entrepreneurs had little inclination to be associated. The turning point here was the above-mentioned 15-storied *manshon* facing the 'symbol road'. The neighbours' protest initiative managed to alert several company presidents, and it helped that one of them – the president of one business assocation – had his own 31 metres tall and architecturally more ambitious headquarters building just steps away from the new *manshon*.

Two of the presidents spoke at protest assemblies and voiced criticism in Kyoto City's advisory bodies. To make more general common cause with the citizens' groups with their (assumed) leftist associations was not an option, all the more since business leaders entertain a self-image of entrepreneurial independence and of solving things among peers instead of dragging in local government agencies or ordinary wage-earners. In this spirit, the presidents of the local chamber of industry and commerce and other business associations visited the *manshon* corporation's headquarters in Tokyo. Despite all appeals, however, the developer only conceded the replacement of ground-floor parking space with shops but would not change the building size. Upon the sobering realisation that a level of moral pressure sufficient to fluster any Kyoto-based company did not work here, the business leaders turned to mayor Masumoto and urged him to find a political solution.

In spite of the many-sided support, there was also resistance against the new building rules, especially when the draft ordinance was made public in November 2006. Kyoto's billboard and neon-sign makers saw themselves threatened by bankruptcy. Real-estate firms and some construction companies likewise deplored the anticipated damages to their businesses but also emphasized those for others, such as the difficulties house owners would face when they no longer had enough space to realise a garage or even a proper house on their own lots, or the anticipated decrease in municipal tax income. Representatives of these sectors also complained about not having been part of the advisory councils that had prepared the new rules (*Kyoto Shinbun Electronic Edition (KSEE)*,[3] 20 December 2006). The head of the chamber of industry and commerce, however, while admitting to divided opinions within their own ranks, emphatically supported the reform, and he also stated what Kyoto City would not, or could not, namely that individual hardships had to be endured (*gaman*) for the common good of the new rules (*KSEE*, 24 January 2007, 3 March 2007).

Resistance also involved the owners of apartments in the no longer legal buildings, and they founded a citizens' initiative that, together with a real-estate business association, published several full-page protest advertisements in the biggest local newspaper. They too deplored an expected slump of property prices and the attendant difficulty to find subsequent loans. The biggest problem in their eyes, however, was that due to the new restrictions, many owners could neither expect sufficient living space upon rebuilding nor adequate compensation. A more general debate about the legitimacy of a preservation-oriented planning regime for Kyoto, however, did not arise, confirming my earlier findings about the extent of *manshon* antipathies. Protests finally reached the city assembly and produced a remarkable picture: during the sessions discussing the draft, the mayor saw himself applauded by the communist opposition whereas his biggest supporting party, the LDP, engaged in unprecedented open quarrels. Given this party's intimate connection to the real estate and construction industry, some display of commitment was apparently called for but in the end, the assembly unaminously adopted the new rules in March 2007 (*KSEE*, 30 November 2006, 31 January 2007, 27 February 2007, 13 March 2007).

One centrally involved bureaucrat told me that not the resistance as such but its weakness had surprised him. The aforementioned newspaper advertisements and one demonstration in front of Town Hall (*KSEE*, 1 March 2007) were already the most dramatic manifestations, and they failed to mobilise people without vested interests. And even real-estate representatives or *manshon* residents would argue less about the measures as such than about the modalities of implementation, such as the speed or the lack of compensation. The resistance of the affected apartment owners appeared orchestrated by the real-estate companies, and LDP support was lukewarm. After all, the city assembly was facing public elections in April 2007, and here, the fact that a large majority of Kyoto's citizens were in favour of the new rules and ready to accept restrictions even for their own properties (*KSEE*, 15 February 2007) was decisive. Among dozens of earlier informants, I did not find a single determined critic, not even among those who had upheld the proprietor's freedom in earlier visits. Thus, Kyoto City got by with a few minor amendments to the first draft (mainly regarding greenery and the sizes of projecting roofs on small lots) and the offer of expert advice for future reconstruction but left the height limits – the central component – untouched and also ignored compensation demands. Against the backdrop of a last-minute construction rush, delaying the coming into effect of the ordinance from summer to autumn (*KSEE*, 8 March 2007) was the only substantial concession. But given the time-consuming necessity to convert the new rules into detailed prescriptions, it was probably unavoidable anyway.

The consequences of the new building code

Three years on, the dust of the last-moment building fever has settled, and citizens are living with the new rules. Debate about their value continues, and real estate, construction and sign-making companies do not stop complaining about their lethal effects (*KSEE*, 25 March 2008, 1 July 2008, 2 August 2008, 13 August 2008, 28 August 2008). Building activity has gone down sharply, and land prices are declining, particularly in the centre (*KSEE*, 1 July 2010). The new rules are a frequently cited factor (e.g. *KSEE*, 2 August 2008) but it is difficult to disentangle their effect from that of the post-2008 global financial crisis that hit Japan full force and that of national-level requirements for new construction tightened around the same time. Building activity in Kyoto has in fact not decreased any more strongly than elsewhere,[4] and the decline of land values in the Shijô Kawaramachi shopping area pales against that of Tokyo's Ginza shopping street (*KSEE*, 1 July 2010) where no zoning changes occurred. Bankruptcies in the sign-making business abound (*KSEE*, 5 May 2008, 21 December 2009) but roofers and tile makers are reporting a brisk trade (*KSEE*, 3 May 2008). And while problems with the older ones among the no less than 650 non-conforming (*fu-tekikaku*) *manshon* are clearly on the horizon, the apartments in recently built 'illegal' structures are gaining value rather than losing it (*KSEE*, 9 May 2008, 20 December 2009). Therefore, it appears premature to assess the overall economic effect of Kyoto's new planning regime at this point, and Kyoto City announced the publication of an annual 'Townscape White Book' (*Keikan hakusho*) analysing the success of its new measures (*KSEE*, 27 December 2009).

As this latter step shows, private gains and losses continue to be seen as a legitimate, non-trivial concern, with local government continuing to argue that in the long run all landowners will profit from value increases. More significant in comparison, however, is the extent to which the townscape has at long last become shared property, rather than just a collection of privately owned plots. Not only criticial citizens' initiatives but all kinds of supportive voices characterise the townscape as a 'common asset' (*kôkyô no zaisan*) and privilege the public interest in this asset over that of private landowners. Equally novel but no less pervasive is a long-term view: proponents stress that the Kyoto of 50 or 100 years ahead is at stake and that this consideration takes precedence over more short-term concerns. As a third novelty, Kyoto's specificity has become an explicit and positive value. For example, instead of seeing Kyoto develop along the lines of Tokyo or Osaka, the mayor now voices his fear that Kyoto could become like any other Japanese city when justifying his own support for the new rules (*KSEE*, 5 February 2007).

Against this long-term, collective and localist perspective, Kyoto City is unwavering in the implementation of the new regime. Detailed prescriptions, guidelines, and collections of exemplary new construction continue to be issued (*KSEE*, 30 March 2009, 6 April 2009),[5] extending the regulatory gaze also to the collapsible summer verandahs of riverside restaurants (*KSEE*, 9 May 2008), solar panels (*KSEE*, 16 April 2009), or wooden grids hiding cooler appliances on *machiya* facades (*KSEE*, 29 May 2008). Personnel of the departments in charge of building permits and counselling have been significantly increased. The exemption clause for special-purpose buildings that was suspected as a potential loophole has been applied only very selectively, with two hospital buildings being the only cases so far (*KSEE*, 16 October 2007, 17 January 2008, 7 March 2008, 23 April 2008, 6 May 2008, 23 November 2010). Concerning billboards and signage, city government also took the gloves off. Conveniently close to the entering into force of the new rules, city officials suddenly alerted themselves to the fact that no less than 80 per cent of the shop signs and billboards on Kyoto's major shopping and entertainment streets were illegal even by the old regulations. They then ordered their immediate removal. Former hotspots of Hong Kong-style visual flamboyance have been completely transformed as a result

(*KSEE*, 21 June 2007, 21 December 2009). The new rules have been slightly attenuated only where provisions were needlessly strict, whereas for new challenges such as suburban shopping centres they have been stepped up even further (*KSEE*, 3 August 2010, 11 November 2010). *Machiya*-inspired design features have been chosen for municipal buildings such as a music school, a police station or a bus stop (*KSEE*, 19 December 2009, 12 March 2010, 5 April 2010). And in the computer simulations of the future urban landscape the city sets up for demonstrating the long-term benefits of the new regime, users are invited to virtually tear down even Kyoto Tower, Kyoto Hotel and the new station building (*KSEE*, 13 May 2010).

Little disturbs the impression of a complete turnaround, and private actors are playing along with it. Several *haujingu mêkâ* ('housing makers') selling prefabricated houses have developed new models in line with the changed rules (*KSEE*, 5 December 2007, 30 April 2008), and actual new *machiya* blending traditional construction methods with modern amenities are being built too (*KSEE*, 8 November 2010). In addition to the many ordinary single-family houses, office buildings and mid-rise *manshon* that now bow to the new demands,[6] within six months traditional-looking design features could be seen used in a nine-storeyed hotel (*KSEE*, 15 April 2010), a new office building in Kyoto's otherwise completely modern research park (*KSEE*, 26 August 2010), the office of a major package delivery service (*KSEE*, 22 June 2010), a suburban railway station (*KSEE*, 29 October 2010) and a new museum for Buddhism (*KSEE*, 6 September 2010). As perhaps the best indication of a new orthodoxy, world star Andô Tadao – the one architect whom informants most often juxtaposed to the world of *kyô-machiya* and vernacular architecture – has also designed a building with *machiya* features. Although confessing his qualms about constructing a gabled roof, he nonetheless reported feeling obliged to honour the *genius loci* of the building's inner-city location (*KSEE*, 17 December 2009). All this happens in clear expectation of broad citizen approval, and indeed, the only one of four candidates for the mayoral election in early 2008 who attacked the new rules and deliberately targeted the inhabitants of non-conforming *manshon* failed miserably (*KSEE*, 10 February 2008, 17 February 2008).

Conclusion

Little had prepared me for all these changes and for the fact that the very informants who had seen more radical moves as premature or entirely impossible in my previous field stays would now express only mild surprise. I had seen signs of a shift in awareness already in 2001, expressing the suspicion that this had simply not found its way into substantive action yet (Brumann 2006:156). This shift must have fostered a process which carried the involved parties beyond what almost any one of them had expected in the beginning, a somewhat vague description for what I, and others, have trouble to explain in detail. The background conditions of the general mood swing are easier to pinpoint. Since 2005, the Japanese population has been shrinking, and offical estimates for Kyoto predict a loss of more than 150,000 inhabitants until 2030. The demand for new construction will decline correspondingly while the competition for visitors, inhabitants and taxpayers increases the pressure on the cities to create livable environments. The boom of Kyoto tourism in recent years contrasts positively with the decline of many traditional sectors such as kimono production, demonstrating the tangible value of history, tradition and visual beauty. Initiatives like former Prime Minister Abe Shinzô's campaign for a 'beautiful country' (*utsukushii kuni*) have increased the legitimacy of an aesthetic gaze on the national landspace. The growing number of Japanese who travel overseas and visit scenic environments will also have an influence.

The new ordinance led the list of 'Kyoto's News of the Year 2007' in the biggest local newspaper[7] but may also prove momentous beyond city limits. In the history of Japanese town planning, I know of no case where landowners' rights have been curtailed as radically. Clearly, there were expectations of more tangible rewards in political circles where Kyoto politicians' lobbying for national support measures and a special law for preserving the city met with only mixed results (*KSEE*, 12 May 2008, 23 December 2009). But even when not every Japanese rushes to support the transition in Kyoto, a precedent has been created and can hardly avoid being taken as a model for historically conscious planning – and, more generally, an aesthetic assessment of urban space – in other cities too. At least in anti-*manshon* movements all over the country, Kyoto is already used this way.

Social patterns have not been overturned to the same extent, however. The major initiative came from the national rather than the local government level, and the distribution of tasks and authority between the levels remained rather conventional. And so also was the political process unfolding in Kyoto, with decisive moves coming from forces maintaining clientelist ties with the mayor and interacting with him in non-public settings. All professed commitment to *pâtonashippu* (partnership) to the contrary, the local bureaucrats drafted the ordinance, seeking the expert input of the usual advisory council but not a wider dialogue with concerned citizens, let alone the critical citizens' groups. Also, the legislative body – the city's assembly – was presented with accomplished facts, attesting to the continuing dominance of bureaucrats over elected representatives. The entire decision process appears no less autocratic than that behind the French bridge copy a decade earlier (Brumann 2002), only better supported by public opinion.

The citizens' groups' most important contribution lay in shaping the public mind. Without their activities, the controversial *manshon* projects would not have found wider attention, particularly not among business leaders. And without the precedent of one neighbourhood initiative that through tireless work managed to unite no less than one hundred households under the roof of a building covenant, it would have been less obvious that even old-time Kyotoites will not reject all measures that affect their property values. Junior bureaucrats also interact most intensely with the citizens' groups, and this provides another point of entry for the latters' views into public policy. State involvement was crucial in accomplishing what the citizens and the associations formed by them could not achieve. Yet for pushing the state to action, the long-term engagement of Kyoto's citizens' groups played a crucial role.

Following future developments will be worthwhile, and placing bets on any specific outcome is still a risky business. As things stand, however, Kyoto is re-united again. Not in the sense of harmony – the complaints of those whose interests were hurt by the new regulations have not yet died down. But for the time being, the city is no longer divided into a myriad of independent single-lot empires whose rulers are free to govern themselves but lack any mechanism to influence each other's decisions. Instead, the townscape has finally come into full conceptual existence as a legitimate object of public policy. The high time of high-rises is over, and Kyoto will be a less conflictive place for it.

(I gratefully acknowledge funding by the Japan Society for the Promotion of Science [JSPS] for fieldwork in 1998/1999 and 2007 and by the German Research Association [DFG] for fieldwork and data analysis in 2001–2003. Heartfelt thanks also go to my academic hosts, Professor Nakamaki Hirochika and the National Museum of Ethnology [Minpaku] in Suita, Osaka.)

Notes

1 I build on participant observation at dozens of relevant meetings and public events, a three-digit number of interviews, the responses to a number of questionnaires I designed and distributed, innumerable casual conversations and documentary analysis.
2 For full details, see www.city.kyoto.lg.jp/tokei/page/0000023511.html.
3 The *Kyoto Shinbun Electronic Edition* (in the following: *KSEE*) is the online edition of Kyoto's largest newspaper *Kyôto Shinbun*. Articles appearing there are usually also published in the printed edition of the same or following day.
4 www.city.kyoto.jp/sogo/toukei/Publish/Monthly/Data/economy-2010.xls.
5 See also www.city.kyoto.lg.jp/tokei/cmsfiles/contents/0000079/79082/guide-4.pdf.
6 See the preceding footnote.
7 www.kyoto-np.co.jp/kp/2007topics/kyoto_back.html.

References

Akizuki, K. (2002) 'Partnership in controlled decentralization: Local governments and the Ministry of Home Affairs', in M. Muramatsu, F. Iqbal and I. Kume (eds) *Local government development in postwar Japan*, Oxford: Oxford University Press.

Brumann, C. (2002) 'Deconstructing the Pont des Arts: Why Kyoto did not get its Parisian bridge', *Senri Ethnological Studies*, 62: 15–24.

Brumann, C. (2006) 'Whose Kyoto? Competing models of local autonomy and the townscape in contemporary Kyoto', in C. Hein and P. Pelletier (eds) *Cities, autonomy, and decentralization in Japan*, London: Routledge.

Dalby, Liza Crihfield (1983) *Geisha*, Berkeley: University of California Press.

Golden, Arthur (1997) *Memoirs of a geisha: A novel*, New York: Alfred A. Knopf.

Hohn, U. (2000) *Stadtplanung in Japan: Geschichte – Recht – Praxis – Theorie*, Dortmund: Dortmunder Verlag für Bau- und Planungsliteratur.

Inoki, T. (2002) 'Staff loans and transfers among central and local governments in Japan', in M. Muramatsu, F. Iqbal and I. Kume (eds) *Local government development in postwar Japan*, Oxford: Oxford University Press.

Itô T. (1993) 'Toshi-shi no naka no saigai', in Y. Takahashi, N. Yoshida, M. Miyamoto and T. Itô (eds) *Zushû Nihon toshi-shi*, Tokyo: Tôkyô Daigaku Shuppankai.

Sorensen, A. (2002) *The making of urban Japan: Cities and planning from Edo to the twenty-first century*, New York: Routledge.

Waswo, A. (2002) *Housing in postwar Japan: A social history*, London: RoutledgeCurzon.

5 Re-imagining public space

The vicissitudes of Japan's privately owned public spaces

Christian Dimmer

Perhaps few other ideas have been more persevering in architecture or urban planning discourses over the past decades than 'public space'. Ironically, its recent, expanded career as a central intellectual concept beyond those academic disciplines, concerned with the built environment, and its extensive use in professional and scholarly debates, in media and everyday language, didn't help to lessen its semantic ambiguities (Gulick 1998; Nadal 2000).

One substantial problem with the concept is its (mis-)conception as static and universal; as transcending the particularities of time, space or culture, thus frustrating meaningful comparative discourses. As a result, examining public space outside one's own cultural context may lead to early conclusions and normative distortions when observations do not match the preconceived repertoire of spatial archetypes, or familiar patterns of appropriation. Neil Smith reminds us thus that '(d)ifferent societies and different modes of production produce space differently; they produce their own kinds of spaces' (1998: 54). He argues that 'specific societies and specific periods have distinctive spatial codes [...that] are integral to the social and spatial practices of a given place and period' (1998: 54). Consequently, public space is better conceived as a complex multi-dimensional notion, perpetually reproduced by local and global actors and discourses, shaped by hard and soft social institutions, as well as specific spatio-culturally induced systems of perception, interaction, representation and language in a particular time and place. The job of theory and empirical enquiry is then elucidating the emergence, performance, and change of those spatial codes, constituting *particular* public space notions, rather than superimposing *a priori* views.

Interestingly, international debates showed hitherto a strong bias toward Europe or North America – underplaying public space in non-Western settings.[1] Referring to the ultimately related and equally abstract idea of 'civil society' Frank Schwartz points out the intricacies of applying concepts across cultures that evolved in distinctively Western milieus (2003: 3). After all, as the etymology of the Latin *publicus* ('of the people') suggests, delineating the social universe in public and private *spheres* or *spaces* has been a recurring concern of Western thought since antiquity. Cultures, however, have always borrowed from one and another in the past and thus rarely constitute homogeneous entities in the present. 'Defying abstract considerations of authenticity and universality, ideas and institutions are constantly spreading beyond their place of origin to take root elsewhere, where they may be reconceived in local terms' (2003: 3). Jennifer Robertson adds that 'culture [...] is every bit as much an ongoing production as it is a constantly transforming product' (1998: 11). With Henri Lefebvre (1991) I suggest that space, or more specifically public space, both reflects and contributes to this process and thus deserves further attention.

The objective of this chapter is therefore to sketch out a more nuanced, flexible and culture sensitive understanding of public space. The key is Lefebvre's influential idea of the social construction of space, after which space is continually and dynamically constructed through a *tria*lectic between *the perceived*, *the conceived* and *the lived*. The chapter elucidates this idea with the example of urban Japan and applies it for a close examination of the underlying socio-spatial and historical processes, leading up to the present public space boom. In order to reduce complexity, the focus is on one particular spatial archetype and its related institutional and discursive context. So-called *privately* owned public spaces (POPS) are quantitatively highly significant as they thrived adjacent to hundreds of downtown skyscrapers since the late 1960s. Moreover, since these privately owned, yet publicly accessible spaces result from a trade-off between bonus floor areas for open space, involving developers *and* local governments, their design and operation reflects how public space was thought about by *both* public *and* private key actors at a specific point in time. This is a fresh perspective, as most writing on the subject focused hitherto mostly on government policies but ignored the motivation of private developers.

Lefebvre's idea is then helpful for deconstructing the public space notion and filtering out 'distinctive (local) codes' (Smith 1998: 54) from generalisable global ones. This facilitates in turn a less biased, cross-cultural, comparative research and opens up the abundant, exiting developments in urban Japan to international discourses.

After decades of standardised production – replicating for instance ever the same neighbourhood parks nationwide through bureaucratic routines – in the late twentieth century the attitudes of politicians, planners, developers and citizens broadly changed. In 2002 the Tokyo Metropolitan Government (TMG) began, for example, accrediting street artists and vendors to systematically stimulate 'bustling public life' (Shinohara *et al.* 2007) in major parks and streets as part of outward-directed tourism promotion campaigns. The same symbolic, highly visual policies served in an inward perspective to prove the governments resolve for successful urban revitalisation to its voters. So-called 'open cafés' (*ôpun kafê*) began to proliferate rapidly in private plazas and public pedestrian malls, parks or sidewalks; deliberately prescribed as remedy for places, which the modernist dogma of efficiency and functionality had turned into mere 'derivatives of movement' or 'dead public space' (Sennett 1992) or to capitalise on newly evolving outdoor lifestyles. Symbolic, beautified public spaces – squares, promenades, waterfronts – became also a panacea for instilling local identity, where past explosive urban growth had levelled all regional characteristics. Moreover, the private real estate sector also realised the importance of public space for image branding of office buildings and whole business districts within a growing location competition among prime office areas in Tokyo. Negative demographics and more competitive budgetary policies urged many universities to brush up their downtown campuses to compete for students and financiers.

Not surprisingly this keen professional interest in the quality of public space corresponds to a surging body of literature on the subject and related topics like civil society, or publicness (*kôkyôsei*). As we will see later, this is not to say that planning experts or citizens haven't long been concerned with public space. In fact Kurosawa's filmic masterpiece *ikiru* (1952), in which residents press local authorities for the creation of a neighbourhood park, proves quite the contrary. Also Hoyt Long shows in his intellectual history of *hiroba* that progressive writers like Hani Gorô have discussed democratic and social ideals with particular reference to squares, or *hiroba* (2007: 196–214) since the early Shôwa period that would be ultimately linked to the broader public space concept in the West. No earlier than the mid-1980s was the umbrella term 'public space' (*kôkyô kûkan*) popularly used. Relevant issues are thus less widely conceived within a theoretical and abstract framework, but restricted to concrete archetypical spatial subsets like squares (*hiroba*) or public parks (*kôen*). Interestingly, the literature on parks and squares increased most significantly with the diffusion of machizukuri-type community planning activities after 1980, where they functioned as loci of community activities and early venues for the formation of civil society. From the mid 1990s on *kôkyô kûkan* came in wide use at a time when related theoretical concepts like civil society (*shimin shakai*) or publicness (*kôkyôsei*) began flourishing (Schwartz 2003; Hasegawa 2004).

Approximating public space

Its varied, imprecise and, often, contradictory use across copious academic fields and in everyday language has rendered public space ambiguous and hard to define. Like a palimpsest it consists of numerous layers of semantic complexity and much depends on one's viewpoint: municipal planners tend to narrow it down to spaces in public property, while social scientists are interested in the public use character of certain spaces, independent of ownership. Often also specific places in the city connote public space like downtowns with their pedestrian malls, passages and piazzas, or a fixed repertoire of spaces like public parks, promenades or plazas. Yet others emphasise green spaces, or open spaces such as parks, urban forests, flood plains and waterfronts, while some find this still too narrow and further include streets, parking lots, railway areas, brownfields or other residual spaces – all *potentially* catering to public life.

John Gulick identifies in his synchronic analysis three major patterns of public space discourses. First, 'public property' debates tend to emphasise physical property, formally owned by the state, such as streets, parks and plazas, and their contested role for marginal social groups to fulfil their basic subsistence needs (1998: 135–6). Second, semioticians and experts, who decode relationships between representations and power, see 'semiotic' public space as 'urban sign systems that ... do not govern or surveil the desires and actions of subjects' (1998: 135–6). Finally, writers of the 'public sphere' view it idealistically as a 'setting where diverse citizens can see and be seen by one another, engage in rational political discourse, and encounter the bond of social solidarity' (1998: 135–6). Often all three views overlap, are normatively charged and easily turn into a 'pervasive narrative of loss' (Crawford 1999: 23); stories of 'dead public space' (Sennett 1992), or declarations of its end (Mitchell 1995). Yet, if post-modern consumption spaces are contrasted with nostalgic, idealised sites of democratic discourse, 'real' contemporary public life must appear in crisis; 'authentic' public spaces as dying or disappearing (Dimmer and Aesche 2001). Margaret Crawford warns therefore that 'this perception of loss originates in extremely narrow and normative definitions (...) that derive from insistence on unity, desire for fixed categories of time and space, and rigidly conceived notions of private and public' (1999: 23).

Moreover, Luc Nadal (2000) demonstrates in his discourse analysis of public space in US American planning that its 'diachronic' representation is also less than fix – even within this relatively confined semiotic system of the spatial disciplines. After the term 'public space' was coined in the early 1960s it never accrued a stable meaning but underwent multiple transformations. In the mid-1970s public space evolved broadly as a powerful device of dissent against the modernist city ideology, conveying alternative conceptions of the 'good city' and 'meaningful' public life (2000: 17). In a second phase, mainstream urban redevelopment practice co-opted this notion, to produce strongly themed 'new public spaces' in large-scale redevelopment projects (2000: 19). From the 1980s on, intellectual critique attacked these as 'pseudo-public spaces' or 'simulacra' with the positively charged term 'public space' cloaking the potent particular interests of the redevelopment sector. Concurrently 'authentic public space' was advanced as antithesis of commodification, privatisation and control (2000: 20). Finally, the late 1990s saw a phase of theorisation and conceptualisation, now spanning beyond the fields of design, planning and social anthropology of space, to include political philosophy, as well as cultural and art theory (2000: 21).

These contesting connotations of the term suggest the improbability of a clear-cut, universal definition. For the purpose of this article Roger Scruton offers a useful working interpretation of public space that he pragmatically conceives as 'space into which anyone may enter, and from which anyone may depart, without the consent of strangers, and without any declaration – however tacit – of a justi-fying purpose' (1987: 15). This acknowledges the social character of public space and avoids the limitations of legalistic views that insist on government ownership and *explicitly* established access; central in an era of public–private partnerships, when the 'great public spaces of modernity' (Zukin 1995: 45) – parks, squares, promenades – have been significantly supplemented by private plazas and shopping malls. The later discussed POPS that are conditioned by government regulations, are open to public access, yet remain in private property, also fall into this hybrid category. In fact, Berding *et al.* question the notion of a clear polarity between public and private spaces altogether, as they show that many spaces, assumed as publicly owned, often consist of heterogeneous property structures (2007). Ownership is thus not important for the everyday experience as long as a wide range of social interactions is permitted among people, who do not necessarily know each other and who engage in an array of public *and* private activities here. Ted Kilian argues furthermore that publicity – the power of access – as well as privacy – the power to exclude the external – are to varying degrees necessary parts of every space – public as well as private (1998: 124).

Social construction of public space

The inherent instability and subjectivity of public space leads to the question how to approach it empirically. Which analytic tools help us understand its dynamic transformation and how do particular spatial contexts, a specific language with its culturally induced systems of perception, interaction and representation, as well as peculiar patterns of everyday life, construct its particular meaning? As noted earlier Henri Lefebvre's idea of the social production of space is helpful here.

Public space is in a given society a space that the generality of a citizenry collectively values, to which it attributes symbolic significance and asserts claims (Goheen 1998). It is clear that such values, meanings and critical awareness are never fixed, but dynamically change over time and across places and cultures. Moreover, public space is not a passive container or theatre stage that exists a priori of its social use, readily waiting for the performance of the societal actors. Instead it is a material product, which includes the people, whose relations and interactions dialectically constitute its functions and meanings. In Edward Soja's words, social life is 'both space-forming and space-contingent, a producer and product of spatiality' (1989: 129).

An untested superimposition of theories that developed in different discursive contexts is therefore critical. Surveillance and social control in public space by means of design (Flusty 1994) are in Japan for example objectively as present as elsewhere, yet their significance within this semiotic system clearly differs from those that Mike Davis found in Los Angeles, his 'city of quartz' (1992). I would suggest that the subjectively *felt* threat of surveillance to civil liberties might be perceived differently in Japan, where concepts like civil society or democracy are seen as relatively young and weak in popular discourses. In an unanimously felt middle class society also the fear of the *other* in public space is less pronounced; open social exclusion is rarely exercised.

Henri Lefebvre (1991) proposed a triadic model for the dynamic social construction of space. He distinguished an ontological triad of space (How *is* space?), consisting of 'the physical' (real space), 'the mental' (planned space/ space of Cartesian cognito) and 'the social' (lived space, the imaginary) from an epistemological one (How is space *known*?) of 'spatial practice' (perceived space), 'representations of space' (conceived space) and 'representational space' (lived space).

Real, or perceived spaces are concrete, physical spatial forms that can be empirically mapped, but are also ultimately socially produced – both mediums and outcomes of human activity, behaviour and experience. This materialised *physical*, yet socially produced, space can be directly sensed and is open to accurate Cartesian description. What is perceived as public space depends thus on concrete physical spaces, in which one was socialised and which are in turn product of collectively mediated values and institutions – laws, regulations, culturally stabilised systems of meaning, or social norms that actors within a cultural system generally respect. Because the very imagery of *physical* public space is seized by such powerful Western archetypes like the Greek agora, the Roman forum, or the Medieval square or common their absence led many to the erroneous conclusion that public space does not exist in Japan. They fail to see that public life exerts itself in different forms and places (Jinnai 1995) and might have a less political character than in the West; more tied to commodity exchange. So strong is their suggestive power as metaphors for idealised, meaningful public spaces that they often appear in the names of commercial redevelopments like Yebisu Garden *Place*, Herbert von Karajan *Platz* (ARK Hills), or Grand *Commons* Shinagawa in order to cloak the banal reality of interchangeable spaces of consumption.

Mental, or conceived, space is constructed in cognitive forms, or imagined. A particular public space notion is conditioned then through particular sign systems, symbols and language, embedded in childhood memories and cultural histories. Conceived space dominates any society and located therein are representations of power and ideology. The signifier 'public' can carry democratic notions in Western languages and thus attaches positive attributes to physical 'public' space. As discussed below the same word signifies officialdom and central state domination in Japan and thus adds negative semantic connotations of state control (Yoshida 1999). Such imagining is constantly reshaped by representations in print and screen media, by direct experiences of foreign cultures and cities, by political, societal, academic, as well as professional discourses, or by changing experiences in the environment of the Japanese city itself. The growing number of design related magazines for architecture, landscape, interior or urban design, the rapid proliferation of Starbuck's-type third spaces with sitting terraces or the swift absorption of the LOHAS (Lifestyle of Health and Sustainability) consumer movement in media and retail-mix of urban developments proves the existence of such alternative conceptions of the Japanese city. Conversely, the engineering dominated planning disciplines have imagined public space through the modernist planning dogma (Uno 1998).

Social, or lived space consists of the actual social and spatial practices, which overlay physical space by making symbolic use of its objects, and whose forms depend on particular socio-cultural traditions. This immediate world of experience and realisation is expressed in systems of nonverbal symbols and signs, that is distinctly different from both physical and mental space. It embodies the real and imagined life world of experiences, emotions, events and political choices. It is directly lived; the space of inhabitants and users, simultaneously containing all other real and imagined spaces (Soja 1996). Lived space of ordinary Japanese people ignores property boundaries and challenges orderly, sanitised mental conceptions of public space administrators with often paradoxical results: *Yatai* (food carts) appear illicitly on nocturnal sidewalks, adolescents rehearse dance in front of mirrored office façades while signs prohibit them from doing so, and shop merchandise persistently encroaches on sidewalks, disregarding regulations. The controversy over the protection of Tokyo's Shimokitazawa neighbourhood from a massive road development shows that bustling alleys are important lived spaces for citizens while modernist planners regard them as traffic bottlenecks and seek to confine public life to separated amenity spaces.

Conceiving the public: officialdom vs. people

What is public or private in a given culture is a social convention or construct and plays a fundamental role in the mental conception of a particular public space notion. Although popular views that directly link the formation of a public sphere or civil society to physical public spaces have been challenged (Barnett 2005), others maintain that such places are a vital precondition (Scruton 1987; Douglass 2003). The idea of public informs furthermore the conception of the relationship between state and civil society and influences the modes through which physical public space is produced, used and imaged. The following section therefore explores the intrinsic Japanese meaning of this concept in Japan.

As frequently suggested, the connotation of public in Japan differs significantly from that in the West, where it tends to refer to the people or civil society instead of to government or officialdom (Berque 1981; Yoshida 1999; Hasegawa 2004). One component of the modern Japanese term 'public' (*kôkyô*), *ooyake* or *kô* signified in feudal Japan 'superior authority' within a system of hierarchically nested 'ruling authorities' (emperor-shogun-feudal lords). Yoshida Shinichi suggests that this use is still deeply embedded in the collective psyche and vocabulary and that the kanji *kô* implies to this day *both* 'ruling authority' as well as 'public'. 'The former connotation is stronger than the latter. Even today, most Japanese ... assume it means 'government' before they think of 'public'. The ... Western sense is still not very familiar in Japan' (Yoshida 1999: 24).

Iokibe Makoto adds that 'officialdom monopolises the public realm while the people, (disregarded as) the masses, are permitted the pursuit of private gain ... and individual happiness insofar as these things lie within the legal and political frameworks dictated by the government' (1999: 51). Consequently, many regulations governing public space reflect this bias and activities opposing a purpose as defined here are *principally* ruled out. The Road Act (*Dôro Hô*) defines for example station-front squares, sidewalks or promenades as places for seamless circulation and therefore more meaningful activities such as festivals, performances or political speeches must be each approved individually. Apart from the control aspect, this monopolisation also resulted in a nationwide repetition of ever the same small parks. Uniform, restrictive design standards and time-consuming bureaucratic procedures encumbered local governments,[2] citizens[3] and designers in realising alternative public space concepts. Moreover, those standards were based on quantitative objectives, prescribing abstract per-capita target figures for cities, but neglecting design quality and participation. Thus, as a result of such automated practices, 'the number of *kôen* keeps increasing, not ... in response to the needs of citizens but as the result of the execution of central or local government plans and the expansion of budget' (Yoshida 1999: 27).

Recently, however, 'drastic changes in the Japanese conceptions of public-ness' are occurring according to Hasegawa Koichi, expressed by a sharp increase of academic writing on themes like 'publicness' and 'civil society' since 1995 (2004: 199). This re-imagination is further underpinned by the evolution of a whole new branch of political philosophy, called 'public philosophy' (*kôkyô tet-sugaku*), in which scholars from different disciplines elaborate on fundamental relations between private individual, civil society or the state, Western concep-tions of public/private, local self-government or alternative public goods (Kim and Sasaki 2001). The influential report 'Japan's Goals in the 21st Century – The Frontier Within: Individual Empowerment and Better Governance in the New Millennium' by the Prime Minister's Commission on Japan's Goals in the 21st Century (2000) also endorsed calls for a 'new publicness' from the highest gov-ernment level. Against the background of privatisation of state property, greater local government autonomy or increased NPO activity, the report urged that the established top-down relationship between state and citizens be reinterpreted to one where the 'citizens ... entrust government with authority ... in the context of a new form of governance, led by citizens as the chief actors' (2000: 2).

Imagining public space in planning

As the article focuses on the production of *physical* public space, its understand-ing in planning needs further attention. How public space is imagined or con-ceived, how it *can* be thought, in its *particular* cultural and institutional context has a profound influence on its concrete spatial production and later use. As we will see, such conceptions can significantly inhibit or expedite the diffusion of new ideas and visions. Herbert Schubert identified three major paradigms of conceiving public space in the physical planning disciplines: first, the paradigm of the built frame; second, that of public *open* space; and third, that of legal titles and rights of disposal (2000: 19–32).

Urban planners and architects who see public space as positively constituted by the façades of surrounding buildings follow the first paradigm. Writers like Christopher Alexander (1977) or Jan Gehl (1987) point out the importance of a 'public–private interface' between buildings and open space, which the urban design guideline of Minato Mirai 21 in Yokohama calls 'activity floors' that 'ensure the liveliness of the town' (MM21 2003: 7). Ground floors are to be turned into shops, showrooms, service facilities and others uses, which stimu-late public use along the designated pedestrian axes. 'Such floors are designed to maintain continuity of street liveliness and to have [a] scale fit for human sensibilities' (MM21 2003: 7). By rendering activities within buildings visible to the street, transparent façades appear to enhance street life; Jane Jacobs' eyes on the street promote a sense of human co-presence, conviviality and security. The articulation of the relation between building and public space depends also always on dominating planning doctrines, like for instance the 'Charta of Athens', which planners of a generation tend to accept as their own design philosophy. Until recently most Japanese planners saw public space from a modernist angle, emphasising effective traffic circulation, functional separation and safety, at the expense of user comfort or quality of life (Uno 1998).

Landscape planners, who focus on non build-up spaces, hold the second paradigmatic view of the public *open* space. They usually engage in planning processes only after urban planners and architects have determined the rough character of public space through the street layout and building allocation. Public art, landscape design and connectivity are means by which to create accessible, safe pedestrian spaces, or ecological networks. In recent years the idea of open space networks was revived and creating water and green networks became a key objective in Tokyo's new green space strategy (TMG 2000). Interestingly, also on a project level public *open* space shifted during the last decade literally from the margins to the centre. Many big developments like Yebisu Garden Place, Grand Commons Shinagawa, Vita Italia Shiodome or Roppongi Hills were designed around significant open spaces that serve as destinations in their own right. The master plan for the housing project Canal Court Shinonome developed in close cooperation between design coordinator Yamamoto Riken, six architect teams and the landscape designer Hasegawa Hiroki, whose elaborate public space network was central in the planning process (Dimmer *et al.* 2005).

Legal titles are a third paradigmatic conception that influences how design, management and control of urban space are thought. In the view of many Japanese planners over-regulation and overlapping jurisdictions are major obstructions for an integrated treatment of publicly, and adjacent privately, owned public spaces.[4] A list by the Urban Design Centre with all regulations limiting the design and use of public spaces shows that their main objective is a seamless traffic circulation and the averting of dangers (UDC 2002). More than only roads, the Road Act regulates also sidewalks, promenades, station-front squares and underground arcades. Ironically, the desperate attempts of Japanese cities to revitalise their atrophied downtowns through events has been thwarted by such limited logic. Only fairly recently attitudes change and in 2002 Tokyo introduced, for example, its Heaven Artist Programme, which now legally permits auditioned artists to perform in designated spots like Ueno Park or Marunouchi at specified times.[5] After progressive cities like Hiroshima or Fukuoka experimented with non-profit organisation models and exceptional deregulations in public parks and promenades in the early 2000s, the Ministry of Land, Infrastructure and Transportation (MLIT) endorsed this with a series of so-called 'social experiment' projects (*shakai jikken*) (Shinohara *et al.* 2007). Based on their positive evaluation it issued a 'Guideline for Facilitation of District Activities utilising Streets' (Kokudo kôtsû-shô dôro-kyoku 2005) that now facilitates revitalisation projects nationwide.

Although the often lamented decay of public space is caused by technological and historical meta-processes that gradually superseded its functions as a venue for everyday activities and communication, its formal marginalisation was institutionalised through the modernist planning dogma that dissected it into functionally isolated units for recreation and circulation, and buildings were apathetic toward it. This was further cemented in professional specialisation with the consequence that different planning disciplines and authorities only perceive public space types in their own domain. In Japan this was particularly pronounced, as planning evolved under the technocratic aegis of civil engineering and only recently has it been thought of more holistically with an integration of built frame, open space and unitary management. Under the catchphrase *nigiwai zukuri* (*creating festivity*) and inspired by pioneering progressive local governments like Yokohama City (discussed below), attractive public space has now moved up the national agenda as a panacea for urban revitalisation, image branding or tourism and business promotion.

Contrary to the West, where public space evolved as common, if vague, theoretical concept, concurrently carrying spatial, sociological, political and philosophical notions, its conceptual foundations in Japan remain relatively weak. In fact only in 2007 a first comprehensive theorisation of *kôkyô kûkan* was published (Shinohara 2007), which introduced the theories of Lefebvre (1991), Sennett (1992), Arendt (1998) or Habermas (1992) but related them only to public space in the West. A recent edited volume with the title 'the city *as* public space' (*kôkyô kûkan toshite no toshi*) is symptomatic for another trend (Ueda *et al.* 2005). Instead of a systematic theoretical treatment of the new concept the contributors tack it with the term '*toshite*', or 'as' pragmatically to familiar, clearly defined spatial archetypes and issues like in 'parks and green spaces *as* public space' (*kôkyô kûkan toshite no kôen ryokuchi*), or 'streets *as* public space' (*kôkyô kûkan toshite no gairo*).

Also the plethora of alternative translations indicates the subject's intricacy.[6] Though *kôkyô kûkan* dominates, frequently other variants are used. *Kôteki (na) kûkan, paburikku supêsu*, or *kôkyô supêsu* are synonymous umbrella terms, emphasising the social character of a place. *Kôkai kûkan* (space open to the public), *kôkai kûchi* (public open space), or *kôkaisei no aru kûchi* (open space with publicness) are planning jargon for spaces, created through incentive planning instruments. The article refers later to these spaces as POPS. *Kôkyô shisetsu* (public facility) marks publicly owned facilities like parks or libraries, used in zoning and public management. In urban planning also green space (*ryokuchi*) or open space (*ôpun supêsu*) figure high as antithesis to hard, built-up urban space, yet broader critical implications like exclusion or control are often underplayed in this context.[7] *Kyôdô riyô kûkan* (commonly usable space), *komon supêsu* (common space), *jun-kôkyô kûkan* (semi-public space), or *jiyû kûkan* (free space) refer to community spaces in the residential sphere. To complicate matters kôkyô kûkan refers beyond physical space to the abstract realm of public discourse and civil society in the sense of Jürgen Habermas' public sphere (1992).

The translation *kôkyô kûkan* in planning discourses implies a legalistic view, referring to publicly owned spaces under direct government control, while bracketing out public spaces in privately owned settings. It is moreover often narrowed down to specific design or management issues and dissected into specified, seemingly unrelated spatial archetypes (park, square, station-front plaza, alleyway, zoning plaza), or particular planning problems (environmental or barrier-free design, downtown revitalisation, public art, citizen participation, maintenance). This specialisation leads to a further imagined, mental segmentation of the physically continuous public realm into strangely disparate academic and professional domains. Addressing public space as abstract notion causes therefore confusion, while discourses rarely transcend disciplinary boundaries.

Japan's privately owned public space (POPS)

The second part of this chapter exemplifies the social production of space through a long-term examination of one particular public space category and its specific institutional context: so-called 'privately owned public spaces' (POPS, or *kôkai kûchi*) are quantitatively highly relevant and have been created at the foot of hundreds of downtown high-rises since the late 1960s through incentive planning. In this public–private partnership the public sector facilitates and regulates the private production, ownership and management of publicly usable space by granting builders bonus floor area that exceeds the limits stipulated by zoning. Although these spaces remain legally in private ownership, the law requires them to be open to the public. Often they are cited as key witness for a supposed privatisation of public space. This notion is however misleading, as it suggests a process, in which previously public assets are given to private hands, thus diminishing the public realm. This is rarely the case with reference to incentive zoning; a planning tool that creates new publicly usable spaces on private land that was not necessarily accessible before. When Loukaitou-Sideris (1993), Cybriwsky (1999) or Sorensen (2003) criticise privatisation of public space in this context, they support this misconception. Clearly, no existing public space is taken away here, but instead a new specific kind of admittedly privately controlled yet publicly usable space is added to the public realm.

Examining POPS is highly significant as they mark a major turning point in Japanese urban governance: the public sector gave up its dominating role as sole provider of urban public space and began systematically delegating it to private actors. This focus allows then the transcending of conventional government-centred perspectives by also being perceptive to values and meanings, attributed to public space by private actors and the market. As Gottdiener suggested, the real estate sector is most sensitive to constantly changing socio-economic trends. Following the logic of profit maximisation, it translates these into new urban form and capitalises on such novel demands, or creates new demands from scratch (1985). Large mix-use redevelopment like Yebisu Garden Place, SIO Site Shiodome, Roppongi Hills, Tokyo Midtown or Marunouchi and their public spaces thus reflect the following four characteristics: first, a fusion of work and leisure; second, a longing for collective memory and shared narratives; third, a heightened awareness for the environment and quality of life; and fourth, a feminisation of urban space. What were the reasons for delegating the creation of public space to the private sector and which necessities and visions of the government shaped this radical system change? How successful has the system been?

The origin of this paradigm shift was the abolition of the absolute height system that had hitherto limited building heights to 20 metres within and 30 metres outside of residential areas and that had forced builders to completely build up sites in order to maximise profitability. Since the early 1960s it was gradually replaced with the floor area ratio (FAR) designation. In 1963 the exceptional 'Specified Block' (*Tokutei Gaiku*) was introduced, which allowed the stipulation of building volumes for specifically designated districts (Ishida 1988: 60). As the FAR only states the gross floor area permitted on a site divided by its net area, it encourages the construction of slim, high buildings and the preservation of (initially private) open space.

This fundamental change was facilitated by the technological progress, now permitting earthquake proof high-rise buildings and by the lobbying of the real estate and construction industry. Interestingly, Mutô Kiyoshi, structural engineering pioneer, who devoted much of his career to developing earthquake resistant structures as professor at the University of Tokyo, joined the Kajima Corporation as executive vice-president, after retiring in 1963. There he led the construction of the Kasumigaseki Building, Japan's first high-rise and catalyser project for incentive zoning. Also among planners it was broad consensus that Le Corbusier's towers in the park were the superior city model and therefore the abolition of the absolute heights, and with it the implicit rejection of the low-rise vernacular city, was uncontested. Decisive was also the environmental degradation after a decade of rampant, unchecked urban growth with a rapid loss of open space. Ishikawa Mikiko details for instance the persistent encroachment on Tokyo's greenbelt, which was finally abolished in 1969 after it had been scaled down 29 times since 1949 (2001: 263–4). Fragmented landownership, lack of funds for urban planning, as well as weak planning powers vis-à-vis private property rights further frustrated the authorities' efforts to create new open space. Much hope was therefore put in the new FAR system and subsequent incentive zoning (Tateishi 1973; Yanagisawa 1973) that was modelled after New York's groundbreaking zoning ordinance of 1961.[8]

From 1964 on the specified block allowed for the production of Japan's first POPS. Based on a directive of the Ministry of Construction (MoC), cities with their own building authority (*tokutei gyôsei chô*) and a population greater than 250,000 were encouraged to offer floor area bonuses and other zoning concessions to builders if they in turn agreed to provide plazas, arcades, atriums and other outdoor and indoor spaces, governed by explicit, yet minimal, design standards. To adapt the system to local conditions, bonuses could be adjusted to favour the creation of certain spaces over others. Generally indoor spaces like atriums, appearing more private, generate less bonus floor area than open air spaces like sidewalk widenings or plazas. In 1969 the 'Intensive Land Utiliza-tion Area' (*Kôdo Riyô Chiku*) designation followed, in 1970 the 'Comprehensive Design System' (CDS, *Sôgô Sekkei Seido*) and in 1988 the 'Redevelopment-type District Plan (*Saikaihatsu Chikukeikaku*). The latter sought to mobilise private capital for the redevelopment of large brownfield sites, vacated through the structural transformation from an industrial to a service economy and also reflected the Nakasone administration's commitment to further deregulation and privatisation (Hebbert and Nakai 1988). All four systems equally encourage the creation of POPS and other amenities[9] but differ in project scale and planning process. Specified block (62),[10] areas of intensive land utilisation (110) and redevelopment-type district plan (63) are used for whole blocks and districts and require a city planning decision to conclude a discretionary review process with public participation. A city planning commission seeks to harmonise projects with their urban context and influences the allocation of public spaces. In con-trast, the CDS applies to smaller developments on single plots. After a non-discretionary review, a building permit must be granted as-of-right, if plans comply with building regulations. An urban design review is commonly not per-formed and its frequent utilisation (694) indicates accordingly its popularity among builders but also reflects the typically small-scale redevelopment conditions.

Evaluating POPS: a missed opportunity?

How has this marriage of private ownership and public use fared in over 40 years? What kind of spaces has it produced? By quantitative measures, the results are remarkable. In Tokyo alone the CDS produced privately owned public spaces at nearly 700 offices, residential and community buildings, totalling 1.88 million m² or equalling 11.6 times the size of Hibiya Park. A closer look reveals that most of these concentrate in the three central wards Minato (22 per cent), Chiyoda (13.5 per cent) and Chûô (16 per cent) and that more than 75 per cent are located outside residential areas. Such downtown areas are however fairly saturated with sidewalks and parks, and the per-capita park supply ratios are high because of low residential densities. Conversely, few POPS were created in the disaster prone areas of the wooden apartment belt,[11] where open space ratios remain despite all planning efforts being extremely low.

Measured in qualitative terms, the results are uneven. At their best, spaces have provided residents, employees and visitors with public places for accidental and planned social, recreational, cultural and utilitarian experiences that are otherwise only accessible within the city's publicly owned parks, or within pri-vately owned privately controlled domains. A comprehensive study in Osaka showed, however, that the majority of POPS users were visitors and employees of the connected buildings during lunchtime (Matsushita *et al.* 2003). Con-sequently, little non-business related activities occur outside working hours. Older spaces in particular are often barren and offer little user comfort. In their accumulation these bleak spaces amplify the negative perception of atrophied central cities. At their worst POPS have been hostile to public use by design and operation because for developers more visitors amount to higher security, maintenance and insurance costs, cause conflicts with the primary building functions and thus reduce the overall profitability.

At this point we revisit the above-discussed notion of three paradigmatic public space views in the planning disciplines that serves as analytic tool for the following evaluation of POPS. Structuring the institutions into those addressing the built frame, open area and attached rights allows for a nuanced analysis.

It is often pointed out that the articulation of the lower building parts in relation to the adjacent public space is crucial for its perception (Whyte 1980, Kayden 2000). If fronted by mirrored glass, blind walls or iron shutters the result can be 'dead public space' (Sennett 1992: 12): 'No diversity of activity takes place on the ground floor; it is only a means of passage to the interior. ... A miniature public square ... is declared ..., but the function destroys (its) nature ..., which is to intermix persons and diverse activities' (Sennett 1992: 12). Roger Scruton adds that publicness, in the sense of attracting public activities, must be the chief condition. 'Spaces do not become public merely by ceasing to be private or by being provided in quantities and shapes that no private purpose requires' (1987: 17). Controlling the relationship between a building and a POPS is hardly possible with formal planning tools in Japan. For better or worse, it is left to the discretion of developers and architects who may 'design out' unwanted activities that they see in conflict with the development's primary function (Whyte 1980; Flusty 1994). This interface is also subject to 'design fashions' and zeitgeist. While modernist designers ignored the relation of buildings to surrounding public space and focused on mere functionality, a new generation of architects uses transparency for a fluent interpenetration of interiors and exteriors.

For the two-dimensional open area, important quality criteria are context integration, legibility, visibility, connectivity between adjacent open spaces, responsive design, cleanliness and a sense of security (Whyte 1980; Gehl 1987; Carr *et al.* 1995). Conventional planning instruments in Japan cannot tackle these parameters proactively. Although rules require POPS to meet minimum design standards in terms of size, layout, physical and visual connectivity to adjacent sidewalks as well as greenery before zoning concessions can be granted (TCDSR 2002), such mechanised check-list-style regulations prevented the worst, but could neither facilitate the evolution of coherent public space networks nor compensate for the lack of urban design expertise, needed for a qualified plan assessment. Interestingly, in the USA detailed design conditions for more context-sensitive zoning were in fact devised (Getzels *et al.* 1988; Kayden 2000).[12] In Japan, however, POPS and connected tower developments can materialise all over the urbanisation promotion area. The open space of the 38-storey Renaissance Tower directly adjacent to Ueno Park earned its owner for example a lavish floor area bonus, is rarely used, but the higher building impairs the cityscape. Despite the absence of proactive open space concepts, few 'accidental' networks developed along Tokyo's waterfront, at Shinkawa, Shibaura or

Tennosû. If and how builders realise possible connections on their building plot depends on each individual case.[13] While office and residential developments tend to produce secluded defensible spaces, shielded from the view of unaware users, retail facilities capitalise on active network integration for safeguarding an unbroken consumer influx.

The rights of disposal mark a third array of institutions that influence the appearance and use of public space and can be approached from two angles: First, how far can private property owners limit the public use of places that were effectively created through government subsidies? Second, which activities does the government implicitly or explicitly permit developers to curate in their POPS? It may come as a surprise that few explicit specifications were made in the first respect. Regulations only vaguely require spaces to be 'generally open to the public' and in agreement with local governments specified nightly closing hours are permissible (TCDSR 2002). The management is also required to file a yearly maintenance report to ensure proper upkeep, but a comprehensive monitoring regime is absent. Reasons for this are overlapping competencies of related public authorities, lack of manpower and critical awareness as well as fundamental doubts about how far to interfere in private property. Management and control issues remain thus effectively in private discretion and consequently the scope of prohibited activities, displayed on signboards and inconspicuously enforced by the ubiquitous security personnel and CCTV cameras, differ significantly from place to place. In newer POPS the standard catalogue lists about a dozen interdicted activities,[14] which raises the question to which degree one can still justifiably talk of public space.

From the second angle, well until the mid-1990s authorities discouraged the creation of more active, shop-lined spaces. As officialdom had primarily defined these as places for disaster evacuation and pedestrian circulation, crowding and bustle would inevitably contradict such objectives. Shinjuku Southern Terrace (1998) marked one of the first deviations from these principles, when TMG permitted the developer Odakyû the introduction of commercial functions within its giant POPS (Dimmer 2008: 203). Apart from such 'hard' design issues, the management was also restrained by the exclusive definition of public. Similar to parks, every event must be authorised out of fear of permanent commercial encroachment. This frustrated attempts to revitalise mono-functional office quarters.

In 2003 the urban renaissance policy of the Koizumi Cabinet and Tokyo's governor Ishihara led to a revised government stance with the aim to brush up the capital's image for international tourists and business people. The 'Tokyo Metropolitan Ordinance for Creating an Elegant Cityscape' (2003, *Tôkyô no shareta Machinamizukuri suishin Jôrei*) aimed among other objectives at the revitalisation of public space by allowing POPS owners in specified cityscape revitalisation districts the formation of a management organisation that can also freely curate commercial events for a period of three years. The model for this legislation was the district development council in Shiodome. Beautification of public spaces and the cityscape as well as staging of events in parks and POPS also became an important part of Tokyo's 'Metropolitan Guideline for Tourism-centred City Planning' (2004, *Tôkyô-to Kankô Machizukuri Kihon Shishin*).

To summarise, by design, size, visibility and location the majority of POPS invite little public use. Against the original anticipations of their inventors, they became imagined as a mandatory requirement in quid pro quo bureaucratic procedures. The underlying understanding was quantitative, as governments were happy enough with ever-increasing open space figures on their balance sheets. Good design and usability mattered little. As incentive zoning is a trade-off of 'building bulk for open space' other urban resources like cityscape, sunlight exposure, microclimate or neighbourhood character were often compromised in the name of a questionable amenity. For developers in turn, POPS were a convenient vehicle to boost the rentable floor area by concurrently curbing maintenance costs.

The spectacular POPS at the heart of more recent developments suggest, however, that these attitudes towards public space have changed since the early 1990s. Interestingly, as the 'hard' institutional framework of planning regulations wasn't significantly modified to account for that, the question arises where this re-evaluation of public space came from? What were the forces that led to the recent revision of government politics and what made private developers spend more effort and funds? The following sections seek to answer these questions by closer examining two influential pioneering cases. First, in a government-led approach of Yokohama City, POPS became part of a comprehensive public space strategy. Second, in Tokyo's prestigious Ôtemachi–Marunouchi–Yûrakuchô (OMY) business district the private landowners equally initiated a far-reaching scheme.

Local government initiative: the Yokohama formula

With 3.5 million inhabitants Yokohama is Japan's second largest city. After the opening of the country in the nineteenth century it became Tokyo's port and Japan's gateway to the West. The city therefore takes pride in a distinct local culture. This identity was threatened by the rapid urban growth since the 1960s and the massive concentration of heavy industries in the Keihin zone. The allied occupation of the historic Kannai centre delayed war reconstruction until the late 1950s, deprived the city of its traditional centre and funnelled urban growth to the fringes. In only two decades the population doubled from 1.5 in 1963 to three million in 1983 and the sprawling suburbanisation led to the factual absorption of Yokohama into the greater Tokyo metropolitan region. The relegation to a commuter town, as well as worsening environmental conditions, increased the political pressure and consequently a top priority on the agenda of the reform mayor Asukata Ichio (1963–78) became countering the marginalisation and promoting sustainable urban growth.

The progressive Asukata assembled a multi-disciplinary team of young professionals from within and outside of the public administration, whom he entrusted with the development of a comprehensive renewal strategy. As head of the restructured urban planning administration he won Tamura Akira over, who had previously served the city as external urban design consultant. In 1965 the team around Tamura presented an integrated, long-term revitalization programme that centred on the famous '6 Big Projects'. Symbolically most significant was the initial restoration of the historical Kannai area and its integration within the new city centre around Yokohama station, from which it had been cut-off by a Mitsubishi shipyard (Yokohama 1965: 48–51).[15] Already the title of the plan was a strong statement against the established top-down governance principles of the time, as it called for 'the citizen to design future Yokohama' (*shimin ga tsukuru Yokohama no mirai*) – 35 years prior to the above mentioned Prime Minister's Commission report that endorsed a new publicness (2000). For a seamless realisation of the showcase projects and to facilitate lateral coordination, the typical vertically segmented municipal administration was reorganised.[16] With unprecedented political support, Tamura established a planning and coordination office in 1968 that sought to align the agendas of all related departments and promote internal teamwork. Two years later Japan's first municipal urban design bureau was set up to safeguard that all major projects would comply with the objective to 'pursue publicness' (*kôkyôsei wo tsuikyû*) and create 'places, where people can come in contact with each other and communicate' (Nishiwaki *et al.* 1992: 25).[17] The backbone of this public space strategy was the vision of a dense network, linking the city's major parks, historical and cultural assets, shopping streets as well as the waterfront. Also, by actively involving the citizens and business community in its planning and management their publicness would be increased. Incrementally this network would be complemented through public projects like promenades, greenways or squares as well as through guided private development.

In order to increase the feasibility of this vision and to provide for a development in line with the urban design principles, the city produced its own variant of incentive zoning. The name 'Urban Environmental Design System' (UEDS, *Shigaichi Kankyô Sekkei Seido*) stressed its unique character but it was only one component of Tamura's ambitious effort to combine all available tools into a far-reaching local planning regime that became known as 'Yokohama formula'.

As the rapid population influx of the 1960s caused unchecked, haphazard development, municipal planning could no longer keep up with providing basic infrastructure such as roads, sidewalks or parks. At the same time the first disputes over access to sunlight had erupted as a consequence of the height regulation abolition. Worse, the tense budgetary situation did not allow countering these conditions through internal financing and Mayor Asukata's objective to curb the central government's influence allowed only minimal utilisation of national subsidies. The city therefore embraced the new incentive planning, which was introduced concurrently with other planning innovations such as the *senbiki* growth control system, new land use zoning and height control areas. Their coordinated utilisation combined with guided private development would help to secure scarce public funds. The UEDS would also add to the city's open space stock, provide greenery and, through *exceptional* exemption from building form restrictions, reward context-sensitive buildings. Without building height caps, however, the system allowed for unpredictably high buildings, depending on how much land developers assembled – thus inevitably compromising other public goods. Unparalleled, Tamura's team designated citywide height control areas and re-established in effect height caps.[18] These were combined with the lowest permissible FAR designations under the Building Standard Act (*Kenchiku Kijun Hô*). Exemptions thereof were only granted if in turn POPS or other bonusable amenities were created or historical landmarks preserved. Height caps and low FAR values meant also that more buildings than elsewhere became subject of a design review process, in which urban designers could exert influence. To preserve the city's character as port town, additional incentives were offered for the provision of POPS facing river promenades or the sea, or natural green space preservation in the hilly woodlands in the north.

Another singularity of Yokohama is an additional, informal planning layer, in which incentive zoning is embedded. Within so-called 'Machizukuri Council Districts' (MCD, *Machizukuri Kyôgi Chiku*) detailed urban design visions were initially developed in public deliberations between the urban design office, local residents and the business community. Informal district guidelines were then legislated to facilitate the incremental realisation; in sensitive areas further backed by district plans. This extra-legal administrative guidance (see Sorensen 2002: 310–11) addresses both, adjacent buildings and public open space, as it stipulates wall setbacks on private land, vitalising building functions in the ground floors, allocation of parking lots off important pedestrian areas, massing of buildings in order to maintain a sense of human scale in public space and reduce shadow fall, promotion of greenery as visual amenity, or control of advertisement signboards around 'dignified' civic spaces. Generally it seeks to complement scarce public space around important parks, symbolic buildings and important intersections. The Yamashita Park vicinity is an early example, where landowners were persuaded to contribute parts of their property for the widening of the adjacent park promenade. The significance for incentive zoning is, that within MCD an additional design review takes place. Before projects enter into the building permit process, proposals must comply with the district rules and respect the local character. Unlike Tokyo, this system enhances the probability that POPS do not materialise out of context but contribute to the city's long-term public space vision.

There has been no bolder municipal attempt to embed the private production of public space into a comprehensive planning framework. Available instruments such as low FAR designations, citywide height control areas, MCD backed by district plans, specified block and UEDS were used to restrict incentive zoning. The Asukata administration politically prioritised good urban form, developed a precise spatial vision around an integrated public space system and readjusted the planning administration to assist its realisation. Compared to other Japanese cities the results of the last 40 years are encouraging. Some 516 POPS were produced citywide up to 2011 at office, residential and community facility buildings, equalling nine times the size of Hibiya Park. Alone in the vicinity of

Yokohama station the UEDS created a cluster of 48 spaces that complement the public space system, while it helped to preserve historical assets in the Kannai area and widen main intersections and the park promenade around Yamashita Park.

However, even within this sophisticated framework certain problems pertain. My own survey of 133 downtown spaces found that many were unsatisfactorily maintained, or did not invite public activities due to small size, adverse layout, hidden location, missing amenities or encroachment by shops and parking (Dimmer 2008: 301). Only one-fifth qualified as destination spaces, offering a pleasant stay and encouraging diverse activities. Four-fifths were pure circulation spaces like substitute sidewalks, sidewalk widenings, through-block connections or arcades. Since their size correlates with that of the overall development, the biggest spaces are found in suburban areas, where residential densities are relatively low and natural green spaces and big parks exist. Downtown POPS in turn tend to be much smaller. Consequently, the best design quality, network integration and maintenance were found in districts, where local business or landowners were keenly interested in high-quality environments, such as the Motomachi or Bashamichi shopping streets, or showcase spaces of citywide importance like Nihon-Ôdori, or Yamashita Park. In Minato Mirai 21 large projects produced some of Yokohama's biggest and most spectacular POPS. Similar to the following case study of OMY, the landowners – among them Mitsubishi Real Estate as owner of the former shipyard and key player in the planning process – developed a detailed design guideline in cooperation with the authorities and concluded a development agreement.

Private initiative in Ôtemachi–Marunouchi–Yûrakuchô (OMY)

Located in a triangle between stock exchange in Nihonbashi, national diet in Nagatachô and state bureaucracy in Kasumigaseki, as well as sandwiched between the landmarks Tokyo Station and Imperial Palace, OMY occupies an exceptionally prominent physical location. As 6,500 companies conducted business here, employing some 240,000 people at its heyday in the late 1980s, and as over one million people pass daily through the 13 Japan Railways and subway stations the area is also central to the everyday experience of many commuters and for the imagining of Tokyo as a whole. In the 120-hectare district 95 corporations own land, of which Mitsubishi Estate Company (MEC) alone holds 30 per cent and consequently has a strong interest in unified development. While one of Tokyo's fanciest shopping locations today, only a decade ago Roman Cybriwsky could describe it justifiably as

> a no-nonsense setting, where the important work of big companies can go on without needless distractions. The streets are laid out in an orderly grid, and the blocks are covered from end to end with big office buildings that are functional, but almost totally without adornment. There are not even many

restaurants or drinking places – highly unusual for a crowded commercial area in restaurant-rich Tokyo.... A walk through Marunouchi reveals its single-minded dedication to work. ... Almost no one speaks. ... The buildings themselves ... all reflect the sameness.

(1998: 119)

Many young Japanese employees and visitors shared this notion. While older workers still held the district in high regard in the mid-1990s, their younger colleagues and especially the increasingly female share conceived it as old-fashioned ('dasai') and boring, offering little beside work (Fukuzawa 2000: 12–13).

Today Marunouchi's image differs remarkably. This is most visible in Naka-dori, the central pedestrian promenade, stretching from Yûrakuchô in the south to Ôtemachi in the north. Where streets were once lined with dull counter rooms of banks and security companies, dropping their iron shutters in the afternoon and on weekends, today fashionable boutiques, cafés and restaurants attract the contemporary *flaneûr*. While the public spaces frequently figure as a trendy backdrop for TV programs, or lifestyle and fashion magazines, one can also enjoy here the rare Tokyo experience of sitting under shady trees and watching people stroll by. The atrium of the Marunouchi Building serves as a popular spot for exhibitions, TV and radio shows, farmers' markets or sports events. Since its privatisation in 2003, the central plaza of the Tokyo International Forum became a stage for concerts, festivals and the popular lunchtime '*neo yatai village*'. The Shin-Marunouchi Building attracts visitors with its public terrace at 30 metres high and a panorama on Imperial Palace and Tokyo Station. The new Maru-nouchi Park Building features an art and water park between the replica of the Mitsubishi No. 1 Building and a massive new office tower.

Besides the exceptional design quality in OMY, the public spaces are all part of one comprehensive urban design strategy, centring on a unified open space network and developed in an unprecedented public–private cooperation or growth regime on equal footing. How did it come to this revaluation of public space within just a decade? How was it possible that a diverse coalition of stake-holders jointly agreed on a future vision and committed to its realisation? To understand the complex socio-political context and the unique urban morphology, a closer look at its development history is necessary.

After housing feudal mansions during the Edo era, the land here was occupied by the Imperial Army headquarters in the early Meiji years. After its relocation and lying wasted for years Mitsubishi purchased it in 1890 and began constructing Japan's first office buildings. The Englishman Josiah Conder planned an initial row of red brick buildings along Babasaki Avenue that became known as 'London Town'. After the completion of Tokyo Station in 1914 large ferroconcrete office blocks followed in its vicinity that were nicknamed 'New York Town'.

The beginning of the high economic growth period, 1955 marked the second development phase. As a response to the rapidly growing demand for office space, the outdated brick buildings were gradually replaced with large profitable office blocks. Sadly, after surviving the Earthquake of 1923 and the bombs of World War II, Conder's famed Mitsubishi No. 1 Building perished on the eve of the 1964 Tokyo Olympics. From the mid-1970s on corporations began consolidating their key functions in Tokyo, while concurrently OMY's office supply could no longer keep up with the demand. At the same time many of the older buildings were no longer state-of-the-art.

In the late 1980s MEC launched the latest development cycle, which became deeply entangled in the ideological battle over the future development trajectory of greater Tokyo and OMY as its central business district (CBD) therein. From the beginning of the decade, plans and policies had been devised by various government entities that identified the main reasons for the worsening quality of life and over-congestion in a uni-polar concentration of business functions around Tokyo Station. Consequently, the long-term development plans 'My Town Tokyo' (1982, 1986) of Governor Suzuki Shunichi (1979–95) proposed a multi-polar metropolitan region with sub-centres along the Yamanote line and in Tama (Sorensen 2001). While these would absorb future development, further CBD growth was curbed. This policy change was symbolically stressed by the relocation of the city hall from Yûrakuchô to Nishi-Shinjuku.

Although over-concentration was stated as severe problem, public policies were equivocal. When the Japan National Railways was privatised in 1987, the National Land Agency (NLA) and several ministries examined ways to utilise the land around Tokyo Station. Incongruous with the decentralisation paradigm, 13 towers were proposed that would add another 145 hectares of downtown office space (OMY 2001: 112).[19] Even the demolition of the historic station building was seriously considered, as it seemed out of tune with the zeitgeist of the bubble years. The heated real estate market with skyrocketing land prices and a seemingly endless demand for office space spurred various development fantasies that seemed to come straight out of science fiction (Sorensen 2002: 285–6) – one of them the 'Marunouchi Redevelopment Plan' (*Marunouchi no Saikaihatsu Keikaku*) (1988), later ridiculed as the 'Manhattan Plan'. Although it was, according to MEC, only meant as a feasibility study based on the capacity of the existing public infrastructure, it shocked the public nevertheless with the simulation of 60 towers, each 200 metres high. This amounted to a FAR of 2,000 per cent, whereas existing regulations allowed no more than 1,300 per cent. MEC rationalised this by arguing that the project would stop further displacement of downtown residences through office functions,[20] improve Japan's economic edge by capitalising on agglomeration effects and it could be realised faster and cheaper than an entirely new international business centre in Odaiba (Taniguchi and Ishida 1988). Unsurprisingly, the bold scheme came under massive public attack, because of its conflict with the decentralisation paradigm and for passing TMG over. It earned further criticism for the visual impact on the cityscape vis-à-vis the Imperial Palace and doubts if the public infrastructure sufficed for doubling the land use intensity (Hara 1989: 149).

Soon after, TMG announced its 'Waterfront Sub-centre Basic Development Plan' (*Rinkaibu Fukutoshin Kaihatsu Kihon Keikaku*) and began the construction of a new business centre on a landfill in the bay (Saitô 2003), effectively shelving downtown renewal for the time being. As redevelopment was stalled at the end of the economic bubble, new state-of-the-art office buildings mushroomed in Nishi-Shinjuku, Nakano Sakaue, Ebisu and Shinagawa that began enticing tenants from OMY with lower rents. At the start of this fierce competition between office locations MEC and other major landowners realised that only a concerted renewal approach could win TMG's approval and maintain competitiveness. Only months after the Manhattan Plan disaster and supported by Chiyoda ward, 74 companies formed the 'OMY District Redevelopment Council' and debated redevelopment strategies before concluding a development agreement for a unified international business centre in close public–private partnership and 'in harmony with the environment and the urban context' (OMY 2001: 116).

The year 1995 brought not only a profound political climate change, but also numerous studies by private think tanks like the City Planning Institute of Japan advocated active downtown renewal. A strong centre would enhance the global competitiveness of the traumatised post-bubble metropolis and revive the ailing national economy. NLA further endorsed this view with its policy 'Grand Design for Downtown Tokyo' (*Tôkyô Toshin no Guran Dezain*). In the same year the newly elected Governor Aoshima Yukio (1995–99) began cutting back the loss-making operations in Odaiba and proposed 'New Development Principles for the Central Wards' (*Kubunchûshinbu Seibi Shishin*) that sought to re-imagine the old mono-functional CBD as a new 'amenity business core (ABC)' by emphasising quality of life and urban beauty. Thereafter TMG took an active stance and set up the 'Advisory Committee on OMY Area Redevelopment'. In this unparalleled public–private partnership TMG, Chiyoda ward, JR East as the owner of Tokyo Station, and the members of the redevelopment council drew up an urban design guideline on equal footing. This was further assisted by external experts from academia and debated in public forums (OMY 2005).

On 3 August 1997 OMY's redevelopment was brought back to public attention when the Nihon Keizai Shinbun opened with the headline 'Twilight in Marunouchi' (*Marunouchi no Tasogare*), with the following points leading to the fatal assessment: first, OMY had developed the reputation of an old-fashioned business location with many big companies – including members of the Mitsubishi group (e.g. Mitsubishi Heavy Industries moving to Shinagawa) – relocating to other areas with state-of-the-art office buildings, low rents and extensibility; second, although MEC reacted to this with the renewal of the Marunouchi Building, the response of the authorities was slow and a long delay was expected, during which the competitiveness would further suffer; third, since the restructuring of Marunouchi would take about 30 years other new districts would spring up in Shiodome, Shinagawa or Roppongi (Shimada 2002: 115). Although the revitalisation of Marunouchi was already under way the article meant a serious blow to the area's image. MEC as chief property owner realised that immediate and accelerated action was necessary. A fresh area image was vital for rebuilding tenant confidence, attracting further foreign businesses, more sensitive to their working environment, or female employees, making up a growing share of Japan's labour market due to demographic trends. A first short-term measure was the renovation of Nakadori as a shady cobble stone promenade, lined with fashionable shops in the ground floors. In a prominent spot the Marunouchi café opened as a 'free-space' for relaxing, free Internet use and events and as a result the media representation began to shift and the revitalization project began to figure positively in magazines aimed at female office workers, and lifestyle magazines like *Hanako*, or *Oggi* (Fukuzawa 2000: 69).

Soon after Ishihara Shintarô assumed office as governor (1999–) and as a result of the devastating Hanshin-Awaji earthquake (1995) that had provided developers with a pretence to 'renewal' for the sake of earthquake proofing, the 'hard' redevelopment commenced. Ishihara took an active stance on the restoration of Tokyo Station in its pre-war state, as a highly symbolic showcase project for the revitalisation of Japan and its ailing economy.[21] His sense of urgency was manifested in the 'Strategy Plan for Overcoming the Crisis' (*Kiki Toppa Senryaku Puran*) and the 'Tokyo New City Planning Vision' (*Tôkyô no atarashii Toshizukuri Bijon*). Both stressed that the revitalisation had to be actively promoted and should hinge on the downtown. In order to safeguard 'dignified' public space Ishihara demanded a comprehensive development plan for the vicinity of Gyôko Avenue that connects the landmarks Tokyo Station and Imperial Palace.

In 2000, the 'OMY District Development Guideline' (*OMY Machizukuri Gaidorain*) was finally released. It demands a harmonious skyline with varying building heights from 100 to 200 metres, environmentally sensitive design respecting cultural and historic assets, induction of mixed functions and an elaborate system of interconnected, attractive public spaces above and below ground (OMY 2005). Nakadori serves as the main amenity axis, while around Ôtemachi, Yûrakuchô and Tôkyô attractive station front squares will cater to public life. In order to create distinct area characters (*merihari*) new planning tools were introduced, such as transferable development rights. In the guideline public space is also no longer treated as two-dimensional open space but additionally active management as well as responsive building forms and vitalising functions seek to animate it. In particular the following three public space related objectives are outlined:

First, representative spaces such as Nakadori, or the sidewalks facing the palace, will be lined with 'vitalising land uses' such as shops, restaurants, cafés or galleries, whereas in other areas office functions dominate. The building design has to safeguard the creation of 'intermediate zones' (*chûkan ryôiki*) at the public–private interface, which stimulate a host of public activities and convey images of 'hospitality' (OMY 2005: 28–30).

Second, as part of this strategy POPS will proactively complement the overall public space network in three different ways: In Yûrakuchô and Marunouchi, which are marked by an exceptionally regular streetscape, bonus spaces will be created only within buildings. To encourage this, the bonus floor area for indoor spaces like atriums and gallerias was raised relative to outdoor-type spaces. In the less regular Ôtemachi area, open air spaces will be concentrated around the station, where they form a central square. Finally, along the Nihonbashi River and at the Yaesu side POPS will contribute to a coherent pedestrian promenade, connecting Tôkyô station with Yûrakuchô station. As a part of the wider Nihonbashi revitalisation, involving the removal of the elevated highway, they will supplement a future riverfront promenade. Around major stations multi-storied atriums or sunken garden-type POPS facilitate the vertical circulation between underground concourses and spaces at ground level.

Third, in order to fully utilise it for area branding, an integrated, total management of public space was developed and a management organisation with NPO status was set up for its implementation. Events like the Cow Parade (2003–present) or the Millenario (1999–2005) brought millions of visitors to the area and their publicity effect was multiplied through exposure in countless magazines and the Internet. 'Hard', coordinated improvement of the physical environment – buildings and privately as well as publicly owned public space – is complemented by 'soft' management techniques like event staging, private policing, cleaning and upkeep of public space, monitoring of customer and tenant satisfaction, unified retail and tenant mix for storefronts and media orchestration (Kobayashi 2005).

The study has shown that the real estate sector increasingly took an active interest in the creation of 'new public spaces' at large mega developments such as OMY, where it served as a distinguishing elements in a growing area competition but also responded to changed socio-cultural values. While quantitative matters like a boost of rentable office space played a chief role in the controversial MEC's Manhattan plan, a decade later more qualitative, soft issues like historical preservation, environmental design and an attractive public realm became equally central to create a distinguished area image. This shift also reflects broader societal trends towards more stimulating work environments that no longer solely cater to middle-aged Japanese businessmen, but increasingly also to young female employees and shoppers, foreign tenants or international city tourists. The result is a 'total landscape of work and leisure' (McDowell 1997: 140), in which boundaries between work and fun blur. Also the recent renaissance of outdoor life styles, expressed in phrases like *machi aruki* (city walking) and expressed through the proliferation of Starbuck's-type open sitting terraces influenced plans and projects like the OMY redevelopment guideline and created a vast body of popular literature and magazines. In a feedback relation the same media feature in turn those 'new public spaces' that again alter lifestyles. The perceived loss of competitiveness of the world city Tokyo vis-à-vis its burgeoning rivals Shanghai, Singapore or Taipei also made the political level aware of the importance of public space for nation branding.

Discussion

This chapter sought to achieve a more nuanced and culture-sensitive understanding of public space by elaborating the intricacies of the concept in Japan. The second part exemplified the dynamic social construction of public space through a longitudinal study of one particular sub-category, namely privately owned public space, and its particular institutional context.

The examples of Yokohama City and OMY both showed that the recent revaluation of public space did not simply stem from a changed mind-set of 'the government' but that it is perpetually reconstructed in a complex interplay between local and global actors and discourses, hard and soft social institutions and a specific spatio-culturally induced system of perception, interaction, representation and language. While the national government began endorsing a new publicness and civil society in the late 1990s, progressive local governments like Yokohama City had already developed a new conception of publicness on the grass-root level three decades earlier. Through differing interactions between public and private actors within planning processes as well as administrative practice this newly conceived public space materialised physically in forms, previously unknown in urban Japan.

Initially local government as well as the landowners had only a minimum interest in the quality of public space and POPS; good design and usability mattered little. The prior were happy to fulfil their quantitative target figures for open space production, while understanding them exclusively as a means to improve disaster prevention and pedestrian circulation while the latter did not spend much money and effort, and conceived them as mere vehicle for boosting the rentable floor area. As incentive zoning is a trade-off of 'building bulk for open space' other urban resources like cityscape, sunlight exposure, microclimate or neighbourhood character were often compromised, in the name of a questionable amenity. Both Yokohama and OMY sought to overcome these side-effects by developing a comprehensive planning vision with public space at the centre. The economical restructuring that had set in with the globalisation had led to an increased local and supra-local location competition, with public space becoming an important distinguishing element. Also its imagining changed by a new representation in print and screen media, focusing on sustainability and quality of life, by growing experiences of foreign cultures and cities, by societal, political and professional discourses but also by changing everyday experiences in the Japanese urban environment.

(The study has been kindly supported through a doctoral scholarship of the Ministry of Education, Culture, Sports, Science and Technology [MEXT] as well as through a JSPS post-doctoral fellowship.)

Notes

1 Only fairly recently researchers began to tackle public space issues outside the 'classical' Western context with varying degrees of theoretical sophistication. See Low (2000) for a thorough discussion of public life on Latin American plazas or Cuthbert

(1995), Cybriwsky (1999), Miao (2001), Douglass (2003), Nguyen (2005) on various examples in East Asia.

2 Sakae Park is central Nagoya's new attraction. Atop an underground bus terminal and shopping centre the city proposed an artificial platform with a stage-like event space that has little resemblance with traditional parks. This caused serious debates in the park department of MoC. Traditionalist wanted to refuse national subsidies because the project negated their Olmstedian ideas of a park as visual antithesis to gridded streets and rectangular buildings. However, when funding was finally approved, the park definition in the Urban Park Act (*toshikôen Hô*) had to be supplemented ex post with a new category: the vertical urban park (*rittai toshikôen*) (Interview with MLIT official, October 2004).

3 In the late 1970s the first alternative adventure playgrounds (*bôkenasobiba*) and wilderness parks (*harappa kôen*) originated from the private initiative of citizens, who had to overcome the resistance of local officialdom. In 1978 Hanegi playpark in Setagaya was completed as Japan's first adventure playground.

4 The Tokyo Central Park NPO advocates a unified design and management of all public spaces surrounding the imperial palace to create a real 'central park' out of disjoint open spaces. A major obstacle is that the nine chief open spaces are controlled by six different public bodies (stated at the founding symposium of the Tokyo Central Park NPO, 9 May 2003).

5 Ishizuka (1988) describes how street activities were gradually outlawed in the Meiji Period. They had to make way for the evolving road traffic but were also seen as detrimental to morals and public order. Such negative and repressive government bias lingered on until the present, further amplified by the violent student revolts of the late 1960s.

6 Such a conceptualisation phase seems typical when foreign ideas meet cultural milieus with different conceptual histories. The public park (*Kôen*, literally 'official garden') is firmly rooted in everyday language today, while in Meiji Japan several alternative terms were concurrently used, depending on if ideas were translated from German, English or French sources.

7 Despite being a major trait in the West (Davis 1992; Mitchell and Straeheli 2006) and increasingly also taken up by Japanese scholars (Aoki 2003), homelessness features only marginally in planning discourses. Their presence is here largely perceived as a design and management problem; an annoyance to 'normal' park users that needs to be 'designed out'.

8 A young Japanese MoC bureaucrat studied at the University of Philadelphia from 1962–63. Among his teachers was Paul Davidoff, who was one of the 'fathers' of New York's new zoning ordinance. After his return to Japan his know-how helped drafting the legislation that would legitimise the already-agreed construction of the Mitsui Kasumigaseki Building.

9 The 'bonusable' amenity menu grew constantly over the past 40 years. FAR bonuses and other zoning concessions are now granted for disaster prevention infrastructure (food storage, potable and fire water), social (community or day care centres), cultural (theatres, museums) and parking facilities, historical landmark preservation, access to subway stations and downtown housing (Kuniyoshi and Senda 2000).

10 Figures in parentheses indicate how often the planning tools were applied in Tokyo until February 2012. See homepage of TMG, Bureau for Urban Development (accessed February 2012).

11 Tokyo's so-called wooden apartment belt (*mokuzô jûtaku misshû*) developed during the suburbanisation phase of the 1910s haphazardly and again in the aftermath of the Great Kantô Earthquake. It forms a zone just outside the Yamanote line from Kôtô, Taitô, Bunkyô, Toshima, Nakano, Setagaya, to Meguro. Even today, these areas are marked by a high concentration of derelict, low-story buildings, fragmented landownership and plot patterns, critical mix of residential and industrial functions,

concentration of elderly and low-income groups and lack of public infrastructure (streets, sidewalks, parks) (Koshizawa 1992: 28–9).

12 Special purpose districts were for example designated in New York to promote the evolution of open space networks. The special park district on the other hand rules out POPS in the vicinity of Central Park, where they are neither needed nor desired, because the higher buildings, they potentiate, impair the user comfort in the park. Seattle earmarked specific areas where incentive zoning is desired and others where it is ruled out.

13 Sometimes landowners abstain from incentive zoning altogether because of the commitment to open the property to the public (interview with Nikken Sekkei project manager, June 2004).

14 Exemplarily for POPS in recent projects, the following activities are prohibited at the City Centre Shiodome Building: 1) entry with bicycles or motor bikes and parking; 2) using skateboards; 3) littering (waste bins are absent); 4) loitering; 5) unauthorized photography; 6) gatherings; 7) sales activity; 8) unauthorized events; 9) distribution of handbills; 9) smoking; 10) drinking; 11) pets. This catalogue is clearly more restrictive than municipal park ordinances, a potential yardstick.

15 The other projects were: 2) land reclamation for relocating and consolidating factories in residential areas; 3) Kohoku new town as a new sub-centre to slow suburbanisation; 4) a subway system as backbone of the public transit network; 5) a highway system to drain traffic from downtown and residential areas; 6) a bay bridge as a link to Tokyo (Yokohama 1965: 52–67).

16 The strictly hierarchical and vertically segmented government in Japan is referred to as *tatewari gyôsei*. Municipal government departments need to communicate directly with the corresponding national ministries and with prefectures as intermediaries. Consequently, local projects have to undergo time-consuming serpentine approval processes, involving multiple ministries and agencies. The vertical administrative strands often pursue antagonistic agendas, even on local government level, with minimum lateral coordination.

17 The seven urban design objectives are: 1) protection of pedestrians in safe and pleasant open spaces; 2) respecting distinctive natural features like topography and greenery; 3) appreciating cultural and historical assets; 4) provision of abundant greenery and open space; 5) creation of open space along rivers and the sea; 6) increasing the places, where people can come in contact with each other and communicate; 7) seeking urban beauty (Nishiwaki *et al.* 1992: 25).

18 Even MLIT officials expressed their doubt concerning the legality of this practice as the instrument was only meant for specific limited areas. Given that it wasn't challenged in court, it has been tolerated to this day (interview April 2004).

19 NLA had published projections, stating that 80 hectares (or five big office towers) of additional office space were annually needed until 2000 to satisfy the demand of the rapidly growing service economy (OMY 2001: 112).

20 See Douglass (1993) and Sorensen (2003) on the dramatic results of the zoning deregulations under the Nakasone cabinet, leading to a displacement of the residential population through a spreading of office functions in central Tokyo.

21 Although restoring Tokyo Station to its pre-war condition fits Ishihara's nationalist agenda, it was not his idea. In 1987 he was confronted by the Tokyo Station preservation movement in his function as Minister of Transport in the Takeshita Cabinet. After the landmark was saved, the movement lobbied for its restoration to its original condition (Tani 2001).

References

Alexander, C., Ishikawa, S. and Silverstein, M. (1977). *A Pattern Language – Towns – Buildings – Construction*, Oxford University Press, New York.

Aoki, H. (2003). 'Homelessness in Osaka: Globalisation, Yoseba and Disemployment.' Urban Studies, 40(2), 361–78.

Arendt, H. (1998). 'The Human Condition.' The University of Chicago Press, Chicago.

Barnett, C. (2005). 'Convening Publics – the Parasitical Spaces of Public Action.' In *Handbook of Political Geography,* eds. M. Low, K.R. Cox and J. Robinson, Sage, London.

Berding, U., Perenthaler, B. and Selle, K. (2007). 'Öffentlich nutzbar – aber nicht öffentliches Eigentum. Beobachtungen zum Alltag von Stadträumen im Schnittbereich öffentlicher und privater Interessen. [Publicly usable – but not public property. Observing everyday use of urban spaces at the intersection of public and private interests].' In *Shopping Malls*, ed. Jan Wehrheim. Wiesbaden: VS Verlag für Sozialwissenschaften.

Berque, A. (1981). 'Analogy in Spatial Analysis: The Case of Japan.' *Ekistics* (289), 268–71.

Carr, S., Francis, M., Rivlin, L.G. and Strone, A.M. (1995). *Public Space*, Cambridge University Press, Cambridge.

Crawford, M. (1999). 'Blurring the Boundaries: Public Space and Private Life.' In *Everyday Urbanism*, eds. John Chase, Margaret Crawford and John Kaliski. New York: Monacelli Press.

Cuthbert, A.R. (1995). 'The Right to the City: Surveillance, Private Interest and the Public Domain in Hong Kong.' *Cities*, 12(5), 293–310.

Cybriwsky, R.A. (1998). *Tokyo: The Shogun's City at the Twenty-First Century*, John Wiley & Sons, Chichester, New York, Weinheim, Brisbane, Singapore, Toronto.

Cybriwsky, R.A. (1999). 'Changing Patterns of Urban Public Space: Observations and Assessments from the Tokyo and New York Metropolitan Areas.' *Cities*, 16(4), 223–31.

Davis, M. (1992). *City of Quartz: Excavating the Future of Los Angeles*, Vintage Books, New York.

Dimmer, C. (2008). 'Renegotiating Public Space: A Historical Critique of Modern Public Space in Metropolitan Japan and its Contemporary Re-valuation.' Graduate School of Engineering, Department of Urban Design, University of Tokyo, Tokyo.

Dimmer, C. and Aesche, J. (2001). 'Myth Public Space – How Public will the City of the Future be? [Mythos Öffentlicher Raum – Wie öffentlich wird die Stadt der Zukunft noch sein?].' In *Faculty of Spatial and Environmental Planning*, Kaiserslautern: University of Kaiserslautern.

Dimmer, C., Golani Solomon, E. and Klinkers, K.V. (2005). 'Shinonome – New Concepts of Public Space,' In *Summaries of Technical Papers of Annual Meeting*, Architectural Institute of Japan, Tokyo.

Douglass, M.C. (1993). 'The "New" Tokyo Story.' In *Japanese Cities in the World Economy*, eds. K. Fujita and R.C. Hill, Temple University Press, Philadelphia, 81–119.

Douglass, M. (2003) 'Civil Society for Itself and in the Public Sphere: Comparative Research on Globalisation, Cities and Civic Space in Pacific Asia.' Second GRAD Conference, Vancouver.

Flusty, S. (1994) 'Building Paranoia: The Proliferation of Interdictory Space and the Erosion of Spatial Justice.' Los Angeles Forum for Architecture and Urban Design, Los Angeles, 16–18.

Fukuzawa, T. (2000). 'The Economics of Marunouchi – This Quarter Is Pulling Forward the Tokyo of the 21st Century – *Marunouchi no keizaigaku – kono machi ga nijûisseiki no Tôkyô wo kenin suru*', PHP Kenkyusho, Tokyo.

Gehl, J. (1987). *Life between Buildings: Using Public Space*, Van Nostrand Reinhold, New York.

Getzels, J., Jaffe, M., Blaesser, B.W. and Brown, R.F. (1988). *Zoning Bonuses in Central Cities*, American Planning Association, Chicago.

Goheen, P.G. (1998). 'Public Space and the Geography of the Modern City.' *Progress in Human Geography*, 22(4), 479–96.

Gottdiener, M. (1985). *The Social Production of Urban Space*, University of Texas Press, Austin.

Gulick, J. (1998). 'The "Disappearance of Public Space": An Ecological Marxist and Lefebvrian Approach.' In *The Production of Public Space*, eds. Andrew Light and Jonathan M. Smith, Lanham: Rowman & Littlefield Publishers.

Habermas, J. (1992). *The Structural Transformation of the Public Sphere: An Inquiry into a Category of Bourgeois Society*, MIT Press, Cambridge.

Hara, T. (1989). 'Rebuilding Tokyo' – *Tôkyô kaizo*, Gakuyô Shobô, Tokyo.

Hasegawa, K. (2004). *Constructing Civil Society in Japan – Voices of Environmental Movements*, Trans Pacific Press, Melbourne.

Hebbert, M. and Nakai, N. (1988). 'Deregulation of Japanese Planning in the Nakasone Era.' *Town Planning Review*, 59(4), 383–95.

Iokibe, M. (1999). 'Japan's Civil Society: An Historical Overview.' In *Deciding the Public Good: Governance and Civil Society in Japan*, ed. T. Yamamoto, Japan Center for International Exchange, Tokyo, 51–96.

Ishida, Y. (1988). 'Chronology on Urban Planning in Tokyo 1868–1988.' In *Tokyo: Urban Growth and Planning 1868–1988*, eds. Ishizuka, H. I. Yorifusa, Tokyo Metropolitan University Press, Tokyo, 37–68.

Ishikawa, M. (2001). 'Cities and Green Space: Moving Towards the Creation of a New Environment – *toshi to ryokuchi: atarashi toshi kankyô no sôzô ni mukete*', Iwanami Shoten, Tokyo.

Ishizuka, H. (1988). 'Amusement Quarters, Public Squares and Road Regulations of Tokyo in the Meiji Era.' In *Tokyo: Urban Growth and Planning 1868–1988*, eds. H. Ishizuka and Y. Ishida, Tokyo Metropolitan University Press, Tokyo, 71–5.

Jinnai, H. (1995). *Tokyo: A Spatial Anthropology*, Nishimura, K. (trsl.), University of California Press, Berkeley.

Kayden, J.S. and New York Dept. of City Planning Municipal Art Society of New York. (2000). *Privately Owned Public Space: The New York City Experience*, J. Wiley, New York.

Kilian, T. (1998). 'Public and Private, Power and Space.' In *The Production of Public Space*, eds. Andrew Light and Jonathan M. Smith, Lanham: Rowman & Littlefield Publishers.

Kim, T.-C. and Sasaki, T. (eds). (2001). 'Public and Private in Comparative Intellectual Histories' – *kô towatakushi no shisôshi*, Tokyo Daigaku Shuppan-Sha, Tokyo.

Kobayashi, S. (ed.). (2005). 'Area Management – Planning and Management through District Organisation – *eriamanejimento: chiku soshiki ni yoru Keikaku to kanri unei*', Gakugei Shuppansha, Tokyo.

Kokudo kôtsû-shô dôro-kyoku (2005): Michi o katsuyô shita chiiki katsudô no enkatsuka no tame no gaidorain. http://www.mlit.go.jp/kisha/kisha05/06/060331/01.pdf.

Koshizawa, A. (1992). 'The Story of City Planning in Tokyo' – *Tôkyô toshi Keikaku monogatari*, Nihon Keizai Hyôronsha, Tokyo.

Kuniyoshi, S. and Senda, M. (2000). 'Image of the Urban Consolidation and Improvement Emerging from the Regulations for the Comprehensive Design System Established by the Special Administrative Agency – *tokuteigyôseichô ga seitei shita sôgô sekkei seido no kisoku ni okeru shigaichi kankyô no seibi kaizen imêji'*. Nihon Toshi Keikaku Gakkai Gakujutsu Kenkyû Ronbun Shû, 35, 925–30.

Lefebrve, H. (1991). *The Production of Space*, Blackwell, Oxford, UK, Cambridge.

Long, H.J. 2007. 'On Uneven Ground: Provincializing Cultural Production in Interwar Japan', University of Michigan.

Loukaitou-Sideris, A. (1993). 'Privatization of Public Open Space.' *Town Planning Review*, 64(2), 139–67.

Low, S. (2000). *On the Plaza: The Politics of Public Space and Culture*, University of Texas Press, Austin.

Matsushita, N., Watanabe, K. and Iwasaki, Y. (2003). 'A Study on Mutual Functional Substitution with Respect to Utilizing Facts between Central City Urban Parks and Semi-Public Spaces – *toshinbu ni okeru toshi kôen to minkan ôpun supêsu no riyô jittai kara mita sôgô kinô daitai ni kan suru kenkyû'*. Journal of the City Planning Institute of Japan, 241, 59–66.

McDowell, L. (1997). *Capital Culture: Gender at Work in the City*, Blackwell, Oxford.

Miao, P. ed. (2001). *Public Places in Asia Pacific Cities: Current Issues and Strategies*, Kluwer Academic Publishers, Dordrecht, Boston, London.

Mitchell, D. (1995). 'The End of Public Space? People's Park, Definitions of the Public, and Democracy.' *Annals of the Association of American Geographers*, 85, 108–33.

Mitchell, D. and Straeheli, L.A. (2006). 'Clean and Safe? Property Redevelopment, Public Space, and Homelessness in Downtown San Diego.' In *The Politics of Public Space*, eds. S. Low. and N. Smith, Routledge, London, New York, 143–75.

MEC (Mitsubishi Estate Company). (1988). 'Marunouchi Redevelopment Plan – *Marunouchi no saikaihatsu keikaku'*, Tokyo.

MM21 (Minato Mirai 21 Town Development Council). (2003). 'Basic Agreement on Town Development – *Minato Mirai 21 machizukuri kyôtei'*, Yokohama Minato Mirai 21 Corp., Yokohama.

Nadal, L. (2000). 'Discourses of Urban Public Spaces – USA 1960–1995, a Historical Critique,' PhD Thesis, Columbia University, New York.

Nguyen Anh, P. (2005) 'Public Spaces, State-Society Relations, and Planning in Vietnam.' 8th International Conference of the Asian Planning Schools Association APSA, Penang.

Nishiwaki, T., Kitazawa, T. and Kuniyoshi, N. (1992). 'Possibilities in Urban Design – 20 Years of Urban Design in Yokohama and Prospects for the Future – *âban dezain no kanôsei: Yokohama nijûnen no kiseki to tenbô'*. SD Space Design, 22(Extra Issue), 25–32.

OMY (OMY Advisory Council for Area Redevelopment WG Compilation Team). (2001). 'The Rebirth of Marunouchi – *Marunouchi no Shinsei'*. Zôkei (Special Issue 3), 110–27.

OMY (OMY Advisory Council for Area Redevelopment). (2005). Ôtemachi, Marunouchi, Yûrakuchô District Development Guideline – *Ôtemachi, Marunouchi, Yûrakuchô chiku machizukuri gaidorain'*, OMY Kondakai, Tokyo.

Prime Minister's Commission on Japan's Goals in the 21st Century. (2000). 'Japan's Goals in the 21st Century – the Frontier Within: Individual Empowerment and Better Governance in the New Millennium – *nijûisseiki nihon no kôsô: nihon no furontia wa nihon no naka ni aru'*, Cabinet Secretariat, Tokyo.

Robertson, J. (1998). 'It Takes a Village: Internationalization and Nostalgia in Postwar-Japan.' In *Mirror of Modernity: Invented Traditions of Modern Japan*, ed. Stephen Vlastos, Berkley, Los Angeles, London: Universtity of California Press.

Saitô, A. (2003). 'Global City Formation in a Capitalist Development State: Tokyo and the Waterfront Sub-Centre Project.' *Urban Studies*, 40(2), 283–308.

Schubert, H. (2000). *Urban Space and Behaviour: Towards an Integrated Theory of Public Space* [Öffentlicher Raum Und Verhalten – Zu Einer Integrierten Theorie Des Öffentlichen Raums], Leske + Budrich, Opladen.

Schwartz, F.J. (2003). 'Introduction: Civil Society in Japan.' In *The State of Civil Society in Japan*, eds. S.J. Pharr and F.J.Schwartz, Cambridge University Press, Cambridge, 1–19.

Scruton, R. (1987). 'Public Space and the Classical Vernacular.' In *The Public Face of Architecture: Civic Culture and Public Spaces*, eds. N. Glazer and M. Lilla, Free Press, New York, 13–25.

Sennett, R. (1992). *The Fall of Public Man*, W. W. Norton & Company, New York

Shimada, A. (2002). *Tokyo Revival Report* － 「Rupo」 Tôkyô saikô, Nihon Keizai Shinbunsha, Tokyo.

Shinohara, O., Kitahara, T. and Katô, G. (eds). (2007). 'Machizukuri for Well Used and Bustling Public Space: Open Cafes, Morning Fairs, Yatais, Events – *kôkyô kûkan no katsuyô to nigiwai machizukuri: ôpun kafê, asaichi, yatai, ibento*', Gakugeishuppansha, Tokyo.

Shinohara, M. (2007). 'Political Theory of Public Space – *kôkyô kûkan no seijiriron*'. Kyoto: Jinbun Shoin.

Smith, N. (1998). 'Antinomies of Space and Nature in Henri Lefebvre's "The Production of Space".' In *The Production of Public Space*, eds. Andrew Light and Jonathan M. Smith, Lanham: Rowman & Littlefield Publishers.

Soja, E.W. (1989). Postmodern Geographies: The Reassertion of Space in Critical Social Theory, Verso, London; New York.

Soja, E.W. (1996). *Thirdspace: Journeys to Los Angeles and Other Real-and-Imagined Places*, Blackwell, Cambridge.

Sorensen, A. (2001). 'Subcentres and Satellite Cities: Tokyo's 20th Century Experience of Planned Polycentrism.' *International Planning Studies*, 6(1), 9–32.

Sorensen, A. (2002). *The Making of Urban Japan: Cities and Planning from Edo to the Twenty-First Century*, Routledge, London; New York.

Sorensen, A. (2003). 'Building World City Tokyo: Globalisation and Conflict over Urban Space.' *The Annals of Regional Science* (37), 519–31.

Tani, S. (2001). '12 Years of Citizen Movement for the Reconstruction and Preservation of Tokyo Station's Red Brick Building – *fukugen hozon undô jûninen: shimin ga mamotta akarenga no Tôkyôeki*'. *Zôkei* (Special Issue 3), 154–7.

Taniguchi, S. and Ishida, O. (1988). 'Marunouchi Redevelopment Plan – Towards the Creation of an International Business Centre – *Marunouchi saikaihatsu keikaku: kokusai gyômu sentâ no keisei ni mukeru*.' *Shintoshi*, 42(4), 47–56.

Tateishi, M. (1973). 'New Land Use Zoning and the Comprehensive Design System – *shinyôto chiiki to sôgô sekkei*'. In *Urban Redevelopment and the Comprehensive Design System – shigaichi saikaihatsu to sôgô sekkei*, ed. Zenkoku Shigaichi Saikaihatsu Kyokai, Zenkoku Shigaichi Saikaihatsu Kyokai, Tokyo, 15–18.

TCDSR (Tokyo Comprehensive Design System Research Group). (2002). 'Comments on the Tokyo Metropolitan Comprehensive Design System Permit Principles – *Tôkyô sôgô sekkei seido kyoka yôkô to sono kaisetsu*', Tokyo Society of Architects & Building Engineers, Tokyo.

TMG Tôkyô-To Kankyô-Kyoku Shizen Kankyô-Bu Hozen-Ka. (2000). 'Plan for a Green Tokyo – Aiming at an Appealing Tokyo with a Network of Green and Water – *midori no Tôkyô Keikaku: mizu to midori ga nettowâkusareta fûkaku toshi wo mezashite*', TMG, Tokyo.

Ueda, K., Nishimura, Y., Jinno, H. and Mamiya, Y. (eds) (2005): *Kôkyô kûkan toshite no toshi [The City as Public Space]*, Iwanami Shoten, Tokyo.

UDC (Urban Design Center). (2002). 'A Research on Use Activation in Urban Public Space – the Example of the Open Cafe System – *toshi kôkyô kûkan no nigiwa riyô ni kan suru kenkyû: ôpun kafê no jirei to seido*', UDC, Tokyo.

Uno, M. (1998). 'The Urban Space We Are Heading from Now – *korekara no toshi kûkan ni mukete.*' Zôkei, 17(10/1998), 24–5.

Whyte, W.H. (1980). *The Social Life of Small Urban Spaces*, The Conservation Foundation, Washington D.C.

Yanagisawa, A. (1973). 'Explanation of the Permission Standards for Comprehensive Designs – *sôgô sekkei kyoka junsoku ni tsuite.*' In *Urban Redevelopment and the Comprehensive Design System – shigaichi saikaihatsu to sôgô sekkei*, ed. Zenkoku Shigaichi Saikaihatsu Kyokai, Zenkoku Shigaichi Saikaihatsu Kyokai, Tokyo, 19–30.

Yokohama City. (1965). 'Yokohama's City Planning – Yokohama's Future Made by Its Citizens – *Yokohama no toshizukuri: shimin ga tsukuru Yokohama no mirai*', Yokohama-Shi Somu Kyoku, Yokohama.

Yoshida, S. (1999). 'Rethinking the Public Interest in Japan: Civil Society in the Making.' In *Deciding the Public Good: Governance and Civil Society in Japan*, ed. Yamamoto, T., Japan Center for International Exchange, Tokyo, 13–49.

Zukin, S. (1995). *The Culture of Cities*, Blackwell Publishing, Oxford.

6 Citizen participation and urban development in Japan and Germany

Issues and problems

Carolin Funck, Tsutomu Kawada and Yoshimichi Yui

From government to governance: the rise of civil society

The idea of government in democratic societies is closely connected to the concept of a representative democracy. However, limitations of this concept have become visible and the necessity to shift from government to governance has been emphasised since the 1990s. Governance has been defined as a move beyond the traditional mode of democratic rule (Evans *et al.* 2005: 33), or, more detailed, 'a process of participation which depends on networks of engagement, which attempts to embrace diversity in contemporary society, which promotes greater responsiveness to service users and, in so doing, seeks to reshape accountability relationships' (Lovan *et al.* 2004: 8). The rather simple system of elections that transfer decision rights from the individual to a representative authority is replaced by complex processes-like engagement, responsiveness, consultation and accountability. Civil society has been used as a term to describe this far more complex system. Civil society is 'the social space in which individuals are able to engage in a range of activities through informal association' (Lovan *et al.* 2004: 8). In another definition, Friedmann and Douglas (1998: 2) describe civil society as 'that part of social life which lies beyond the immediate reach of the state and which must exist for a democracy state to flower'. However, it is not only the space between the state and the economy, where citizens can engage and associate themselves freely; the actions taken within this space should be influencing the structures of government and also business. In the case of urban development and urban planning, civil society thus 'is a collective actor in the construction of our cities and regions, in search of a good life' (Friedmann 1998: 21).

In accordance with the rise of concepts like governance and civil society, the paradigm of urban planning has also changed 'from technical skills and regulatory powers to advocacy of the disempowered or at least a process of finding common ground' (Friedmann and Douglas 1998: 3).

These somewhat idealistic definitions leave some questions unanswered. Even Friedmann (quoted in Abu-Lughod 1998: 237), a well-known advocate of civil society, distinguishes between the different roles of civil society, a social maintenance role and a role as a generator of social movements. In the role of social maintenance, civil society ends up filling the gap between organised government and free markets. As it takes over low profit functions in welfare, education, maintenance of public space and other areas that so far had been covered by the state, the first question is whether civil society functions mainly as an ally in the withdrawal of the state from public policy.

The second question concerns the processes of governance. Certainly, in urban planning as in other sections of public policy, procedures to guarantee a certain degree of citizen participation and of accountability have been introduced. However, is participation only a set of procedures or does it also include any specific content?

Finally, as civil society includes a range of different actors with conflicting interests, the question remains: who is civil society? The system of a representative democracy had given one solution to the problem of how to translate the interests of citizens into public policy. If, as mentioned above, civil society in the context of urban planning aims for a good life, who then defines what a good life is? Who defines the public good?

These questions will form the background for an analysis of recent changes in citizen participation in the urban planning system of Japan and Germany. Rather than concentrating on the system of planning itself, the multiple realities of citizen participation in the construction of urban space were examined using examples from major urban centres and peripheral towns.

Urban planning in Japan and Germany

Both countries are known for an elaborated system of urban planning and detailed planning regulations. In the urban planning law, citizen participation is included at two steps in the formal process, once in the early stage and once after the plan is drafted.

However, there are also many differences between the two countries. The highly centralised system of urban planning in Japan has been accused as one reason for the undifferentiated character of Japanese modern cities. On the other hand, the federal system in Germany has allowed for a variety of planning regulations in states and municipalities. Moreover, the detailed German *B-Plan* (*Bebauungsplan*) contains strict regulations on height, type of roof, building type etc. that can't be found in Japanese urban planning.

As can be seen from this difference, urban planning is conducted within the framework of the regional administrative system and therefore strongly influenced by its structure. Although Japan set up an elaborated system of central, regional and local governance after the Second World War, local autonomy has been restricted by a lack in financial resources and mechanisms to ensure the influence of central administration on the regional and local level. However, recent years have seen similar trends in the development of local government and governance in both countries. Foljanty-Jost (2009: 8) analyses the deterioration of local government finances and the loss of credibility of the representative democratic system, which is mirrored in the decrease of election participation, as the background for political reforms on the local level. The shift to strengthen decentralisation occurs as a double-strategy that combines accountability, privatisation of public services and quality control of the public sector with elements of direct democracy.

A comparison between Japan and Germany can thus help us to examine conditions for a stronger civil society, as both countries share similar structures and problems of local government. The very strong tradition of communal independence in German has been frequently used as a model in the discussions on decentralisation in Japan. However, comparing examples of citizen participation in urban planning will show that while a simple transfer of structures is impossible, as has been pointed out by Foljanty-Jost (2009: 13), limits and possibilities of citizen participation can be discovered and in consequence enrich the debate on civil society.

Four places were chosen for comparison, two from a metropolitan and two from a regional context. Berlin and Kobe have been compared before as 'imperfect cities' (Hirayama 2003), left with scars of German separation and reunification on the one hand and the devastating 1995 Hanshin-Awaji Earthquake on the other. In consequence, both cities have turned to citizen participation for solutions of urban crises and social inequality.

The choice of the two smaller cities might seem less obvious. While Freiburg is famous for its environmental policies, it is less well known that the same social and political elements that promoted environmental issues also pushed for reforms of social and political structures. The creation of a model district, as described below, therefore included environmental and social elements, making it a rare example for active citizen participation from the planning stage. Tomonoura, on the other hand, is part of an 'ordinary' industrial city in western Japan. However, the fact that in October 2009, for the first time in Japan, a court judged Tomonoura's citizens' rights to preserve their townscape as more important than a harbour development project shows the importance of the citizens movement in this town and the impact it has had on the national discussion. Both Freiburg and Tomonoura thus form suitable examples to illustrate developments of civil society in smaller cities and towns in the twenty-first century.

Citizen participation in Japan

In Japan, the space between the state and the economic sector, where civil society is supposed to be located, is said to be very narrow (Schwartz 2003: 5).

On the other hand, administrative reforms and efforts to reduce the role of the state in recent years have created a vacuum similar to the situation in many European countries. Space for the maintenance role of civil society has definitely widened, but how about the role as a generator of social movements?

Traditional citizen organisations like resident's organisations, women's, children's and senior citizens' associations have been based on the place of living.

However, these organisations mainly serve to fulfil administrative functions at the neighbourhood level and to rubber-stamp decisions that need the formal agreement of local inhabitants, like public construction projects. Since the 1970s, when environmental pollution and rapid destruction of traditional townscapes initiated a surge in citizen activities, citizen participation in urban planning has been summarised under the keyword of *machizukuri*, a term that would be literally translated as 'town making', but includes strong aspects of community development or neighbourhood building. A narrow definition restricts *machizukuri* to activities of the inhabitants of a certain area with the aim of creating a better living environment for themselves, while a wider interpretation can include all activities to make an area more attractive to live in (Sawamura 2004: 15, 20). The introduction of district plans set up by *machizukuri* councils in the urban planning law in 1980 provided citizen groups with a planning tool for the first time, although the measure of control is not particularly strong. *Machizukuri* has taken on a range of activities that have virtually been ignored by Japanese urban planning (Sorensen 2002: 325) and serves therefore mainly to fill the gaps in urban planning created by the absence of regulations that could contribute to a distinctive townscape or the improvement of residential areas.

The law for the introduction of non-profit organisations (NPOs) in 1998 resolutely widened the possibilities for citizens to form associations on a legal basis. Although fraught with many problems (Schwartz 2003: 16), these new actors, together with a vogue for voluntary activities after the Great Hanshin-Awaji Earthquake Disaster in 1995, redrew the map of citizen participation, as has been illustrated by Itô (2007) and Funck (2007). The following three examples, two from Kobe City, which together with the surrounding Hyôgo Prefecture became the avant-garde of *machizukuri* in Japan after the earthquake, and one from a more peripheral area, the town of Tomonoura in Fukuyama City, Hiroshima Prefecture, will be used to examine issues, forms and problems of citizen participation and cooperation in urban planning and in the improvement of urban life.

Improving urban neighbourhoods: Nishisuma (Kobe)

Nishisuma is the western part of the Suma ward, situated in the west of Kobe City. Just before the earthquake, citizens in Nishisuma had declined a land readjustment project suggested by Kobe City (Nishisuma Machizukuri Kondankai 1997). Suma ward was not affected as severely by the earthquake as the neighbouring Nagata ward and therefore not included in any of the urban renewal projects. The ward was left with some city planning road projects designed in the 1960s and still had to recover its pre-earthquake population in 2004. It is caught in the typical downtown area dilemma between narrow lanes, where houses cannot be rebuilt due to high building costs, legal restrictions and widened roads, where the construction of apartment buildings destroys the character of the area.

On the other hand, since the conflict about land readjustment, the area can look back on a vivid and multiple structure of citizen participation, displaying almost all possible forms of organisation in one area.

These organisations can be divided into resident-based and theme-based groups (Shaw and Goda (2004), which are loosely connected through a roof organisation, the Machizukuri Meeting in Nishisuma (*Nishisuma Machizukuri Kondankai*). Three neighbourhood associations cover the district, the most active one being Tsukimiyama *Jichikai*. It has nine thematic and four local subgroups, a system to elect and rotate officials regularly, and forms the core of the Machizukuri Meeting in Nishisuma.

The theme-based groups developed in close connection with the issues that had to be confronted in the area. The first issue was the confrontation on three City Planning Roads promoted by Kobe City. With the elevated Hanshin Expressway already cutting through the area, an increase in pollution was feared. A separate group was founded that is still running a court case against Kobe City. In the meantime, one of the roads has been almost completed, as many houses along the planned route were destroyed during the earthquake and it became easier to readjust land-lots. As a compromise neighbourhood associations were for the first time included in the planning of road design and succeeded in reducing the number of lanes from four to two.

A second issue was the reconstruction of a local park below the Hanshin Expressway that had been used for temporary housing after the quake. Tsukimiyama *Jichikai* had a subgroup that was in charge of parks. In negotiation with the city, they designed a biotope park. Now, a separate park management group takes care of this park.

As reconstruction proceeded and some roads were broadened, apartment buildings started to spring up in the area. Different groups were formed to oppose construction – only rarely was the opposition successful. Japanese building regulations allow for higher buildings along wider roads, and opposition to individual projects has been a rather frustrating experience for citizen groups not only in Kobe, but also in other Japanese cities.

With a large percentage of senior residents in the area, the issue that keeps coming up is the provision of welfare services for the elderly. Here, an NPO called Nishisuma *Danran* was formed with support from Tsukimiyama *Jichikai*. It uses a building provided by the neighbourhood association to conduct day care salons, lunch meetings and volunteer services for senior residents. This NPO has become the most constant part of citizen activities in the area.

If we analyse problems and potential of citizen activities in this area, the largest potential can certainly be found in the close cooperation between resident-based and theme-based groups. However, this cooperation was based on good personal relations, for example between the leader of the Tsukimiyama *Jichikai* and the leader of the NPO. When a new leader was elected for the *Jichikai*, trouble occurred concerning the use of the *Jichikai* building by the NPO. For the NPO securing regular funding is a constant problem and support by the *Jichikai* is vital.

As in the case of Nishisuma, all issues concerning urban planning, like the construction of parks and roads, are still basically decided by the administration. However, after the earthquake, citizens requested and were able to secure a role in the actual design of public space.

A survey of civil society organisations, mainly NPOs, in Hyôgo Prefecture in 2005 (Table 6.1) shows that welfare is the main theme of activity. Nationwide, NPOs in the category welfare and health make up for 39.3 per cent of all NPOs in 2003, followed by the categories culture, arts and sports (10.8 per cent) and environmental protection (10.8 per cent) (Sawamura 2004: 36). Combined with the example of Nishisuma, this proves that although citizen groups have achieved new forms of organisation and new fields of activities, their main function is to fill the gaps the state has left in public policy, especially to care for the weaker members of society.

Supporting citizens groups

After the NPO law came into effect, NPOs have spread rapidly throughout the country. Because each prefecture has a different support and management system (Pekkanen 2000: 141), numbers per population vary according to prefectural policies, issues and the strength of citizen movements in each area. The increase has been made possible by the existence of intermediate NPOs, organisations that support citizen activities. They offer advice and training for all kinds of groups, but also conduct their own projects. Supporting activities by the administration, as publishing information on existing groups or creating networks, are often entrusted to intermediate NPOs. Such entrusted projects are an important source of income and require a public competition.

In Kobe, some volunteer groups that sprang up after the earthquake developed into intermediate NPOs. Each of them has a different focus of activity, so while they often compete for entrusted projects, they have also been able to network and share projects. To introduce some of them we can take Kobe Empowerment Center (KEC), for example. In 2005, it started to operate a centre where it was easy to find information on citizen activities for those interested in getting

Table 6.1 Civil society organizations by subject of activity in Hyôgo Prefecture, 2005

Type	Number
Welfare	230
Education	85
Human rights	82
Machizukuri	55
Group support	55
International	42
Environment	40
Culture/sport	30
Work	30
Disaster prevention	29
Women	15

Note
Shimin Katsudô Sentâ Kôbe (2005), *n*=247, multiple answers.

involved. *Machizukuri Kenkyû* Center (Machizukuri research) developed from a group of architects who first created *Fukkôjuku* (a cram school) as a study group for themselves. Now they offer professional advice and run workshops on *machizukuri*. CS Kobe differs from these two groups in that it has a strong local focus. Located in Higashi-Nada Ward, it cooperates with neighbourhood associations and local volunteer groups.

CS Kobe has three kinds of projects. First, support projects help to start new groups and make them capable of working independently as community business. In seven years, it has encouraged over 40 groups who are active in a variety of sectors.

Second, original projects include services like advice and training, e.g. accounting for NPO staff. Although it originated in the welfare sector, CS Kobe also has an emphasis on environmental issues. Compared to welfare activities, environmental themes require a long-term, regional approach that is often neglected in *machizukuri*, but necessary to ensure future life quality (Nakamura *et al.* 2004: 35). It has created a local solar energy plant, partly with citizen investment, to provide environmental friendly energy in the area.

Third, entrusted projects include the management of a local community centre and of a day care salon for senior citizens. These projects generate the biggest share of income, 67 per cent in 2004 (Community Support Center Kobe 2005).

Although it has slightly decreased since 2001, CS Kobe handles a large budget. The large variety of projects is hold together by the concept of *kurukuru commyûniti*, a 'spinning' or 'cycle' community where all fields of activity are connected with each other (Community Support Center Kobe 2005).

CS Kobe is recognised as an innovative NPO with strong connections to the local area, so it has the potential of bridging the gap between traditional, neighbourhood based organisations and NPOs. The complex concept of a circulating community is also unique. However, like other intermediate NPOs that have to support professional staff and act as a reliable provider of funds and information for other groups, it has problems in securing regular funding. There is also the danger of spreading activities too far. In the immediate years after the earthquake, funds sprang up easily, seducing intermediate NPOs into constantly widening their activities. Ten years after, many of the funding programmes were stopped and some organisations realised that they had lost their focus of activity during this expansion phase that might be dubbed the 'NPO bubble'. In the case of CS Kobe, for example, research had been started on a community bus project, but the group finally was unable to continue the project and its realisation was left to the local citizens and professional town planners supporting them. The above-mentioned KEC decided in 2003 to reduce applications for government funded projects and concentrate on their original activities, even though this meant a significantly reduced budget. Caught between the dilemma of securing funds and losing their originality, intermediate NPOs nevertheless have consolidated themselves as an important actor in civil society.

Improving a historic district: Tomonoura (Fukuyama)

While the distribution of NPOs nationwide roughly correlates with population numbers, so that their spread cannot be called an urban phenomenon, differences in the social fabrics of conurbations and small towns are still considerable. In provincial areas, the public good is defined by the administration and not perceived as something that citizens construct as a common activity among themselves. If therefore citizens have the impression that their interests are not considered sufficiently by the administration, confrontation is often unavoidable. The process of redefining the public good proves to be difficult as those opposing the administration are accused of persecuting their private interests at the expense of 'the general public' (Sawamura 2004: 71).

The town of Tomonoura in Fukuyama City, Hiroshima Prefecture, is a case in point. Once an important port town where ships had to wait for the tides to change and trade flourished, it houses the only preserved complete port ensemble from the eighteenth century. Nineteen temples and about 80 buildings from the Edo Period are witnesses to a past glory. In the twentieth century, iron and steel industry, shipbuilding and tourism became the pillars of the local economy. The town is known not only for its rich historical heritage, but also for the scenic beauty of coastline and islands, which were designated as part of the Seto Inland Sea National Park in 1934. However, since the train connection was abolished and the town merged into Fukuyama City in 1956, it started to lose population and now has a high percentage of senior citizens. In 1983, a plan by Fukuyama City became public to move the main road from the historic centre into the harbour. To this purpose, part of the harbour is to be reclaimed as a landfill and the other half spanned by a bridge. Since the plan became known, citizen groups have opposed it vehemently. However, the plan had achieved the approval of the heads of the residents associations and was therefore proclaimed by the city as a 'public good'.

In the long process of opposition, citizen groups in town have been trying to suggest alternatives like a road tunnel behind the town while at the same time seeking support for the appreciation of Tomonoura's heritage. During the long conflict, which cannot be explained in detail here, a variety of institutions and individuals have come to support the opposing groups with research, advice and financial means. Academic and research support comes from architectural seminars of Tokyo University and the University of Japan, who regularly hold fieldwork courses in town were students not only examine the structure of historic buildings but also conduct events and suggest new activities. The leader of a well-known, internationally active NPO in Tokyo has provided not only the incentive to create a NPO, but also political support as well as new ideas for small-scale business in town. International organisations like the World Monuments Fund and ICOMOS also became involved. For the reason that the harbour development 'will radically alter its waterfront, increase traffic within the city, and adversely affect its inhabitants' way of life', the World Monuments Fund has put Tomonoura twice on its yearly list of 100 worldwide heritages in danger

(World Monuments Fund 2004) and also provided funds for the renovation of an Edo Period house. ICOMOS appealed to the mayor of Fukuyama City in 2005 to preserve the historic district and cancel the development project.

In 2003, citizens created an NPO called *Machizukuri Kôbo* (*machizukuri* factory) to move from a stance of opposition to an active role in reviving the town. As many of the historic buildings in town fall empty when their owner dies, one of their main tasks is to put vacant houses to new uses. Projects include a coffee shop, information, a rest house and the arrangement of rent contracts. With funds from the World Monuments Fund it was possible to buy and reno-vate an Edo Period house that opened as a restaurant and pension in 2008. In 2005, the group received two awards for these projects.

There is probably no other heritage conservation movement in Japan that has received such an amount of attention nationwide as well as internationally. The degree of networking as well as the variety of activities is certainly unique. The accumulation of local knowledge that was achieved during the process, a key to setting up successful structures of governance (Evans *et al.* 2005: 29), is also considerable. However, the planned public development project poses a constant threat to these activities. After 20 years of protest, the infamous 'iron triangle' between industry (in this case construction industry), bureaucrats and politicians still holds tight at least in this provincial city, restricting possibilities of govern-ance. In this discourse, 'participation' is defined as the approval of projects by traditional resident associations, which can easily be gained through the leaders of the associations.

When citizens opposing the project finally went to court, they appealed for a reconsideration of plans and a 'right for landscape', arguing that the destruction of the historic harbour would deprive them of future possibilities to enjoy their townscape and make use of it as a cultural and tourism resource. The district court in Hiroshima judged in their favour and demanded that Hiroshima Prefec-ture and Fukuyama City reconsider the development plans. Shortly after this decision, the newly elected governour of Hiroshima Prefecture started a process of negotiation between different citizen groups in Tomonoura, departing from his predecessors' top-down implemenation of urban planning.

Citizen participation in Germany

In contrast to Japan, finding an organisational form for their activities has not been a problem for citizens in Germany. The *Verein* (society) is a well-established part of German society. Those recognised as *gemeinnützig* (charit-able, for the benefit of the public) even enjoy tax exemptions. When in the 1970s movements addressing issues of peace, environment and third world problems sprang up around the country, many immediately established themselves as a *Verein*. The German proportional election system also made it easy for these movements to develop into a political party, *die Grünen*, which at least in the beginning supported ideas of direct democracy and advocates citizen participation.

The traditional concept of urban planning as an expression of broad, long-term interests of the people sanctioned by the relevant political body (Friedmann 1998: 19) was shaken during the squatter movements against urban redevelopment in the late 1970s and early 1980s. These movements were particularly strong in the cities of Berlin, Freiburg and Köln.

In 1976, law amendments obliged local authorities to make the early drafts of planning documents available to the public for comments and objections. In reality, however, planning authorities can be quite skillful in presenting documentation that they have met the legal requirements for citizen participation without making major changes to the original plans (Levine 2004: 102). Since then, opportunities for citizen participation in urban planning have not only been widened legally, but have also been endorsed in a variety of forms that exceed the minimum legal requirements. Especially since the late 1990s, integrated urban development programmes like *die Soziale Stadt* (the Social City) or European Union (EU) sponsored programmes like Urban 2 aim for improved living conditions through the involvement and eventually independent action of residents. In this phase, the term of participation is replaced by cooperation (Bundesamt für Bauwesen und Raumordnung 2003: 18).

Two examples from the cities of Freiburg and Berlin will illustrate the involvement of citizens in the planning of a new development on a former military site and in districts designated under the programme *Soziale Stadt* as districts with special development needs.

Creating a new neighbourhood

The City of Freiburg in the state of Baden-Württemberg, with about 200,000 inhabitants, has a reputation as an environment-friendly model city. Since the late 1970s, integrated programmes to improve public transportation and to achieve independence from nuclear energy have been promoted by the city, supported by a large variety of citizen groups and research institutes engaged in environmental issues as well as a high percentage of green votes in the local assembly. When in 1992 an area of 38 ha located 3 km south to the city centre was vacated by its former user, the French military, the city decided to create a sustainable model district. This included integration of living and working, a district centre with shops for daily use, conservation and extension of existing natural spaces, priority for public transport, cyclists and pedestrians, energy-efficient buildings, family friendly institutions like schools and nursery schools and last not least expanded citizen participation above the legally required minimum (*erweiterte Bürgerbeteiligung*) (Sperling 1999: 19). The Vauban District was to provide housing space for 5,000 people and jobs for 500. In 1995, the outline of the project was decided on by an architectural competition, which favoured a design of three- to four-storeyed terraced housing. The same year, coordination of citizens' interests in the development process was officially entrusted by the administration to a group called *Forum Vauban* to enable a process of learning planning (*lernende Planung*). This group was founded in

1994 by citizens interested in the chances to realise new social and ecological ideas in the district. Forum Vauban received regular funds out of the development budget and took part in the Vauban District Committee of the local assembly, where all decisions concerning the district were prepared for the assembly. It organised working groups and information for future residents of the district and actively promoted cooperative housing. Self-organised *Baugruppen* (building groups) were seen as a possibility to build up to 30 per cent more cheaply than development companies; these groups were also considered effective in expressing residents request and forming connections between future neighbours (Sperling 1999: 130). Forum Vauban also conducted research on practical concepts for a sustainable urban model district financed by the European Union LIFE programmefrom 1997–99. Since 1999, when the first construction phase came to an end, community building became the focus of activities.

The original *B-Plan* was decided in 1998; afterwards, however, it was changed four times to adjust to changing circumstances and to accommodate citizens' requests. Both sides, administration and citizens, emphasise the success of this process of learning planning. On some issues, Forum Vauban succeeded in promoting their ideas; on others, the administration did not compromise. For example, there was a difference in opinion about the traffic concept. The first *B-Plan* already included certain areas without private car parking. While cars are allowed into the area, they have to be parked in two district garages at the edges of the district. As the law in Baden-Württemberg State requires a parking lot for every apartment built, costs for a parking space in the district garage were included in plot prices. To encourage a lifestyle without owning a car, Forum Vauban suggested that households without a car would not be required to pay for garage parking space, but this was not accepted by the administration. In the end, a combination of the two concepts, 'no parking' and 'no cars' was accomplished through the creation of a Society for Car-free Living (*Verein für autofreies Wohnen*). Households that sign a contract with the city and become a member of the Society for Car-free Living upon acquiring a plot in the area are exempted from paying garage costs. The Society holds a special plot in case additional parking space is needed when its members decide to buy a car someday and the district garage has no space available.

Another issue connected to the traffic concept was the main boulevard that forms the spine of the district. Originally planned with two traffic lanes on both sides of the streetcar line, car traffic ended up being restricted to one side and the other side reserved for cyclists and pedestrians.

Apart from environmental issues, public space was also a topic of conflict. The original design had included a peripheral public square, in front of the school. Citizens demanded a more centrally located square and also suggested that one of the original buildings left by the French military should be remodelled as a community centre. While both ideas were realised, part of the new square is still designated as potential building land.

As Vauban was promoted as a sustainable model district from the beginning, it attracted mainly citizens with a strong interest in social and environmental issues. According to a citizen questionnaire conducted by Freiburg City in 2001 (Stadt Freiburg i.Br. 2002), it developed a rather unique resident structure. Table 6.2 shows some social indicators and opinions compared to the city in general.

The unbalanced population structure with many young families and a distinctive lifestyle certainly has positive aspects like strong community ties and a high level of citizen participation. On the other hand, this poses problems for residents of other age groups and opinions. Accordingly, the core members of Forum Vauban can be perceived either as 'people with dreams' or as 'eco-fascists'. As the group was founded before most residents lived in the district, the question arises whether it was an adequate representation of citizens' interest.

Similar to Japanese NPOs, Forum Vauban also faced funding problems, although of a different kind. In 2003, the EU stated there were irregularities in the accounting of the research project conducted from 1997–99 and requested about €160,000 back, forcing Forum Vauban to declare bankruptcy and dissolve itself in 2004 (Forum Vauban 2004). As EU funds increasingly form an indispensable part of citizen activities in Germany and other EU countries, problems stemming from the overly bureaucratic handling of funds increase.

On the positive side, the cooperation between administration and citizens certainly helped to create an environment-friendly model district that is now regularly visited by professional groups from all over the world. A new model of expanded citizen participation was successfully tested as the result is a district with a decisively individual profile. However, this result could be achieved because of the peculiar political structure of Freiburg City, the first major German city to elect a Green Party mayor in 2002.

In a further attempt to widen citizen participation in urban planning, the city introduced several elements like forums, working groups and hearings when it revised its F-plan (*Flächennutzungsplan* or land-use plan) in a three-year project from 2003 to 2006.

Table 6.2 Social indicators and opinions in the Vauban District and Freiburg City

	City	Vauban
Living space per person	38 m²	28 m²
Households with children	18%	69%
Number of cars per 1,000 persons	427	150
Green Party voters (2005 national election)	26%	61%
'I think population density is too high.'	14%	47%
'I think my neighbourhood is safe.'	57%	74%
'There are many children in the neighbourhood.'	17%	47%
Community ties in the district (1 = weak, 5 = strong)	3.4	4.0
Citizen participation (1 = weak, 4 = strong)	2.0	3.3
Regular Internet users	38%	61%
Participation in volunteer activities	25%	44%

Source: Compiled from Stadt Freiburg i.Br. 2002, data requested from the Amt für Statistik (Statistics Office) in 2005.

Improving urban neighbourhoods

Berlin, the old and new capital of Germany, has some similarities to Kobe in that its urban structure experienced radical, sudden changes – not by natural hazards, but by political circumstances when it was first divided by the wall in 1961 and then unified again in 1990. During the years of division, the eastern part formed the capital of the German Democratic Republic, while the western part was surrounded by the wall and led a somewhat artificial, heavily subsidised existence as the West's outpost against communism. After the unification, problems from both sides of the wall, like high percentages of migrant population, high levels of unemployment, inner city desolate prewar housing stock and cheaply built high-rise suburbs, concentrated in some districts, while others were quickly renovated and gentrified. Urban renewal through renovation rather than reconstruction played a prominent role in the gentrification process. According to Krätke (2004), the erosion of Berlin's industrial base after unification as well as the relatively weak presence of corporate headquarters are undermining Berlin's economic potential. It could therefore be said that 'in terms of the urban social fabric Berlin is a globalising city with an internationally mixed population, as well as a city with growing socio-spatial divides. It is quite a problematic challenge to obtain the socio-spatial divides of a global city without attaining the economic power of a global city' (Krätke 2004: 522). For districts with a high percentage of unemployed, of households living on social welfare and with low purchasing power, the tool of district management (*Quartiersmanagement*) was introduced in 1999.

Quartiersmanagement (QM) is part of the above-mentioned programme *Soziale Stadt* that was introduced in cooperation of the federal and state governments in 1999. Its aim is to counter tendencies of urban social segregation through integrated, district-based strategies. Integration of citizens in the process of district management is to be encouraged in order to develop independent, sustainable structures of citizen activities.

Nationwide, more than 200 areas were designated under this programme. The City of Berlin choose 15 QM-areas in 1999 and added two more in 2002, covering inner-city districts with desolate housing stock as well as urban renewal districts or large-scale suburban public housing complexes. In 2005, after the results of the monitoring process were deemed positive, 16 more areas were designated so that the programme now covers about 385,000 inhabitants. However, three areas were judged sufficiently stabilised to gradually phase out the programme.

QM aims to provide equal chances in all districts. Nine strategic goals were set to improve living quality in the area, enhance the chances of residents in life and foster networks in the area. These goals consist of improvement of living spaces, social infrastructure adequate for residents, improved cultural activities, better chances to find a job, education, improved health, improved security, fostering a tolerant community and increasing participation of residents (Krumm 2005: 127).

The process of citizen participation is enabled mainly through the local QM-office, a team of consultants or planning professionals selected by the administration through a competition. They are in charge of coordinating local groups and actors, activating citizens to participate and to support the realisation of projects. One distinct feature of QM was the introduction of *Quartierfonds* in 2001. These funds, one million DM for each district for two years, were available for projects suggested by residents and local groups; distribution was decided by a citizen jury in the area. For larger infrastructure projects like parks, which were financed through general funds, workshops were held to include residents' suggestions.

To get a closer look at issues and projects taken up in the QM process, the Falkplatz District will be taken as an example. It is located in Pankow Ward and forms part of the Prenzlauer Berg, a former eastern area that with its cheap housing, trendy reputation and central location in a unified city soon became the target for gentrification, at least in its southern parts (Levine 2004). Adjacent to the former *Mauer* (Berlin Wall) and not designated for urban renewal, the Falkplatz area was lagging behind this development and therefore included into the QM programme, although it has, for example, a low percentage of migrant population (12 per cent) compared to the average of QM districts in 2002 (28 per cent, Krumm 2005: 124), one of the social indicators used for the designation of QM districts. Falkplatz has not a particularly high percentage of children under 18 (10 per cent compared to 15 per cent in Berlin as a whole) and a very low percentage of elderly, but a large percentage of 25- to 35-year-old residents. To keep this age group in the district and avoid strong fluctuations, a good infrastructure for child-rearing is essential.

A range of projects were implemented during the six years of QM, mainly concentrating on the improvement of green areas. The large *Mauerpark*, which runs along the former wall, threatened to become a gathering place for drug addicts. A society, Friends of the *Mauerpark*, was initiated through QM and now looks after the park. School yards were redesigned, integrating art projects by the children themselves. In contrast to Japan, where most extracurricular activities also take place inside schools, children in Germany are normally out of school in the afternoon. Providing adequate facilities for children and teenagers is therefore an important task of urban management. As there is no public youth centre in the Falkplatz district, infrastructure for children and young people to enjoy out of school activities is supplied by private sector organisations. To improve these facilities, a youth centre and a children's farm were supported by their activities. Tivoli, a centre for voluntary activities, was set up as a mutual help network for residents in the area. Rent for this centre was supported through QM funds, so the future is unclear after funds run out.

One of the biggest conflicts during the years of QM occurred when a large supermarket chain opened a shop in the district. Although the supermarket itself was welcome, residents feared increased traffic in the rather quiet district. The QM team was active in negotiating a compromise so that the street to the market was restricted to one, winding lane.

Generally, public space and greenery in the area have been improved and projects for young people have helped easing social tensions. As renovation of desolate housing gradually proceeded, both QM districts in Pankow Ward were chosen for a phase-out of the QM programme in 2005. Without the QM team as coordinators, the QM office as a place to gather and exchange information and funds to support local groups, it will be difficult to secure the continuation of activities. Another problem pointed out during interviews with QM teams was the role of QM offices between administration and citizens, as they also had to support the stance of the administration. Even though QM was designed to promote cooperation between different sections and levels of the administration, this did not prove easy in reality. Concerning funds, a new problem surfaced in the latest phase, when the administration introduced the regulation that projects decided on by the residents had to be allocated through a citywide competition to avoid local advantages. This was difficult to accept for residents who had suggested the projects.

In the official evaluation of the first phase of QM until 2004, it was acknowledged that improvements of living conditions like public space or green areas are relatively easy to measure. Changes concerning the second aim of QM, better chances in life for residents, are much harder to evaluate. Generally, evaluation results were positive, especially in the case of the *Quartiersfonds* (district funds), which presented strong incentives for residents to become involved (Krumm 2005: 130). As the City of Berlin does not have the financial means to continue this special type of funding, EU funds will probably take over this role.

In a city undergoing such radical changes as Berlin, market forces will always be stronger than neighbourhood improvement activities. However, 'at the neighborhood level, not at the strategic project level, a new culture of citizen participation has begun to emerge in Berlin. Still, the new planning culture in Berlin has not placed power directly into the hands of citizen groups as much as it has shifted decision making to a more community-oriented group of planners' (Levine 2004:14). This quote points to the important role planners and consultants have played in urban renewal projects and QM teams. In the latter, staff with a background in social working or pedagogy has often been involved, thus facilitating the role of a coordinator.

Summary

This short survey of four case studies from Japan and Germany has introduced a range of experiments in different forms of citizen participation and cooperation. The different economic background and the uniqueness of the urban social fabric in each city make a comparison difficult. However, as a first step, it is possible to identify common issues that get citizens involved in improving living conditions.

The first issue is to secure, design and manage public space. Parks, squares and community centres form the nexus of local activities. Deindustrialisation and other changes in land use, as some rather radical ones like the earthquake in Kobe or the demolition of the Berlin Wall, have made space available in urban areas. Stagnating and in the future shrinking populations in Japan and Germany will also offer new chances for citizens to control some common urban space. Projects like in Tomonoura, where formerly private houses that fell empty are being used for public purposes now point in this direction. While it will be easier to secure public space in the future, shrinking budgets will increasingly force the administration to involve residents in the management and thus also give them a role in decisions on design issues.

The second issue for all kind of civil organisations is to secure sufficient, continuous and flexible funds. In Japan, the increase in NPOs has lead to an increased outsourcing of welfare and other activities from the administration to these groups. However, this creates a tendency for NPOs to adjust their activities to the tasks and funds available through the administration rather than their own policies. In some prefectures, small, unbureaucratically handled funds for regular activities are also available. In Freiburg, costs for managing a process of widened citizen participation were financed out of the development budget for the new district. QM funds in Berlin are a unique experiment in that they allow for a jury of citizens to decide on the use of the budget. In Europe, EU money plays an increasing role in the budgets of civil society organisations; this however requires a large amount of bureaucratic knowledge.

The third task is to evoke sufficient interest among citizens and find methods of consensus building. As participation is based on the voluntary initiative of individual residents, it is difficult to create structures that secure a broad participation and prevent the so-called 'professional citizens' from pushing their own interests. This is even more so when not only urban management, but also urban planning becomes the matter of cooperation between citizen and administration. As the mayor of Freiburg emphasised in a forum, the city assembly has to be careful not to hide behind citizen participation, but to fulfil its democratic role as a representative body. On the other hand, an ordinance on citizen participation introduced by Hyôgo Prefecture that included not only rights, but also duties, was criticised by NPOs as ascribing citizens to a role of supporting the administration, therefore contradicting the concept of civil society.

Another important issue concerns the professional and semi-professional staff that support citizens. Citizen participation requires a broad knowledge that can only be provided by professionals. Architects, urban planners and other consultants played an important role in *machizukuri* after the earthquake and also in the QM teams in Berlin, but sometimes found themselves in an awkward position as mediators between the administration and citizens. The fact that most professionals involved tend to be architects or urban planners leads to an emphasis of improvements in the hardware of the urban fabric, in the hope that this will positively influence the urban social structure. Intermediate NPOs in Japan have taken over some of the tasks of professional advisers, which they can fulfill more independently; Forum Vauban in the case of Freiburg or many of the large environmental societies perform a similar role in Germany. Such civil society organisations put a stronger emphasis on social and environmental issues. However, the role of consultants, mediators and coordinators in the process of governance deserves further research.

In general, the urban planning system in Germany and Japan offers citizens the right to comment and suggest, but not to decide. Only on the small-scale, local level has this structure been changed to allow for new forms of governance. For the administration, a lack of funds and staff are still the main reason for increased citizen participation, combined with the experience that plans and development projects are easier to implement if they have been discussed with citizens in advance.

Limits to governance differ between the two countries. In Japan, the famous iron triangle between politicians, bureaucrats and industry, especially construction industry, still controls public work projects. Many of the large-scale projects were planned years ago, but there exists no formal process to re-evaluate and rescale or even stop them. This puts citizen organisations in a position of permanent opposition and leaves little room for creativity. The weak legal base of NPOs on the one hand and the undemocratic structures of traditional resident organisations on the other hand leave few possibilities for citizens to organise themselves effectively.

In Germany, citizen organisations have a strong base and therefore a tendency to establish and defend their own vested interests, sometimes forming a hindrance for wider participation. The framework for governance has been changed through the increasing influence of the EU. Urban planning now has to respect not only state and federal, but also EU laws and regulations; most funds available for local and regional projects include some EU money. As a large, multinational organisation, the very existence of the EU somewhat contradicts ideas of direct democracy and citizen participation.

To come back to the questions posed in the beginning, civil society in Japan and Germany certainly mainly serves to fill the gap created by the withdrawal of the state from urban management, especially where the maintenance of the urban social fabric is concerned. It has, however, been able to assume a more active role on the local level, where the creation and management of public space form the operational basis for a large variety of civil society organisations.

Procedures to ensure some degree of representative participation certainly receive a lot of attention. Often, the fact that a workshop or forum was held is considered more important than the actual results. It is only by the constant control of independent groups and organisations that a formalisation of participation processes can be prevented. Evaluation of participation by citizens themselves is an important task that has not been tackled yet.

Finally, the question of who defines the public good is impossible to answer. Generally, the right of definition lies with the various levels of government and is confirmed by means of democratic procedures. However, a wider variety of organisations and new forms of connections between the state and civil society have slightly improved channels between citizens and the government. On the very small-scale level, the right of definition by the government has been relinquished, either through deregulation or through an active policy of encouraging governance.

(This research has been supported by the Ministry of Education, Culture, Sports, Science and Technology Japan [Grant-in Aid for Scientific Research B 16320114]).

References

Abu-Lughod, J. (1998): Civil/Uncivil Society: Confusing Form with Content. Douglas, M. and Friedmann, J., *Cities for Citizens*. Chichester, New York, Weinheim, Brisbane, Singapore, Toronto: John Wiley & Sons, 227–237.

Bundesamt für Bauwesen und Raumordnung (ed.) (2003): 3stadt2 – Neue Kooperationsformen in der Stadtentwicklung. *ExWoSt-Informationen* 3(7). Bonn: Bundesamt für Bauwesen und Raumordnung.

Community Support Center Kobe (2005): Community Support Center Kobe www. cskobe.com/ (accessed 19.10.2005).

Evans, B., Joas, M., Sundback, S. and Theobald, K. (2005): *Governing Sustainable Cities*. London/Sterling: Earthscan.

Foljanty-Jost, G. (2009): Einleitung: Kommunaler Reformdruck aus vergleichender Perspektive. Foljanty-Jost, G. (Hrsg.): *Kommunalreform in Deutschland und Japan*. Wiesbaden: Verlag für Sozialwissenschaften, 7–15.

Forum Vauban (2004): *Vauban actuel: die Stadtteilzeitschrift* 2004–3.

Friedmann, J. (1998): The New Political Economy of Planning: the Rise of Civil Society. Douglas, M. and Friedmann, J., *Cities for Citizens*. Chichester, New York, Weinheim, Brisbane, Singapore, Toronto: John Wiley & Sons, 19–35.

Friedmann, J. and Douglas, M. (1998): Editors' Introduction. Douglas, M. and Friedmann, J., *Cities for Citizens*. Chichester, New York, Weinheim, Brisbane, Singapore, Toronto: John Wiley & Sons, 1–6.

Funck, C. (2007): Machizukuri, Civil Society, and the Transformation of Japanese City Planning: Cases from Kobe. Sorensen, A. and Funck, C. (eds), *Living Cities in Japan*. London/New York: Routledge, 137–156.

Hirayama, Y. (2003): *Fukanzen toshi. Kobe – Nyûyôku- Berurin*. Kyoto: Gakugei Shuppansha. (Imperfect Cities. Kobe, New York, Berlin).

Hohn, U. (2000): *Stadtplanung in Japan*. Dortmund: Dortmunder Vertrieb für Bau- und Planungsliteratur.

Itô, A. (2007): Earthquake Reconstruction Machizukuri and Citizen Participation. Sorensen, A. and Funck, C. (eds), *Living Cities in Japan*. London/New York: Routledge, 157–171.

Kiguchi Hyôgo NPO Sentâ Kenkyûkai (2005): *Hyôgo CSO Meibô*. Kobe: Author.

Krätke, S. (2004): City of Talents? Berlin's Regional Economy, Socio-Spatial Fabric and 'Worst Practice' Urban Governance. *International Journal of Urban and Regional Research* 28–23, 511–529.

Krumm, W. (2005): Evaluation des Berliner Quartiersmanagementprogramms. *Informationen zur Raumentwicklung* 2005–2/3, 123–132.

Levine, M.A. (2004): Government Policy, the Local State, and Gentrification: The Case of Prenzlauer Berg (Berlin), Germany. *Journal of Urban Affairs* 26–1, 89–108.

Lovan, W.R., Murray, M. and Shaffer, R. (2004): Participatory Governance in a Changing World. Lovan, W.R., Murray, M. and Shaffer, R., *Participatory Governance: Planning, Conflict Mediation and Public Decision Making in Civil Society*. Aldershot/Burlington: Ashgate, 1–20.

Nakamura, J., Mori, A. and Kiyohara, K. (2004): *Hinotori no joseitachi*. Hyôgo Futasho: Kobe (Women of the Phoenix).

Nishisuma Machizukuri Kondankai 1997: *Jûmin shutai e no chosen*. Kobe: Epikku (Challenging residents as actors).

Pekkanen, R. (2000): Japan's New Politics: The Case of the NPO Law. *Journal of Japanese Studies*, 26–1, 111–148.

Sawamura, A. (2004): *Machizukuri NPO no riron to kadai*. Hiroshima: Keisuisha (Theory and tasks of machizukuri NPOs).

Schwartz, F.J. (2003): Introduction. Schwartz, F.J. and Pharr, Susan J., *The State of Civil Society in Japan*. Cambridge: Cambridge University Press, 1–19.

Shaw, R. and Goda, K. (2004): From Disaster to Sustainable City Society: The Kobe Experience. *Disasters* 28–1, 16–40.

Sorensen, A. (2002): *The Making of Urban Japan*. London/New York: Routledge.

Sperling, C. (1999): *Nachhaltige Stadtentwicklung beginnt im Quartier*. Freiburg: Öko-Institut e.V.

Stadt Freiburg i.Br.(2002): *Bürgerumfrage 2001 in Freiburg*. Freiburg: Author.

World Monuments Fund (2004): *World Monuments Watch List of 100 Most Endangered Sites*. www.wmf.org/html/programs/watchlist2004.html (accessed 2.6.2004).

7 Indifferent communities

Neighbourhood associations, class and community consciousness in pre-war Tokyo

Katja Schmidtpott

A crucial aspect of urban spaces everywhere is the way their residents perceive and appropriate them, which space precisely they define as the territory of their local community, how they govern it and how they organise social interaction on the local level. This is Henri Lefebvre's *espace vécu* (see Introduction), and while it is often an absent dimension in urban planners' and other specialists' visions, it is nonetheless vital for the human experience of the city past and present. In Japan, a key factor in shaping this dimension has been the neighbourhood assocations (*chôkai, chônaikai, jichikai*) that encompass nearly all urban households of a district (*chô*) for administrative and social purposes. Although they lack legal status and thus are to be considered as private organisations of volunteers, they clearly serve administrative purposes in so far as they cooperate with the local authorities by, e.g. forwarding official notes from town-hall to the individual households or by keeping streets and park areas of their districts clean. In addition, they also provide a framework for social life, mainly by organizing social and cultural events for the local community.

Recently, both political and scholarly interest in the neighbourhood associations is on the increase. As regards politics, in view of the financial difficulties many municipalities are facing, how the honorary co-operation of the citizens can be used to keep up the quality and quantity of public services is discussed (Nawata 2004: 63). In the current scholarly debate on the role of the citizens in urban governance (Sorensen and Funck 2007), or on the nature of civil society in Japan as such (Pekkanen 2006), neighbourhood associations are often noted as organizational networks integrating a large part of the population, whose potential to provide a wide range of community services and to engage in a variety of social and cultural activities should not be underestimated.

Discussions about the present or even the future role of the neighbourhood associations often include assumptions about their past. Although most neighbourhood associations were established in the 1920s and clearly are a phenomenon of the modern Japanese city, the idea that neighbourhood associations are an expression of a strong sense of community prevalent in Japanese urban neighbourhoods since premodern times (e.g. Kurata 2000: 68), or that Japan has a 'long and vital tradition of local self-help and strong neighbourhoods' (Sorensen 2006: 121) still remains widely accepted.

This idea is enmeshed in descriptions of Japanese urban neighbourhoods as village communities, which are encountered in many works by both Western and Japanese literary and scientific authors over several decades (Smith 2006). In urban sociology, the idea of Tokyo as an agglomeration of villages can be traced back to the influential social scientist, Fukutake Tadashi (1917–1989), whose works were widely received also by Western scholars. Fukutake (1982: 6) conceived of the pre-war *chô* as socio-spatial entities similar to the rural village, with inhabitants considering themselves as part of 'a "community of fate"', held together by 'emotional bonds of union and harmony'. This implied the view that in contrast to the development of the Euro-American societies, pre-modern or even rural patterns of social life persisted in modern urban society in Japan.

However, in his ethnographic study of a present-day urban neighbourhood in Tokyo, Bestor (1989) takes issue with 'the implicit thesis [that] in those communities that *today* manifest strong communal institutions and identity', the present can be accounted for by the past 'through assertions of direct (but not clearly specified) links of historical continuity' (Bestor 1989: 259). In fact, although much has been written about the alleged community consciousness of past urban residents, little of this has been written by historians, and even less has been written based on the analysis of sources that can actually report people's perception of their local communities.

In general, English-language historical research on the development of the modern Japanese city is rather scarce (e.g. Allinson 1975, Hastings 1995), as compared to ethnographic research on postwar Japanese urban community life (e.g. Dore 1958, Bestor 1989, Ben-Ari 1991, Robertson 1991). Of course, there is ample literature on Japanese urban history in Japanese, which reveals that Japanese historians suggest the idea of the 'city-as-village' should be abandoned, and even question whether *pre*modern urban neighbourhoods can actually be called communities (*kyôdôtai*) (Yoshida 1991, Harada 2002).

As regards the modern city, like many others, Narita Ryûichi (2003) suggests we should explore variety and multilayeredness of urban society more strongly, in order to emphasise not the adherence to alleged traditions such as that of the 'village community', but the modernity, which in his opinion has characterised Japanese urban society as well as Euro-American societies. Influenced by theories of space, he introduces the concept of the *espace vécu* (*ikirareta kûkan*) of urban residents, describing its gradual homogenization due to the emergence of the nation state.

However, it can hardly be noted that Japanese urban history has undergone a 'spatial turn'. It is often criticised that in research based on this approach, the notion of 'space' remains abstract and the social structure of local urban society is often unconsidered (e.g. Saga 2007: 13). Recent research on the modern Japanese city focuses on the interaction of social groups on the local level and further connects it to the bigger frame of urban politics and administration, so that Narita's suggestion is seen as a chance to further enrich the history of urban self-governance (*toshi jichishi*) in combination with socio-historical approaches (Ôishi and Kanazawa 2003: 10).

While the weaknesses of this approach can hardly be denied, one of its strengths is that urban space is to be understood as socially constructed. In fact, as regards the history of neighbourhood associations, the existence of a *chô*-community as a socio-spatial entity has often been taken as a given fact. From the principle of all-comprehensive membership it has often been concluded that neighbourhood associations were both the source and the result of community consciousness, community solidarity and a sense of identity shared by urban residents in view of the demographic changes that rapid urbanization brought upon the *chô* (Downward 1976: 218, Smith 1978: 66). Another argument runs that the neighbourhood associations were also intended as 'melting pots' in order to integrate migrants from rural areas into the *chô* community. While some authors (THHI 1979b: 270, 290) assume that this process of integration was intended to create a new 'village community' for the migrants in order to make them feel at home in the metropolis, others interpret the principle of all-comprehensive membership as an expression of Taishô-era liberalism and a rising consciousness for social equality (e.g. Nakamura 1979, Hastings 1995, Amemiya 1997). However, individual perceptions of the *chô* or of the neighbourhood associations by urban residents have remained largely unexplored, so it is unclear whether the alleged *chô* communities actually existed or how they came into being.

Taking the social structure of urban society into account, it is clear that the local social elite played a key role in the establishment of neighbourhood associations (Ishizuka and Narita 1994: 167). Looking at urban society in Meiji and Taishô periods, historians tend to make a rough division between the general population (*minshû*), i.e. those roughly 70 per cent of the urban population who were living as tenants, and the social elite of the 'dignitaries' (*meibôka*) or 'influential personalities of the city' (*toshi no yûryokusha*), i.e. land-owning or home-owning families, ranging from big capitalists (*dai-shihonka*) down to the owners of small businesses (*shô-keieisha*). Until the end of the nineteenth century, they usually came from old established families (Harada 2002: 10–12), then in the following decades of urbanisation they gradually became replaced by migrants who purchased property in the *chô* (Tamano 1993), indicating that the power structure in the *chô* became less based on geographic origin, while class remained strongly relevant.

By focusing on the 1920s as the formative period of the neighbourhood associations, I want to show how the *chô* as a socio-spatial entity and as a focus of identification and community sentiment was deliberately constructed by the local social elite and by municipal administrations in order to mobilise the cooperation of urban residents for administrative purposes and to create social cohesion in a fast-changing local society under the influence of urbanisation, and how they were perceived by the rank-and-file members.

The main sources that were used were a collection of model charters published by the Social Bureau of the city of Tokyo in 1924 in order to promote the establishment of neighbourhood associations (TSS 1924), a survey conducted by the Tokyo Institute for Municipal Research in 1925 (TSC 1927) which contains short reports written by the leaders of neighbourhood associations about the problems they encountered with their rank-and-file members and two diaries written by the wives of landlords in Kyoto and Tokyo at the turn of the century (Nakano 1995, Kobayashi 1991).

Urban problems, the local social elite and the idea of *chô* associations (1880s–1910s)

Urbanisation and its related problems, which shaped the living conditions in Tokyo as well as in other big cities in Japan at the turn of the century, led to the emergence of the forerunners of present-day neighbourhood associations, i.e. the sanitation associations and the early neighbourhood associations with exclusive membership for landowners.

After half of the roughly one million inhabitants of Tokyo (Edo) had left the city subsequent to the Meiji Restoration, the population started to increase again when urbanisation began in the 1880s. At the end of the century, Japanese industrialisation entered into a new stage with the rapid development of heavy industry (*jûkôgyôka*) after the war against China (1894/1895). Huge factories were built in the urban areas and attracted labour from rural areas in great numbers. The populations of Tokyo and of the other five 'big cities' (*daitoshi*) Yokohama, Nagoya, Kyoto, Osaka and Kobe doubled or even tripled during the years between 1898 and 1920, with Tokyo alone growing from 1.44 million inhabitants to 3.35 million (Yazaki 1968: 420).

The systems of urban infrastructure, which had been inadequate even before the onset of urbanisation, lagged behind this rapid growth, and the Japanese cities faced the same problems as their counterparts in Europe and the USA. Infectous diseases, fires, poverty and crime increasingly threatened health and safety of large parts of the urban population. In its residential areas, Tokyo was a city with unpaved streets that were dark at night, with almost no sewage system or waste collection, inadequate police, fire service and medical care. Most people still had to take their daily water from wells, which led to frequent outbreaks of epidemics. Between 1890 and 1903 there were 13 outbreaks of infectous diseases such as cholera, diphtheria and typhus registered in Tokyo, each causing several hundreds or even thousands of patients and deaths (THHI 1979a: 719–720).

The improvement of urban infrastructure made only slow progress, since the state considered the development of industry and military as more important. According to the basic political dictum of the Meiji government to 'enrich the nation and strengthen the army' (*fukoku kyôhei*), huge parts of the tax revenue were used for the wars against China (1894/1895) and Russia (1904/1905) as well as for the development of the Asian colonies. What is more, due to the strict centralisation of the Japanese administrative system, urban infrastructure was being planned on the national level, while the needs of local urban residents were hardly considered (Yazaki 1968: 411–417). To the urban residents, this meant that could not expect substantial help from the state, leaving them to take the initiative to improve their living environment on their own.

In premodern times, the local level had been regulated by the administrative institution of the *goningumi* ('group of five'), groups of landlords who were made responsible for the administration of the neighbourhood in which they lived by the central government. These groups were officially abolished by the Meiji government and gradually disappeared in the course of the 1870s. They were replaced by a modern system of local administration, which, as it was finally established in 1888, reached down only to the *ku* ('ward') level, leaving the neighbourhoods underneath untouched. However, as a stable social elite, in some places landlords continued to control their neighbourhoods in an informal way (Smith 1986: 369–370), and in some parts of Tokyo, they founded special associations (*jinushikai*) in order to achieve that purpose (Hiraide 1979: 27). Most of the members were venerable old families, whose ancestors had been members of the premodern *goningumi* (Yazaki 1968: 455). These landlords' associations carried out certain administrative tasks which were not sufficiently provided by the city such as keeping the streets clean, street lighting or crime and fire prevention. They also hired manual workers for certain tasks.

These associations were not related with the idea of a *chô* community, since at that time, the *chô* could hardly be recognized as clear-cut socio-spatial entities. The premodern *chô* with its clearly defined boundaries and a population which could easily be overlooked had been recognisable as communities. The boundaries of the modern *chô*, however, had been altered several times due to the administrative re-organisations at the beginning of the Meiji era. At the turn of the century, the *chô* only mattered as a geographical denomination to the inhabitants, which was a part of their postal address (Yazaki 1968: 333; Hastings 1995: 70). Moreover, due to rapid population turnover in the course of urbanisation, in about 1909, migrants surpassed the indigenous population of the capital (Smith 1986: 367). In addition, with around 70 per cent of the urban population being tenants, many of whom, since long-term employment was still uncommon, changed jobs every couple of months and with it their residence, urban residents could hardly develop a clear idea of who was actually living in their neighbourhood.

Therefore, it cannot be assumed that local landlords were motivated by some *chô*-related community consciousness, and rather, it seems that as members of the former *goningumi*, they were inclined to share the common understanding of the term self-government (*jichi*) as it 'implied a commitment to the national good', an idea which harked back to the Edo era when 'local governments performed certain tasks out of dutiful loyalty to the state' (Smith 1978: 63). Even those who might not have shared this view, in everyday life they certainly felt that it was simply necessary to protect their homes and businesses, as urban living conditions worsened. As they belonged to the upper stratum of the old middle class, i.e. mainly land-owning merchants and manufacturers, they had good reason to feel responsible for providing for a healthy and safe neighbourhood, since their home-ownership and their business bound them continually to the place where they lived and worked.

What is more, the range of their social contacts by far exceeded the shifting boundaries of the *chô*. They were not determined by space, but by class. The examples of the Nakano family (Nakano 1995), who were pharma dealers and politicians in Kyoto in 1910, and of the Kobayashi family, who were landlords in Tokyo and whose head was a high ranking employee in a big international trade company in 1898/1899 (Kobayashi 1991), show that the social contacts of urban landlords were mainly restricted to a few other families of their own social class. Since both families were considerably wealthy, they did not need to ask their neighbours for help, and in daily communication, relatives, business partners and friends were most important. Both families hardly knew their neighbours next door, and relations to them were confined to the basic actions that custom required, that is, giving a small present when moving in and joining in funeral ceremonies. The Kobayashi family did not even appear in person on these occasions but sent their servants. While they had almost no contact with the general population of their neighbourhoods, landlords were usually active members of various local organisations with exclusive membership, e.g. shrine associations (*ujiko dantai*), young men's associations (*wakashûkai, wakaishû*), culture associations, women's associations or military associations (Komori 1973: 88). The head of the Nakano family, for example, sat on the board of two shrine associations, one temple association and the local elementary school, a pharma dealers' association and a literary circle. These memberships, which demanded that he participated in meetings several times a week, occupied much of the time he dedicated to his social life (Nakano 1995). These associations, however, did not necessarily overlap with the boundaries of a *chô*.

Soon, the landlords' initiatives came under the influence of the state. In fact, the modern state had never completely given up the premodern idea that urban residents were responsible for the maintenance of their neighbourhoods by themselves. When the regulations concerning the modern system of local administration were published in 1888, they contained a passage that said that local dignitaries should engage in public affairs (Harada 2002: 113), be it as elected members of prefectural or municipal parliaments, or as the holder of a honorary office. Shortly after, in 1890, the prefecture of Tokyo began to call the landlords together in elementary schools, where medical doctors, policemen and representatives of local administration explained to them about methods of disease control. They were instructed to forward the information to their tenants and to report to the authorities if their tenants were suffering from an infectous disease (Narita 2003: 51). Obviously, the cooperation of urban residents, i.e. local landlords, with local administration was considered crucial in solving the urban problems of that time.

Further seeking to institutionalise the cooperation of the urban population, at the turn of the century local authorities introduced the idea of associations with an all-comprehensive membership on the *chô* level whose purpose was to support municipal administration in the field of disease control. In 1897 the national disease prevention law (*densenbyô yobôhô*) was passed, which ordered local authorities to make urban residents found sanitation associations (*eisei kumiai*) (Tanaka 1910: 11–12). On the base of this law, the prefecture of Tokyo obliged the heads of all the households in each individual *chô* to found sanitation associations in 1900 (TSS 1924: 81). The same had already taken place in 1897 in Kyoto (TSC 1927: 218) and in Osaka (Kawata 1991: 250), and other cities followed suit.

The legally defined tasks of the sanitation associations included the regular cleaning and disinfection of streets and homes and the killing of rats and insects (THHI 1979a: 722), and they were closely linked to the municipal administration. They had to report the names of their members and their activities to the ward mayor (*kuchô*), who in turn had to report annually to the governor of the prefecture about the sanitation associations in his ward (TSS 1924: 82, 84). Although it was ordered by law that sanitation associations with an all-comprehensive membership of all the households were to be founded on the *chô* level, in practice they were a failure due to a lack of members and funds (Nakamura 1979: 13). Most of the 445 sanitation associations that were still registered in Tokyo in 1923 (TSC 1927: 84) had long since been inactive (THHI 1979a: 722). Although the sanitation associations were only a short-lived phenomenon, they are to be noted for the fact that they were the first associations on the *chô* level based on the principle of all-comprehensive membership. It has to be underlined, though, that the idea of such *chô*-wide associations regardless of social status was introduced by the state, not by urban residents themselves, and that their sole purpose was to serve the municipal administration, and not to strengthen the local community.

Parallel to the sanitation associations, local authorities promoted yet another kind of *chô*-wide association. When the post of a lord mayor was created in Tokyo in 1898, local authorities started to promote the model of multi-purpose *chô* associations which should function as support units of municipal administration (Komori 1973: 91). Starting in 1907, they advised the leaders of the sanitation associations to change their associations into general neighbourhood associations, and from 1911 in some places they distributed pamphlets that contained written instructions on how to found a neighbourhood association as well as a model charter (Komori 1973: 91–92). It can be estimated that in 1917, more than 200 of these early neighbourhood associations existed in the then roughly 1,300 *chô* of Tokyo (THHI 1979a: 274, Komori 1973: 86). Some of them already bore the name *chôkai* or *chônaikai*, which gradually became widely accepted in the following decades.

Those multi-purpose associations actually carried out a variety of tasks – both for the municipal administration, as for their members. They provided mutual assistance and fostered friendship among their members as well as cooperating with local authorities in various respects. They forwarded official notices to the individual households, kept the neighbourhoods clean and cooperated in disease control, and crime and fire prevention. Like the sanitation associations, many of them had only a few members (TSS 1924), and thus represented only a small part of the population. Membership was restricted to landowners. For example, when the head of the Nakano family became the president of the local neighbourhood association, the association had only 24 households as members. One of the members, who received a wedding present from the association, was an umbrella dealer or manufacturer (Nakano 1995: 71–72). The members met once a month in a restaurant where they enjoyed good food and drink, got together on the occasion of certain festivals and held memorial ceremonies for deceased members or farewell ceremonies for young recruits leaving for military training (Nakano 1995: 110, 179, 210). Their activities clearly centred around strengthening the ties of friendship among each other, while no social interaction of any sort with the rank-and-file residents of their neighbourhood is mentioned.

In sum, it has to be noted that both the sanitation associations as well as the early neighbourhood associations were groups of the social elite. There is no indication that either of these organizations was an expression of or a means of creating local communities on the *chô* level. Rather they were an expression of the persisting tradition of cooperation of local landlords with the authorities.

The expansion of the neighbourhood associations, their increasing tasks and activities and the need for funds (1920s)

The 1920s saw a fast expansion of the multi-purpose neighbourhood associations in combination with an increase in their tasks and acitivites, which, again, was closely related to the persistence of urban problems in the course of an accelerated urbanisation. Between 1920 and 1930, the proportion of the Japanese population living in cities increased from 18 to 24 per cent (Karan 1997: 13), and the population of Tokyo prefecture annually increased by an average of 3–4 per cent (THHI 1979b: 61). From its 3.35 million inhabitants in 1920, the city of Tokyo grew to more than five million inhabitants in 1932 and became the biggest city in the world after New York (Fujino 2002: 146–147).

However, the living conditions in the metropolis improved only gradually. After the nationwide rice riots (*kome sôdô*) of 1918, when around 700,000 people protested against the sharp rise in living expenses after World War I (Ishizuka and Narita 1994: 130; THHI 1979b: 1067), the Japanese government acknowledged that it was necessary to introduce social policy measures in order to calm social unrest. The most prominent measure taken to improve the living conditions of the urban population was the first Japanese City Planning Law (*toshi keikakuhô*) of 1919, which applied to the six biggest cities of Japan. This law should not only foster the economic development of the citites, but also improve the quality of life of urban residents. To accomplish this, the law stipulated the construction of streets, pavements and parks, the provision of street lighting and street cleaning, etc. Due to financial restrictions, however, only a few of these projects were realised. The Ministry of Finance mainly supported the construction of big infrastructure such as main roads, harbours, railroads, canals and schools, while it gave only very little funds for the improvement of urban neighbourhoods (Sorensen 2004: 109–111).

Thus, the expansion of urban infrastructure made only slight progress during the 1920s. While a municipal waste collection service covering the whole city area was established in 1919 (THHI 1979a: 712–713, 1979b: 847), sewage systems covered only one-tenth of the city area (THHI 1979b: 817–818). Up to

30 per cent of the urban population still had to take their drinking water from wells or running waters (THHI 1979b: 810). Most of the roads remained unpaved, and the inadequacy of the fire service became apparent when 44 per cent of the built-up area of Tokyo burned down after the big earthquake in 1923 (BRHO 1929: 7). As regards poverty relief, the city established a Bureau of Social Affairs (Shakaikyoku) in 1919 in order to coordinate certain relief measures, which were, however, far from sufficient to eradicate poverty, homelessness or unemployment (Hastings 1995: 52). In sum, while in some parts of the city the improvement of the living environment made some progress, a comprehensive solution could not be achieved due to financial restrictions. Since public services remained largely inadequate, the cooperation of urban residents continued to be indispensable.

In fact, the bureaucrats who created the City Planning Law shared the understanding of the term citizen (*shimin*), which implied that urban residents had to be loyal to municipal administration (Smith 1978: 63), and held the view that urban residents had to improve their living environment to a great extent by themselves (Sorensen 2004: 111). The prominent Japanese legal scholar, Hozumi Shigetô (1883–1951), argued that the modern Japanese system of local government could only unfold its full potential through the cooperation of the neighbourhood associations. In his view, 'true communal life' of the citizens, as incorporated by the neighbourhood associations, should serve as the base of the modern government system (Hozumi 1924: 7). As a consequence, politicians and bureaucrats launched a campaign to promote the establishment of neighbourhood associations.

At the local level, police officers and ward mayors advised urban residents to found neighbourhood associations (Nakamura 1979: 20), and on the occasion of the founding ceremony of a neighbourhood association in Koishikawa-*ku* in 1922, greetings of the Mayor of Tokyo and of the Minister of Interior Affairs were being delivered, in order to commemorate the event before the eyes of the public (Nakamura 1979: 30).

Consequently, the number of neighbourhood associations increased rapidly in Tokyo as well as in the other big cities (TSC 1927: 230–231, 233–234). Between 1922 and 1924, the number of neighbourhood associations in Tokyo doubled from around 450 to more than 900 (TSS 1924: 188) and continued to increase until finally, around 1930, most part of the capital area was covered with neighbourhood associations.

Although there were many individual reasons that led to the foundation of a single certain neighbourhood association, in general, just like in the past decades, the establishment of neighbourhood associations can be described as motivated by a combination of administrative purposes as well as political or economic reasons of the local social elite.

Many of the new neighbourhood associations were former sanitation associations: 90 per cent of the 445 sanitation associations that were registered in Tokyo in 1923 had been transformed into neighbourhood associations by 1925 (TSC 1927: 84), that is roughly one-third of the neighbourhood associations extant in that year had been created under the influence of the authorities. The reason for their transformation might have been that the neighbourhood associations could combine sanitation activities with other functions considered necessary both by the municipal administration as by the urban residents.

Other neighbourhood associations were founded in view of certain acute crises that threatened the livelihood of urban residents. The charters of some neighbourhood associations disclose that they had been founded in order to cope with the galloping inflation after the First World War (e.g. 'No. 10', TSS 1924: 19), while others were founded after the big earthquake, although its influence was not so great as sometimes stated (Ishizuka and Narita 1994: 166–167; Dore 1958: 271), since most neighbourhood associations had already been founded before it occurred (TSS 1924: 188).

Another factor was the introduction of universal manhood suffrage in 1925, which made it attractive to persons with political ambitions to found a neighbourhood association in order to use their position on the board to boost their political career (Tamano 1993). As president or vice-president of a neighbourhood association they could present themselves as local benefactors who in return could hope for the support of the voters. Of the 181 members of the ku-parliaments, who were elected in Tokyo in 1925/26, 140 had acted as a president, vice-president or board member of a neighbourhood association (TSC 1927: 105–106), which underlines the close connection between a career in local politics and commitment in a neighbourhood association. In other cases, established businessmen founded a neighbourhood association and invited businessmen who had recently moved in to the area to become members, in order to be able to control their new competitors (Tamano 1993: 176–177, 183–184). Individual interests like these in some places even led to the establishment of several neighbourhood associations covering the same area, which were consequently competing for members (TSC 1927: 10).

With the expansion of the neighbourhood associations, the range of their tasks and activities also widened. At the beginning of the 1920s, among an already wide variety of activities, more than half of the associations carried out the following five tasks:

1   congratulations and condolences: making money presents to the members on the occasions of marriages, births or ceremonies for the deceased, etc.
2   sanitation: support for the extension of the public water supply and sewage systems, cooperation in epidemics control, emptying and disinfection of cesspits, waste disposal, organizing inoculation campaigns, etc.
3   military affairs: farewell or welcome ceremonies for recruits leaving for or returning from military training or war, moral support for their families for the time of their absence
4   festivals: organisation of the annual shrine festival and other public festivals or private celebrations, etc.
5   protection: desaster prevention, crime and fire prevention, nightly neighbourhood patrols, etc.

(TSS 1924: 115–116)

In the following years, the proportion of neighbourhood associations in Tokyo that carried out these five standard tasks rose to 94 per cent in 1933 (Nakamura 1979: 27).

At the same time, the municipal administrations more and more tried to bring the associations under their control by tying them to the structure of the municipal administration, in a similar manner as had been the case with the sanitation associations. First, the administrations grouped the neighbourhood associations in leagues (*rengôkai*) on the levels of the *ku* and of the cities. The first of those leagues was founded in 1923 in Shitaya-*ku*. Its rules stipulated that the bureau of the league was located in the town hall of the ward (*kuyakusho*), and that a ward official acted as its vice-president (TSC 1927: 115–116). In Osaka, all the neighbourhood associations were grouped in one big league in 1925 (TSC 1927: 230), and the neighbourhood associations in Nagoya were grouped on the level of the wards in 1929, with the ward mayors acting as presidents of the leagues (Nagoyashi 1954: 88, 91–92). In Yokohama, the league of the neighbourhood associations was controlled by the governor of the prefecture, by the ward mayors and by the police (Narita 2003: 274). In so doing, the municipal administrations established a hierarchical communication structure that allowed them to coordinate the administrative activities of the neighbourhood associations.

Second, the municipal administrations tried to standardise the structure and the functions of the neighbourhood associations by the dissemination of collections of model charters. The city of Tokyo was the first to publish such a collection in 1924 (TSS 1924), Nagoya followed in 1926 (Nagoyashi 1954: 88) and Yokohama in 1927 (Narita 2003: 275). In addition, the prefecture of Tokyo published a bi-monthly newspaper called *Chôkai jihô* [News of the neighbourhood associations] starting in 1924 (TSC 1927: 7) as a channel of communication with the neighbourhood associations.

Some of the tasks and activities of the neighbourhood associations caused considerably high expenses. Apart from the annual shrine festival, those activities that served to support the administration were particularly costly. For example, for certain sanitation activities, such as inoculation or disinfection campaigns, the associations had to purchase medical or chemical substances. Some neighbourhood associations also employed night watchmen or other personnel for various manual works. All the related expenses had to be completely borne by the neighbourhood associations, because, in legal terms, they were private associations of volunteers. This, however, meant that many neighbourhood associations faced the same problems as the former sanitation associations, which had often failed to fulfill their tasks due to a lack of members and funds.

Since they were obviously considered as support units of the municipal administration, many neighbourhood associations, such as a neighbourhood association in Kôjimachi-*ku*, tried to solve their problems by asking for 'financial support by the city or by the ward' (TSC 1927: 150). The leaders of the neighbourhood association of Ichigaya Tamachi in Ushigome-*ku* also demanded financial support and explicitly pointed at the wide range of administrative tasks they carried out:

> We always keep close contact with the town-hall of the city, with the town-hall of the ward and with the police, and we carry out their orders without exception, [we assist them with] statistical surveys, [we forward] information ... etc. We do wish that at least we receive some financial compensation for postage or other commuications fees.
>
> (TSC 1927: 163)

However, demands like the above were in vain, since the authorities maintained the position that legally, the neighbourhood associations were nothing but private associations on a voluntary basis, and therefore not entitled to demand public funds. In fact, politicians and bureaucrats often praised the work of the neighbourhood associations while referring to them as private and voluntary organisations. The Director of the Office for Public Education in the Bureau of Social Affairs of the City of Tokyo (Shakaikyoku Shakai Kyôikuka), Ikekuni Tetsutarô, wrote in October 1924:

> the neighbourhood associations have never received any kind of order by the local authorities, and of course, they come into being without any kind of support. They are the expression of the beautiful custom of mutual neighbourly assistance, they are self-government groups that developed from true self initiative. In no way are they ruled by law ... they are extra-legal units of self-government of the citizens.
>
> (TSS 1924: 2)

Although the neighbourhood associations clearly served the interests of the state, the state did not create a legal framework for them, thus shifting the responsibility for the functioning of these organisations completely upon the leaders.

The opening of the neighbourhood associations to all-comprehensive membership and the invention of the '*chô* community'

Faced with the problem that the wide variety of tasks and activities required funds and helping hands in order to keep up the operations of the associations, the leaders of the neighbourhood associations opened the formerly socially exclusive associations to all-comprehensive membership of all the households regardless of their geographic or social origin. Since no help was to be expected from the authorities, the only way for the neighbourhood associations to improve their financial situation was to raise membership rates in order to be able to collect a higher amount of membership fees. Like many others, the leaders of a neighbourhood association in Akasaka-*ku* reported:

> Since we have only a few members, the expenditures are bigger than the income, which causes problems when fulfilling our tasks. We wish that all households in the *chô* shall join our association as soon as possible.
>
> (TSC 1927:154)

Under these circumstances, it is clear that the opening of the associations to the general population was neither an expression of community consciousness, nor was it meant as a friendly invitation for everyone. Actually, the goal was not to unite as many inhabitants as possible, but to make literally every household a member, because only with a membership rate of 100 per cent could the associations carry out their central administrative tasks such as fire prevention and epidemics control. Consequently, some neighbourhood associations, such as the following in Kanda-*ku*, considered it 'problematic ... that there are persons who refuse to join the association' (TSC 1927: 134). Since the services of the associations had to be provided for the whole *chô* population, it was considered only natural that everyone became a member. While in theory it was a voluntary act to join the associations, in practice membership was more considered as a duty for the good of the *chô*, and, ultimately, for the good of the nation, since becoming a member was considered as a necessary precondition for the functioning of the Japanese local administration system as a whole.

However, the leaders of many neighbourhood associations obviously doubted that the general population would cooperate voluntarily and thus tried to convince the municipal administration to introduce a special legislation which would make membership compulsory. Again, since the neighbourhood associations willingly served the needs of the local authorities, the leaders felt entitled to demand from the municipal administration to be given a legal status similar to that of public servants. This, they hoped, would enable them to force all the inhabitants to join, to pay their fees and to carry out the necessary tasks.

The leaders of a neighbourhood association in Ushigome-*ku* wrote:

> We want the neighbourhood associations to be acknowledged on a legal basis, so that the mayor can lend them the authority to raise membership fees and to make all inhabitants of the *chô* become members, and also to punish those who do not pay membership fees as well as those who refuse to become members, in an appropriate way.
>
> (TSC 1927: 137)

It is striking that the leaders sought to forge an alliance with the municipal administration in order to take legal steps against their fellow *chô* inhabitants in case they refused to cooperate. Obviously, they felt closer to the local authorities than to their neighbours and did not identify with the general population very much. Referring to the bad paying habits of their members, the leaders of a neighbourhood association in Hongô-*ku* wrote:

> It is only natural that the neighbourhood associations are facing difficulties when collecting membership fees, since neither the central government nor the municipal administration has created a legal framework for them. Consequently, they suffer from a complete lack of authority.
>
> (TSC 1927: 156)

Since the authorities refused to give the neighbourhood associations legal status, social policy bureaucrats, moral education propagandists and local leaders who organised neighbourhood associations were mobilising traditional values (Smith 1978: 64) in order to raise membership rates and to gain the cooperation of urban residents in connection with the introduction of a '*chô* community', which encompassed all the inhabitants of a *chô* under the leadership of the neighbourhood association.

To explain this concept, some leaders referred to the older idea of the urban neighbourhood as a family, with the landlords as parents and the tenants as children, which had been formulated in the Edo era and was expressed in literary works as well as in popular *rakugo* story-telling even after the Meiji restoration (Smith 1978: 51–52). The idea of the family was further intertwined with the idea of the modern nation, which demanded the loyalty of the citizens. Thus, the idea of the *chô* as a hierarchically structured community was evoked in the charters of the neighbourhood associations, where terms such as 'family' (*ie*, *kazoku*), 'community' (*kyôdô*), 'communal life' (*kyôdô seikatsu*), 'solidarity of the community' (*kyôdô itchi*) or 'love for the *chô*' (*aichô*) were frequently used to explain this concept.

For example, it says in the charter of neighbourhood association 'No. 14':

> The neighbourhood association is an image of the family (*ie*), and all of you, who are its members, shall be the children. In case these children do not know their rights and duties and are ignorant of their social position, no healthy system of self-government and no healthy state can be established [on the base of the] neighbourhood associations. [...] [T]he neighbourhood association is a big household encompassing all of you as a family [...]. There can be no doubt that you already understood that you are all members of the neighbourhood association, and that it is an expression of your duty towards the state, that you carry out the public services as described above.
>
> (TSS 1924: 25–26, 30)

The leaders of this association made it clear to their fellow *chô* inhabitants, that it was not only their patriotic duty to join the association, but that in fact they already had become members in the very moment when they had moved into the *chô*, just as children become members of a family in the moment of birth. They suggested that membership was not a matter of choice but a matter of residence. The official act of becoming a member was suggested to be nothing more than a formal confirmation of a given fact.

Leaders of other associations, such as those of 'No. 10' evoked the image of a 'communal life' (*kyôdô seikatsu*) and asked 'all the inhabitants of the *chô* to join the association' (TSS 1924: 19), and, in a similar way, the leaders of neighbourhood association 'No. 13' wished that 'a truly peaceful and happy life in communal solidarity (*kyôdô itchi no seikatsu*) will be created through their association' (TSS 1924: 25). Some associations such as 'No. 1' appealed more to the emotions of the *chô* inhabitants: 'we want you to join in order to foster the love for the *chô* and in order to create a prospering *chô* where it is enjoyable to live' (TSS 1924: 11).

Neighbourhood association 'No. 12' used a somewhat more idealistic and emotional tone:

> [I]f neighbours interact with each other intimately based on honesty, on the priciples of moral and in the spirit of a harmonious community (*wachû kyôdô no seishin*), and if the inhabitants of a *chô* form a well-knit community and help each other, this will serve the good of the *chô*-inhabitants as well as the good of the state.
>
> (TSS 1924: 21–22)

Thus, by the opening of the neighbourhood associations, the idea of the *chô* as a socio-spatial entity began to take form again – at least on paper, i.e. in the charters of the neighbourhood associations.

Indifferent members, rising social conflicts

The opening of the neighbourhood associations was a huge success in terms of membership rates. In 1924, already more than 250,000 of the 417,353 households in Tokyo had joined the neighbourhood associations. This equates to a membership rate of 60 per cent (TSS 1924: 188; THHI 1979b: 60). In the following year of 1925, more than 360,000 of the then 429,852 households had become members, equating to a membership rate of almost 84 per cent (TSC 1927: 7; THHI 1979b: 60). Thus, as soon as the middle of the 1920s, the opening of the neighbourhood associations was complete with the result that the vast majority of the households in Tokyo had become members. However, these numbers can hardly be interpreted as an expression of a growing community consciousness among the urban population since they do not disclose anything about the nature of the social relations between the *chô* inhabitants or about their perception of the neighbourhood associations.

To be sure, the leaders tried to evoke emotional belonging in the *chô* inhabitants in order to fill the propagated *chô* community with life. They invented special symbols to make the association and its activities for the good of the inhabitants visible. Among others, those were the flags of the *chô*, which were presented at certain occasions such as farewell or welcome ceremonies for recruits or funerals (e.g. charter of Hongô 5chôme chôkai (TSS 1924: 45–49)).

Furthermore, a part of the social activities of the neighbourhood associations also aimed at fostering a community sentiment among the inhabitants, with the annual shrine festival being often mentioned as the most prominent measure in this respect. However, it is hard to estimate how big the influence of the shrine festival actually was. After all, the festival took place only once a year, and the borders of the shrine parish did not always correspond with the borders of the *chô*. The festivals doubtlessly attracted many people, but it seems hard to equate an enthusiastic participation at a shrine festival with the existence of a community consciousness in everyday life.

Actually, leaders of many neighbourhood associations in Tokyo complained about the indifference of their members and about their general lack of community consciousness. While it must have been comparatively simple to make most of the people join the associations – after all, how could they refuse to join when being asked by the leaders, who often were their landlords? – it was obviously not so easy to gain their active cooperation, including the payment of membership fees.

The survey conducted by the Tokyo Institute for Municipal Research in 1925 showed that it was quite common for members not to pay their monthly fees, to refuse to take over certain tasks and not to comply with the rules of the associations. In fact, the lack of community consciousness was seen as the most urgent problem by the leaders, since it hampered their efficiency.

Similar reports came from associations from all over Tokyo, such as the following four examples:

Most of the members do not care about the association (TSC 1927: 130).
[The inhabitants] lack a sense of community (TSC 1927: 139).
The majority of inhabitants are indifferent towards us (TSC 1927: 141).
If someone moves out, the rules of our association ask that the member concerned come to the office and declare his withdrawal from the association, but regrettably so far nobody has complied with this rule (TSC 1927: 134).

In sum, the attitude of the rank-and-file members towards the neighbourhood associations as displayed in the letters collected by TSC 1927 strikingly reminds of the findings of Ronald Dore (1958), who in his seminal book 'City Life in Japan', characterised the attitude of the inhabitants of Shitayama-*chô* towards their neighbourhood association in 1951 as 'negative acceptance', i.e. they accepted they had to join and enjoyed the benefits, but were often reluctant to pay membership fees.

There were several reasons for this obvious lack of community consciousness. First, in spite of the charters calling for 'love of the *chô*', in many places the *chô* still had not developed into clear-cut socio-spatial entities one could easily identifiy with. Administrative reorganizations continued, with a big change taking place after the earthquake of 1923, when the municipal administration of Tokyo altered the boundaries and, consequently, the names of many *chô* yet again in order to form areas of almost equal size (BRHO 1929: 125–126; THHI 1979c: 62). What is more, in most cases, the boundaries of the neighbourhood associations and of the *chô* did not correspond. Due to a lack of members and funds, many leaders of neighbourhood associations in smaller *chô* tended to expand their association into neighbouring *chô* or they merged with neighbouring associations (TSC 1927). As a result, in 1938, only one-third of the neighbourhood associations in Tokyo did actually operate within the boundaries of one single *chô* or *chôme*, the sub-unit of a *chô* (Nakamura 1980: 4–5). Consequently, it must have been difficult for the members of many neighbourhood associations to project a feeling of belonging upon a certain *chô*, since it was difficult to know exactly what spatial area this *chô* actually occupied.

Then, due to the ongoing urbanisation, the population grew dramatically. *Chônaikai* statistics (TSC 1927) show that by the beginning of the 1920s, there were several hundred families living in one *chô* totalling between 1,000 and 2,000 persons. In view of these numbers, it was hardly possible that a substantial number of the inhabitants of a *chô* would know each other personally, let alone interact with each other on a daily basis. The sharp rise of the urban population was also reflected in the size of the neighbourhood associations. The size of the neighbourhood associations in Koishikawa-*ku*, for example, ranged from 45 households up to 1,400, with an average of 315 households per association (TSS 1924: 168–170). While face-to-face communication was possible in the smaller neighbourhood associations, social cohesion could hardly be created in those that had several hundred households as members. This is reflected in the following report by a neighbourhood association in Yamabukichô in Ushigome-*ku*:

> With its more than 1.480 households, Yamabukichô is the second biggest *chô* in Ushigome-*ku*. [...] Not even half of the inhabitants has been living here for more than ten years. Although board members were appointed regardless of the duration of residence, and although they were assigned tasks for the administration of the *chô*, the organisation does not completely take root in the *chô* due to diverging interestes and other differences.
>
> (TSC 1927: 138)

Furthermore, the opening of the associations did not change the realities of class divisions and social inequality prevalent in the *chô* and in urban society as a whole. Whereas, for example, in one charter it said that 'a neighbourhood association should absolutely not consist of only the wealthy', combined with a call for all the inhabitants of the *chô* to join (TSS 1924: 25), it has to be noted that social hierarchy remained a characteristic of the associations, since the boards remained reserved for property owners. This is reflected in a list of the professions of the presidents (*kaichô*) and vice-presidents (*fukukaichô*) of 50 neighbourhood associations in Ushigome-*ku* in 1924 (TSC 1927: 26–29). Among 45 presidents, whose professions are known, there were six landlords who were living on the income of rents or leases, 15 merchants, among them four wholesalers, one owner of a construction company, one owner of a printing shop, one owner of a brewery, one owner of a tea-house and one owner of a pawn shop. Further, 19 presidents were public servants, employees or self-employed, among them the Minister of Interior Affairs of Japan [*sic*!], two members of parliament, one economist, two chief executives, three lawyers and four doctors, one of them the director of a hospital. Their vice-presidents had similar professions. The findings of Hastings (1995: 80–81) about the professions of 153 persons who acted as presidents of the 78 neighbourhood associations in Honjo-*ku* between 1925 and 1935 underline the impression that they belonged to the upper strata of urban society.

What is more, since many neighbourhood associations suffered from financial difficulties, it was necessary to collect special donations in case bigger expenses had to be made, for example for street repairs, for the construction of an assembly hall or for the provision of street lighting. This meant that some wealthy 'bosses', who were able and willing to give such donations, tended to dominate the activities of the associations (Iwamoto 1995: 218). Although the charters stipulated that decisions about bigger concerns should be made by all the members during the annual general assembly in a democratic way (e.g. charter of Hongô 5chôme chôkai, TSS (1924: 45–49)), in practice most of the decisions were made by the financially influential benefactors of the associations. Thus, the opening of the associations led to the result, that the boards, which continued to be dominated by the local social elite, received a fundament of rank-and-file members from the general tenant population. Most of them belonged to the old middle class, who lived as tenants, e.g., craftsmen such as roofers or coppersmiths or shop tenants such as *dagashiya-san* (sweets and toy sellers). Their involvement with the association was confined to the monthly payments of the fees and sometimes lending a helping hand.

And finally, despite the charters evoking images of harmonious, well-knit communities, in fact the overall difficult economic situation led to social tensions and lingering conflicts that shook urban society in the course of the 1920s. Major social movements emerged, such as the labour movement, the tenants' movement and the consumers' movement, and affected the local level of the *chô*: workers opposed their employers, as depicted in Tokunaga's documentary novel (Tokunaga 1930; Hastings 1995), tenants opposed their landlords (Narita 1981), and the rise of consumption cooperatives posed a threat to the numerous small shop-owners (Ogata 1925, Katsube 1994). Thus, the social relations between the *chô* inhabitants were frequently characterised by conflicting interests, which hampered the emergence of a community consciousness.

What is more, the social structure became more heterogenuous by the emergence of the new middle class and the workers. Both classes changed their residence quite often and had a very distant relationship to the neighbourhood associations. Members of the new middle class, i.e. public servants or employees in large companies, had a strong desire for privacy and tried to avoid membership in a neighbourhood association. This was often criticised by board members like those of a neighbourhood association in Kôjimachi-*ku*:

> The majority of our members do not care about the association, but the members of the middle class are especially indifferent about it.
>
> (TSC 1927: 130)

Instead, they preferred other types of local associations like culture or leisure clubs, and in some places they established consumer cooperatives and other associations which more resembled citizens' movements. For example, the inhabitants of the Western suburb of Senzoku founded a neighbourhood association called Senzokukai, which mainly organised cultural activities like lectures and cinema shows and which demanded that the construction company that had developed the estate should also build an elementary school (Tamano 1993: 217).

In a similar way, factory workers avoided the neighbourhood associations and preferred to establish their own types of local organisation, mainly trade unions or tenants' associations. In his documentary novel, Tokunaga (1930) describes that neighbours helped each other when someone fell ill, that they took part in each others' funeral services and that they had formed a trade union which helped during a strike. He also describes how members of the neighbourhood association in the *chô* patrolled at night together with the police in order to spy on the workers.

And finally, in some places there were also individual reasons for inhabitants not to join or cooperate with the neighbourhood association, as described in the following report from Hongô-*ku*. The population of that *chô* was quite heterogeneous regarding the professions of the household heads, among whom there were public officials, bank clerks, landowners, doctors, merchants with residential property and workers. The board members wrote that it was difficult to unite all these different groups in one association, since many inhabitants ranked their own interests higher than the interests of the association:

> [W]hen the neighbourhood association has to collect money for disinfection or inoculation campaigns, the doctors say that there is no need for them to pay the fee since they can do the job by themselves at home. Same with the fire patrols: some say that their houses were fire-proof or that they had a fire insurance. And some merchants say that they could not cooperate because the president or the board members had never bought anything at their shops. In this way, they all display their individualism in an inconsiderate manner.
>
> (TSC 1927: 147)

The 'individualists' mentioned in this report who refused to cooperate obviously had no feeling of 'dutiful loyalty' and showed no community consciousness, but considered rationally what benefits membership could bring them.

Summary

In sum, the notion that Japan has a strong tradition of urban residents living together in village-like *chô*-communities from pre-modern to modern times is a fiction. After the Meiji Restoration, the *chô* in the capital ceased to exist as socio-spatial entities, since their boundaries were altered several times while the population fluctuated and increased due to urbanisation. However, at the turn of the century, their revival was sought after by the state, which, due to diverging financial priorities, sought to shift the social costs of urbanisation on to the individual households and expected urban residents to provide a safe and healthy living environment in the cities by themselves.

For this purpose, municipal administrations used the tradition of the local social elite cooperating with the municipal administration and initiated the establishment of *chô* associations, be it sanitary associations or multi-purpose neighbourhood associations. These, however, did not encompass all the households in a *chô* – which was difficult to recognise as a spatial entity, anyway, since its boundaries were altered several times – but more resembled the socially exclusive landlord's associations which in some places had existed since the last decades of the nineteenth century. Thus, they were neither expressions of nor a means to create *chô* communities.

After the upheavals of the rice riots and with urban problems persisting in the 1920s, the local authorities continued to successfully propagate the model of neighbourhood associations, which rapidly spread across the cities and were opened to all-comprehensive membership, encompassing all the households in a *chô*. Yet, the boards remained reserved for the local social elite, who were not so much motivated by community consciousness in creating neighbourhood associations, but by a mixture of reasons, ranging from a feeling of dutiful loyalty to the state, the necessity to protect their homes and businesses to political or economic ambitions.

At the same time, the associations sought to integrate all the households in a *chô* in order to overcome financial difficulties. While the opening of the associations was thus due to administrative necessities, the idea of the *chô*-community was created, and the charters show that it was envisioned as as a well-knit local community characterized by harmonious social relations based upon traditional values. Although the *chô* was thus deliberately constructed as a focus of identification and community sentiment in order to mobilize the cooperation of urban residents, in reality they were hardly perceived as such, since the boundaries of the *chô* were altered again and in most cases did not overlap with the boundaries of the associations, while populations in the *chô* increased in a way that made it hardly possible to know all the people who were living there. Many urban residents could have only a vague idea of the '*chô* community' as propagated by the leaders of the associations, who consequently complained about their indifference and lack of community consciousness.

From the viewpoint of the rank-and-file members, neighbourhood associations were barely more than an additional level of administration where the property owners and landlords of the *chô* cooperated with local authorities. They accepted becoming members, but they did not cooperate more than was necessary. Some social groups, such as the new middle class or the workers, avoided the neighbourhood associations completely.

This means that even in Japan, where the membership in a neighbourhood organisation has been a substantial part of the historical experience of urbanisation, many urban residents neither had a strong community consciousness nor did they emotionally identify with the *chô* in which they lived. Japan can thus not be viewed as an exception, which would be characterised by the persistence of rural or premodern social patterns in the midst of urbanisation.

Finally, present expectations of an increasing role of the neighbourhood associations in urban governance based upon the assumption that they are expressions of a strong tradition of community consciousness among urban residents, should not be too high. On the other hand, it is obvious that, although the commitment by the general population has never been too strong, the neighbourhood associations were generally able to fulfil their tasks sufficiently and might continue to do so in the future.

References

Allinson, Gary D. (1975): *Japanese Urbanism: Industry and Politics in Kariya, 1872–1972*. Berkeley/Los Angeles/London: University of California Press.

Amemiya Shōichi (1997): *Senji sengo taisei ron* [On the war and postwar systems]. Tokyo: Iwanami Shoten.

Ben-Ari, Eyal (1991): *Changing Japanese suburbia: A Study of Two Present-day Localities*. London, New York: Kegan Paul International.

Bestor, Theodore C. (1989): *Neighborhood Tokyo*. Stanford/California: Stanford University Press.

BRHO (The Bureau of Reconstruction, Home Office) (ed.) (1929): *The Outline of the Reconstruction Work in Tokyo and Yokohama*. Tokyo: The Sugitaya Press.

Brown, Philip C. (2003): 'New Frontiers in Japanese Urban History', *Journal of Urban History* 29(2): 198–206.

Dore, Ronald P. (1958): *City Life in Japan: A Study of a Tokyo Ward*. Berkeley: University of California Press.

Downard, Jack Douglas (1976): 'Tokyo: The Depression Years, 1927–1933'. Ph.D dissertation, Indiana University.

Fujino Atsushi (2002): *Tōkyōto no tanjō* [The birth of Tokyo prefecture]. (Rekishi bunka raiburarii [Library of History and Culture]; 135). Tokyo: Yoshikawa Kōbunkan.

Fukutake Tadashi (1982): *The Japanese Social Structure: Its Evolution in the Modern Century*. (Trans. Ronald P. Dore). Tokyo: University of Tokyo Press.

Harada Keiichi (2002): *Nihon kindai toshishi kenkyû* [Historical research on the Japanese modern city]. Kyoto: Shibunkaku Shuppan (First edition: 1997).

Hastings, Sally Ann (1995): *Neighborhood and Nation in Tokyo, 1905–1937*. Pittsburgh, London: University of Pittsburgh Press.

Hiraide Kôjirô (1979): *Tôkyô fûzokushi* [History of the manners in Tokyo]. (*Meiji hyakunenshi sôsho* [100 years since the beginning of the Meiji period series]; 78). Second edition. Tokyo: Hara Shobô (1st edition 1968, reprint of the original edition publ. 1901).

Hozumi Shigetō (1924): 'Chōkai to jichisei' [Neighbourhood associations and self-governing system]. In: TSS (1924): *Chōkai kiyaku yōryō* [Collection of model charters of neighbourhood associations]. (Kindai shiryō kankōkai (ed.): Tōkyōshi shakaikyoku chōsa hōkokusho (1920–1939) [Research reports of the Social Bureau of the City of Tokyo, 1920–1939]; 11). (Nihon kindai toshi shakai chōsa shiryō shūsei [Surveys on modern Japanese urban society]; 1). Tokyo: SBB Shuppankai, pp. 1–9.

Ishizuka Hiromichi/Narita Ryūichi (1994): *Tōkyōto no hyakunen: Kenmin hyakunenshi* [100 years of Tokyo prefecture: 100 years history of the prefecture's citizens]; 13. Second edition. Tokyo: Yamakawa Shuppansha.

Iwamoto Michiya (1995): 'Shōka no shikumi to itonami: Shōnin no nichijōteki sekai'

[Customs and enterprises of the merchants: The everyday life world of the merchants].
In: Miyata Noboru *et al.* (ed.): *Toshi to inaka: Machi no seikatsu bunka* [Town and
countryside: The life culture of the towns]. (Nihon minzoku bunka taikei [Compendium of Japanese folk culture]; 11). Tokyo: Shōgakkan, pp. 151–186.

Karan Pradyumna Prasad (1997): 'The City in Japan'. In: Karan, Pradyumna Prasad/Stapleton, Kristin (eds): *The Japanese City*. Lexington/Kentucky: The University Press of
Kentucky, pp. 12–39.

Katsube Kin'ichi (1994): *Niji no ayumi: Seikyô shôhisha undô 50nen: 21 seiki e heiwa to
kurashi no kyôdô o kangaeru* [The form of the rainbow: 50 years consumers' movement: Imagining a twenty-first century of peace and cooperative living]. Tokyo: Hon
no ki.

Kawata Chieko (1991): 'A Historical View of People's Involvement in Health Care in
Modern Japan'. In: Kawakita Yosio/Sakai Shizu/Otsuka Yasuo (eds): *History of
Hygiene: Proceedings of the 12th International Symposium on the Comparative
History of Medecine – East and West*. Tokyo, St. Louis: Ishiyaku EuroAmerica,
pp. 247–264.

Kobayashi Shigeyoshi (1991): *Meiji no Tôkyô seikatsu: Josei no kaita Meiji no nikki*
[Everyday life in Tokyo during the Meiji era: A diary from the Meiji era, written by a
woman]. (*Kadokawa sensho* [Kadokawa anthology]; 217). Tokyo: Kadokawa Shoten.

Komori Takayoshi (1973): 'Tōkyō ni okeru chōnaikai no hensen ni tsuite' [About the
development of the neighbourhood associations in Tokyo]. In: *Nihon rekishi* 2.297,
pp. 81–96.

Kurata Washio (2000): 'Komyuniti katsudô to jichikai no yakuwari' [Community activities and roles of self government associations]. In: *Kwansei gakuin daigaku shakai
gakubu kiyô* 86, pp. 63–76.

Nagoyashi (ed.) (1954): Taishō *Shōwa Nagoya shishi: Shiseihen* [The History of the city
of Nagoya during the Taishô and Shôwa eras: Municipal administration]. Nagoya:
Nagoyashi.

Nakamura Hachirô (1979): *Senzen no Tōkyō ni okeru chōnaikai* [Neighbourhood associations in Tokyo in the prewar era]. Tokyo: Kokusai rengô daigaku.

Nakamura Hachirô (1980): *Chônaikai no soshiki to un'eijô no mondaiten: Senzen ni
okeru Tôkyô no baai* [Problems in the management and structure of neighbourhood
associations: The case of pre-war Tokyo]. Tokyo: Kokusai rengô daigaku.

Nakano Makiko (1995): *Makiko's Diary: A Merchant's Wife in 1910 Kyoto*. (Trans.
Kazuko Smith). Stanford/California: Stanford University Press.

Narita Ryûichi (1981): '1920nendai zenhan no shakkanin undô: Shakkanin dômei o
chûshin ni' [Tenants' movements in the first half of the 1920s: With an emphasis on
the Tenants' Alliance]. In: *Nihon rekishi* 394, March, pp. 54–72.

Narita Ryûichi (2003): *Kindai toshi kûkan no bunka keiken* [The cultural experience of
modern urban space]. Tokyo: Iwanami Shoten.

Nawata Yoshihiko (2004): 'Chiiki shakai no gôi keisei to jichitai seisaku hômu' [Consensus making in local community and legal policy making of municipal government]. In:
Toshi mondai 95 (5), pp. 63–76.

Ogata Kiyoshi (1925): *Die Genossenschaftsbewegung in Japan* [The Japanese cooperative movement]. Berlin: R.L. Prager.

Ôishi Kaichirô and Kanazawa Fumio: 'Joshô: Kadai to hôhô' [Preface: Problems and
methods]. In: Ôishi Kaichirô and Kanazawa Fumio (eds) (2003): *Kindai Nihon toshishi
kenkyû: Chihô toshi kara no saikôsei* [Studies on modern Japanese urban history: A
restructuring from regional cities]. Tokyo: Nihon Keizai Hyôronsha, pp. 3–52.

Pekkanen, Robert (2006): *Japan's Dual Civil Society: Members without Advocates*. Stanford: Stanford University Press.

Robertson, Jennifer (1991): *Native and Newcomer: Making and Remaking a Japanese City*. Berkeley/Los Angeles/Oxford: University of California Press.

Saga Ashita (2007): *Kindai Ôsaka no toshi shakai kôzô* [The structure of urban society in modern Osaka]. Tokyo: Nihon Keizai Hyôronsha.

Smith, Henry D. (1978): 'Tokyo as an Idea: An Exploration of Japanese Urban Thought until 1945', *Journal of Japanese Studies*, 4 (1), pp. 45–80.

Smith, Henry D. (1986): 'The Edo-Tokyo Transition: In search of common ground', in: Jansen, Marius B. and Rozman, Gilbert (ed.): *Japan in transition: From Tokugawa to Meiji*. Princeton: Princeton University Press, pp. 347–374.

Smith, Henry D. (2006): 'Mura (birejji) to shite no Tôkyô: Henten suru kindai Nihon no shuto zô' [Tokyo as a 'Village': Changing Perceptions of Japan's Capital City], in: Suzuki Hiroyuki *et al.* (eds): *Shiriizu: Toshi · kenchiku · rekishi 6: Toshi bunka no seijuku* [Series: City, architecture, history 6: The maturity of urban culture]. Tokyo: Tokyo University Press, pp. 201–237.

Sorensen, André (2004): *The Making of Urban Japan: Cities and Planning from Edo to the Twenty-first Century*. London, New York: Routledge.

Sorensen, André (2006): 'Centralization, Urban Planning Governance, and Citizen Participation in Japan', in: Hein, Carola and Pelletier, Philippe (ed.): *Cities, Autonomy, and Decentralization in Japan*. London, New York: Routledge, pp. 101–127.

Sorensen, André and Funck, Carolin (eds) (2007): *Living Cities in Japan: Citizens' Movements, Machizukuri, and Local Environments*. Abingdon, New York: Routledge.

Tamano Kazushi (1993): *Kindai Nihon no toshika to chônaikai no seiritsu* [Urbanisation and the emergence of neighbourhood associations in modern Japan]. Tokyo: Kôjinsha.

Tanaka Yasuke (ed.) (1910): *Densenbyō ni kansuru hōrei ruisan* [Collection of regulations on infectuous diseases]. Seritamura (Nagano pref.).

THHI (Tôkyô hyakunenshi henshû iinkai) (ed.) (1979a): *Tôkyô hyakunenshi* [History of 100 years of Tokyo]; 3. Tokyo: Gyôsei.

THHI (1979b): *Tōkyō hyakunenshi* [History of 100 years of Tokyo]; 4. Tokyo: Gyōsei.

THHI (1979c): *Tôkyô hyakunenshi* [History of 100 years of Tokyo]; 5. Tokyo: Gyôsei.

Tokunaga Naoshi (alias: Sunao) (1930): *Die Straße ohne Sonne. Ein japanischer Arbeiter-Roman* [Street without sun]. (Trans. K. Itow and A. Raddatz). (*Der internationale Roman* [The international novel]; 5). Berlin, Wien, Zürich: Internationaler Arbeiter-Verlag.

TSC = Tôkyô shisei *chôsakai* [Tokyo Institute for Municipal Research] (1927): *Tôkyô-shi chônaikai ni kansuru chôsa* [Survey of the neighbourhood associations in the city of Tokyo]. Tokyo: Tôkyô shisei *chôsakai*.

TSS (Tôkyôshi shakaikyoku shakai kyôikuka) (ed.) (1924): *Chōkai kiyaku yōryō* [Collection of model charters of neighbourhood associations]. (Kindai shiryō kankōkai (ed.): Tōkyōshi shakaikyoku chōsa hōkokusho (1920–1939) [Research reports of the Social Bureau of the City of Tokyo, 1920–1939]; 11). (Nihon kindai toshi shakai chōsa shiryō shūsei [Surveys on modern Japanese urban society]; 1). Tokyo: SBB Shuppankai.

Yazaki Takeo (1968): *Social Change and the City in Japan*. San Francisco, New York, Tokyo: Japan Publications.

Yoshida Nobuyuki (1991): *Kinsei kyodai toshi no shakai kôzô* [The social structure of the premodern metropolis]. Tokyo: Tokyo Daigaku Shuppankai.

8 Who cares about the past in today's Tokyo?[1]

Paul Waley

Commemorating, preserving and broadcasting the past

In cities around the world a tense game is played out between those who would plug into global modernity (and maximise profits on available land) on the one hand and others who prefer to manipulate the existing urban landscape to engender a sense of cultural and/or national identity on the other (with the potential collateral benefit of rising property values). In many European cities, the regulatory framework tends to encourage preservation, while in Asian cities there has generally been a prioritisation on development activities. Along this admittedly rather sketchy spectrum, Japanese cities, and Tokyo above all of them, find themselves nearest to the development pole. Tokyo is an extreme case, a city founded some 400 years ago with very few substantial structures over 50 years old. This is not however to say that Tokyo has no visual reminders of its past nor that conservation activities are entirely absent. But it does raise a number of questions about history, identity and memory and about conservation and tourism and the role of the state and of civil society. This chapter brings together these concerns within the spatial context of Tokyo. I argue here that the state is not seriously interested in 'referencing' the nation's past in its capital city. This is true of the central state, and to a surprising extent true too of the metropolitan state. Instead, conservation becomes the preserve of citizens groups, who occasionally skirmish with the state but in general work compliantly within the regulatory framework that the state has set up. In Tokyo, this situation plays itself out to the great advantage of those whose main concern is to exploit the urban territory for profit.

The substantive sections of this chapter reflect the engagement with these two sets of themes, oriented around memory and identity on the one hand and the state and civil society on the other. They start with an examination of current tourism policy at national, metropolitan and local level. From there, the chapter narrows its focus to Taitô Ward, northeast of the city centre, where Tokyo's oldest and most important historical sites are located. These include a famous temple and its precincts in Asakusa and nearby Ueno Hill, a site of great significance in the city's history and the location of many important national and metropolitan museums. Tucked in behind Ueno is one part of Tokyo that would appear to enshrine the qualities that tourists are likely to find appealing. With its narrow lanes and attractive temples, Yanaka of all places might seem an appropriate location for some form of official intervention in conservation. Not so, however. The work of trying to retain characteristic elements of the townscape is left to civil society groups, which approach these issues obliquely, seeing themselves as ill equipped to take on a more interventionist role. Meanwhile, sitting beside Yanaka and Ueno Hill is Shinobazu Pond, the second of the two case studies examined in this chapter. Here, civil society groups have pitted themselves against each other in a struggle that was portrayed by one side in terms of livelihood issues against historicist conservation and on the other as unthinking and unnecessary development against preservation of a natural site of historical importance. The conclusion brings these various themes together and argues that Tokyo has made little space for its own past.

Nevertheless, the past can never be eliminated. 'Remembering the past,' David Lowenthal has written, 'is crucial for our sense of identity …: to know what we were confirms that we are' (Lowenthal 1985, 197). Our relationship with the past is a complex one, and there at least three different ways in which we act to keep present before our eyes a reading of the past. First, the past is commemorated in monuments and memorials; these inevitably reflect current ideas about past occurrences, casting in stone specific readings of past events. Sometimes these readings are contested, as in a number of prominent sites across Europe, where sharp divergences lead to competing claims of suffering on behalf of victims of fascism and communism (Azaryahu 2003; Purvis and Atkinson 2008). This has a particular pertinence in the case of Tokyo, as we shall see below.

Second, the past is preserved as heritage through conservation activities. But the questions that inevitably follow are these: which past, whose past? In many cities of East Asia, from Seoul to Jakarta (but, significantly, not in Tokyo), preserving the past involves some sort of compromise with colonial history (Logan 2002). In Seoul, the colonial past has been dismantled where possible, but in Singapore, which was after all a colonial foundation, it forms a defining framework for national heritage. In the case of Jakarta, Kusno has argued that current administrations are attempting to present the sense of order they identify in colonial urbanism as a vision of how the city should be today (Kusno 2004). In Taiwan, the preservation of old buildings is an important means of expressing a sense of Taiwanese – as opposed to mainland Chinese – identity and culture. A recent emphasis on the preservation and revalidation of historical buildings has occurred as part of a policy of underscoring Taiwan's 'different-ness' from mainland China (Tan and Waley 2006). In Singapore, a 'heritage landscape' has been created, 'provid[ing] the nation with a sense of historical continuity' (Kong and Yeoh 2003, 135). Ethnic parcels of the past have been fenced off and preserved, and as a result arguably divorced from ambient living cultures (Chang and Yeoh 1999).

Third a vision of the past is broadcast by promoting tourism, reinforcing a sense of nationhood and national identity in the process. But tourism too is built around a selective view of history. Light (2001) has shown how in Romania, as elsewhere in east and central Europe, specific buildings and views of the city have been promoted for the purposes of tourism so as to portray a view of the country as being located within a European mainstream that sidesteps, or jumps over, the 'non-European' Socialist period. In Beijing, the Old Summer Palace, on its lake just outside the city, has been turned into a sort of Chinese historical Disneyland in order to appeal (ironically in view of its history) to the foreign tourist hordes (Broudehoux 2004, 75).

In many countries (especially strong state countries) the state sees itself as having a central role to play in defining national identity, in building nationhood and also therefore in preserving the national heritage; one need only think of the associations of the French concept of *patrimoine*. States are rooted in capital cities, normally the largest city within a state's territory, and here the rituals of state are played out, at special sites that enshrine national memories, such as the Cenotaph in London or the Champs-Elysées in Paris. The state uses its capital city as a stage on which both to bind inwards (nation-building) and to stretch outwards (selling place, establishing global city status, etc.). But what happens when the state finds it too contentious to have its capital city enshrine national memories? Or when the state has absolved itself of this responsibility? What happens when civil society fills in the holes? In many if not most circumstances and conditions, it is not either/or. The state and civil society work together. To be effective as advocates of various positions, civil society needs to work within a framework provided by the state.

Looking for history in Tokyo

In Tokyo everything is coloured by the short lifespan of buildings. Wooden buildings withstand the test of time with difficulty. Stone and brick buildings, many of which might be thought to have considerable historical cachet, have only sparsely been preserved. The city has been largely destroyed on two occasions over the last 100 years through fire, and is constantly being knocked down and rebuilt. Not only in Tokyo but throughout Japan, development pressures are extremely strong; this is, after all, the archetypal construction state (*doken kokka*). A discourse of disaster prevention on the one hand and impermanence on the other dominates research and policy on the built environment.

Even taking into account the depredations of disaster and bulldozer, there would be few buildings and monuments that pronounced an authoritative view of Japan's past. However, there is no such authoritative view – many crucial periods of the past are mired in ideological controversy, not least Japan's role in the Second World War. Almost from the city's foundation, it never had a strong landmark to denote the centre of power. The Shogun's Castle lay concealed behind its walls, as did subsequently the Emperor's Palace, which occupied the same central site, hidden from the gaze of imperial subjects. This absence in the centre of the city has been thrown into relief in recent years because various politicians, including prime ministers, have chosen to commemorate the past (pay respect to the war dead) at Yasukuni Shrine (Takahashi 2006). This has caused immense controversy and hostility both within Japan and among Japan's immediate neighbours, as the shrine memorialises the spirits of Japan's wartime leaders. There is, then, no official place in Tokyo where national acts of commemoration are held. This contrasts with a basic (but far from total) consensus over the memorialisation of the Hiroshima A-Bomb (Saaler and Schwenter, 2007). In Tokyo even popular sites of historical memory have been obscured (as with Nihonbashi Bridge, centre of old commercial Tokyo, and now covered by an expressway) or all but crowded out, as with Hachikô, the statue of a loyal dog at Shibuya Station.

Nor has the state been much involved in preserving Japan's past through conservation. As we shall see below, there is a legal framework and limited state involvement. But much of the country's architectural heritage takes the form of Buddhist temples, and the early Meiji governments, after the overthrow of the shogun, were hostile towards Buddhism, while in the post-war period Japanese leaders have, at least until recently, preferred to abide by the strict separation of state from religion. However, the state has not been totally inactive. It has done a number of things by way of manipulating the past in the present: it has fenced it off and packed it elsewhere; it has encouraged it to be subsumed within events and people; and it has allowed it to be commodified.

As far as promoting tourism and broadcasting the past is concerned, Tokyo has been seen as a largely sender city – tourism happens elsewhere, in Kamakura, Nikkô and in Kyoto, not in Tokyo. In the 1980s, domestic tourism was promoted, both in hard terms through legislation to encourage investment in tourism infrastructure (Rimmer 1992) and in soft terms through the cultivation of a vision of a purer, rural 'Japan of the hometown', or *furusato* (Creighton 1995, 446). Only in the last few years have the Japanese authorities appeared to become seriously interested in promoting in-bound tourism. In 2003 the national government introduced a campaign to double tourist arrivals by 2010, while the Tokyo Metropolitan Government (TMG) published a new strategic vision to boost tourism. The former was instigated, in part, by ex-Prime Minister Koizumi Junichi's advocacy of tourism. The latter was driven by Tokyo's candidacy for the 2016 Olympics. Both were built on the perceived success of the 2002 football World Cup and the quality of the impression made on visiting football fans from around the world. Neither campaign, it must be said, was notable for its inventiveness or its sense of conviction.

None of this is to say that Tokyo is a city that has lost its sense of its own history. On the contrary, new-found national self-confidence in the 1980s led to a rediscovery of the city's history, and this history was recreated principally through a celebration and commodification of Edo (as Tokyo was called when it was the capital of the Tokugawa shoguns until 1868) and Shitamachi, the name given to the old centre of the merchants and artisans' part of the city (Sand 2001; Waley 2002). But that sense of history is not visible and the iconic landmarks that Kong (2007) sees as an indispensable part of a city with global aspirations are simply not present in Tokyo – unless, that is, one sees the whole of the cityscape as possessing the qualities of iconic landmark. Unlike in some other 'strong-state' countries in the region such as Malaysia, the Japanese state has in recent years shown little interest in involving itself in the business of city-building, leaving that task largely to big business (Waley 2007). Property developers and big business more generally have not been concerned about realising the commodified value of historical space; culturally little value is ascribed to old buildings, and in economic terms it is the land on which buildings stand that is valuable. There are no incentives for business to be interested in conservation.

Where the state has withdrawn and capital is uninterested, there is room for civil society to be active. But civil society is generally seen as rather weak beside a strong state that has the tendency to co-opt it whenever it can to act as its sub-contractor or its 'local office' (Pekkanen 2006). One way of understanding the nature of civil society in Japan is to divide it into old and new. The old civil society is compliant with the state. It is old because many organisations that form part of it date back before World War II. They are male-dominated and traditionalist in outlook. They form a strong presence in many spheres, more so in Japan than in other industrialised countries. Neighbourhood and shopkeeper associations are just two examples of compliant, old civil society groups, place-based and generally conservative and hierarchical, working closely with local government as a matter of routine. New civil society, which relates more closely to equivalents in Europe and North America, is sometimes confrontational but more often consensual. Where it is confrontational, groups tend to be issue-oriented, the issues often involving development and perceived threats to the environment (Vosse 2000). Generally but not always, their actions are moderate in scope and limited in effectiveness. Groups operating on the basis of consensus may be involved in campaigns and consciousness-raising exercises, often led by a 'soft elite' of academics and government officials (Waley 2005b). Or they may be active in social welfare and other areas where the state prefers to sub-contract, dependent for their survival on state patronage.

These definitions of civil society hinge on relations with the state. The state, however, is largely absent in the spheres of activity under consideration here. Civil society groups have as a result had more room for manoeuvre, as for example in the sort of conservation efforts that are discussed below in the context of Yanaka. But equally, some of the contradictions stemming from the existence of a largely state-dependent civil society sector have surfaced in the dispute over what to do with Shinobazu Pond, the second of the two case studies examined here.

Conservation, tourism and community involvement

Civil society groups have only recently become involved in conservation of the built environment, and even more recently still in tourism. The following section provides a brief synopsis of some of the ways in which the 'organized, nonstate, nonmarket sector', as Pekkanen (2006, 3) defines civil society, involves itself in these spheres of activity.

Neither sphere has been defined by the strong presence of the state, although the state has set the tone of conservation efforts. Early legislation, the 1897 Law for the Preservation of Ancient Temples and Shrines, was directed towards the preservation of religious buildings (Henrichsen 1998; Hajdu 2002; Yamasaki 2003). Not until 1929 was protection extended to cover other sorts of buildings. such as castles and town houses, through the Law for the Preservation of National Treasures. The third major legislative landmark, the Law for the Protection of Cultural Properties, enacted in 1950, recognised the need to protect not only objects but also (intangible cultural properties and people involved in traditional pursuits, and it corresponded thus to a more sophisticated understanding of a wider range of meanings of conservation. It was, however, very much a child of its times in reflecting a static view of the meaning of 'the traditional' and a dualistic idea of Japanese culture – Japanese vs Western, traditional vs modern. It was influenced both by the work of Japanese folklorists and by the accent on democracy engendered in the wake of defeat in the Pacific War.

The last 50 years or so have seen a number of trends develop, many of them around the introduction of Important Preservation Districts for Groups of Historic Buildings (IPDs) as a result of a revision in 1975 of the Law for the Preservation of National Treasures (Hohn 1997). The designation of such a district needs enabling ordinances to be passed at the municipal level, but there has been a growing responsiveness to public pressure on designation. IPDs and other forms of preservation district have grown out of local campaigns. Particularly in the 1990s, there has been an increase in the number of local residents' groups keen both to protect local environments and livelihoods and to encourage tourism. However, designation remains a bureaucratic process, with ultimate control exercised by central government. The situation is not helped by a funding structure that mixes regional and central subsidies but remains insufficient to encourage further designations. Despite the introduction of more generous subsidies in the 1990s for the management and repair of buildings in IPDs, procedures are still regarded as too cumbersome and the subsidies insufficient, with the result that property owners, all of whose permission is needed for designation to go forward, often prefer not to be involved in the procedure. A further point, one that is of particular interest in the context of this chapter, is that tourism has increasingly become an incentive for the submission of applications for IPD status. The media have played an important role in focusing attention on specific locations, to the point where in some cases the size of the tourist influx has led to saturation and caused problems of sustainability.

While the built environment has been largely left prey to profit-led processes of development, conservation policies have come to reflect an emphasis on human activity, on work, on occupation, on crafting objects with the hands. The person is more important than the setting. Traditional crafts and artisans have been supported through various measures at a local, metropolitan and national level. The same sort of points can be made about tourism. As has already been intimated, IPDs are the result of a lot of hard work and enthusiasm on the part of private citizens, who will inevitably have joined together in groups. Many of the members of the Japanese Association for Townscape Preservation (Zenkoku Machinami Hozon Renmei) are non-profit organisations registered as such under Japan's 1998 NPO law. One such is the Kawagoe Kura no Kai, which campaigned for over 20 years for the centre of the town to be declared an IPD, the first and so far the only one in the Tokyo conurbation. This is a representative situation, in that the proclamation – and after that, the supervision and safeguarding – of IPDs has generally been the work of determined local enthusiasts and community leaders (Hohn 1997). The successful registration of IPD status has a direct link with tourism in that it leads to a large increase in tourist numbers. For example, the village of Shirakawa in Gifu Prefecture, with its distinctive high thatched roofs, has had to contend over a long period now with all-but overwhelming numbers of tourists.

The central government attempted a few years ago to involve local communities in tourism promotion, and the TMG followed suit with similar ideas. The policy was built around three drivers of sustainable tourism development: resources, living environment and visitor satisfaction (OECD 2002). However, there is little indication that this policy has been consistently pursued, and at the metropolitan level it appears to have been relegated in the TMG's new tourism promotion plan of 2007.

Local communities are, however, active in various ways in place-based activities. Civil society activity in Tokyo matches the typology set out above – old and new, compliant, consensual and confrontational. It is occasionally confrontational, as when it attempts (usually unsuccessfully) to douse rampant development, especially construction of high-rise apartment blocks (Fujii *et al.*, 2007). More often, it is consensual, working with local (ward-level) governments to attract interest, raise consciousness or support local activities or economies. The urban scenery in Tokyo is full of such place-making activities, which form part of what is known as *machi-zukuri*, community planning or 'soft' town planning. Finally, it is compliant where it endorses and promotes development projects sponsored by the state, sometimes in coalition with outside business interests. Compliant civil-society place-based activities elide often into consensual community planning. The difference is in the institutional base – groups here categorised as 'old', such as neighbourhood and shopkeeper associations, being more likely to be involved in compliant activities, new and ad-hoc groups in consensual ones.

This, then, is the contextual setting within which the past is made present in contemporary Japan, and more specifically in Tokyo. The state has played a rather withdrawn role, and indeed could be said to have been more or less absent. However, local communities have promoted conservation plans in the form of IPDs, and are active in place-based and place-making activities. This is the picture throughout urban Japan. In the following sections, the focus is narrowed to Tokyo and then again to one of Tokyo's wards, Taitô Ward, in which are located Yanaka and Shinobazu Pond, the two case studies that are considered in more detail here.

Tokyo, tourism for the Olympics

Conservation and tourism in Japan both have specific thematic and geographic foci. Objects of the tourist gaze still tend to belong to conventional views of a Japanese tradition. And they tend to remain clustered in certain locations, principally of course Kyoto, Nara and other sites of historical primacy. Tokyo is excluded from this activity. As already mentioned, the national government of Japan launched a Visit Japan campaign in 2003 with the aim of doubling the number of incoming tourists to 10 million by 2010 and of redressing the huge disequilibrium in tourist flows and therefore in the balance of trade. The core of the campaign, which is run by the Ministry of Land Infrastructure and Transport, (MLIT), remains the pulling power of traditional images of the country, although there are excursions into 'Cool Japan', which it locates primarily in Tokyo (www.vjc.jp/). This was followed by a revised Basic Law for Tourism (2006), designed to create an appropriate environment for the promotion of tourist activities, and a new Tourism Master Plan, which was in the consultation and drafting stage in the summer of 2007. At the time of writing, it was not clear what the impact of the campaign would be, other than that of contributing to an increase in tourist incomers.

To the extent that the Visit Japan campaign relies on the pulling power of tradition, Tokyo is largely excluded. Tokyo cannot draw tourists by highlighting its historical attractions as these are few in number and, for the main part, not considered to be worth conserving. For its part, the Tokyo Metropolitan Government published its second tourism promotion plan in March 2007, under the title, 'Tokyo, Aiming to be a Dynamic and Stylish World City' (TMG 2007). The main impulse behind the plan was to support Tokyo's candidature for the 2016 Olympics, a personal crusade of the long-serving metropolitan governor, Ishihara Shintarô. The tourism promotion plan was also designed to address Ishihara's concern that Tokyo should compete effectively as a world city with other regional hubs such as Shanghai and Singapore. There are seven main thrusts to the plan, the first two of which are the 'formation of a beautiful landscape' and 'improvement of the attractiveness of waterside space'. The sixth is entitled 'tourism that makes the most of history, culture, sports, etc.' The order here is surprising, given Tokyo's lack of visual distinction and the particular poverty of its waterside scenery. The emphasis on waterside locations was reinforced through the publication in 2005 of a 30-year 'General Framework for the Improvement of the Attractiveness of Waterside Space' (TMG 2005). There is however much disagreement within the Tokyo Metropolitan Government (reflecting disagreements at the national level) as to the best approach to waterside space, with strong pressures from some quarters to retain existing (normally industrial) functions along canals and other waterways.

It is significant that at the national government level tourism is handled by MLIT, and at the metropolitan level by the Industry and Labour Bureau of the TMG. Neither of these organisations is noted for its sensitivity to conservation and culture; they deal predominantly with engineering projects and economic affairs respectively. It is not surprising therefore that conservation has not been a priority in Tokyo, where the emphasis has been on safety, community and economic dynamism. Recently TMG policy has linked tourism to community planning, the mantra of planners and politicians in Japan. Community planning is indeed an appropriate vehicle both for conservation and sustainable tourism. In 2004, the TMG published its *Basic Guidelines for Urban Planning and Tourism Promotion in Tokyo* (TMG 2004b). This involves, in the words of the guidelines, 'Aiming for urban planning which allows proactively-involved communities, [and helping] them realize a vital town that makes residents proud of it and tourists feel like visiting again and again' (2004b, 4). And indeed community planning at a ward level (approximately equivalent to a city level elsewhere in Japan), through the consultative and/or participatory processes that it involves, has led to increased consideration for local livelihoods and sustainability in development. This has in some areas facilitated conservation activities, although this does not apply to the case studies examined below. The policy link between tourism and community planning was downplayed in the 2007 tourism promotion plan.

At a more strategic level, two considerations dominate. In the first place, making Tokyo an attractive city for foreigners represents an important part of the policy of the Tokyo Metropolitan Government's drive for international competitiveness in the face of competition from cities like Shanghai. And second, current tourism policy was very much oriented around Governor Ishihara's 2016 Olympic bid. This is perhaps fitting, given the success of the 2002 football World Cup in bringing people to the city. The event is seen to have energised both local communities and tourist authorities, spreading a more expansive view of the varieties and potential of tourism, including budget tourism.

Taitô Ward: tourism without conservation or gentrification

In other cities of the world, Taitô Ward would likely be a prominent centre for tourism. In the middle of the ward stands the temple complex of Sensôji, with its avenue of shops and its series of annual events. This is the fulcrum not only of popular religion but more broadly it is the associative touchstone for many of the city's residents. And yet, however full the temple grounds might get, they are surrounded by a somewhat depressed urban landscape. Like Tokyo itself, Taitô Ward has only recently awoken to the potential for urban change that tourism brings. In 2007, the ward office created a department for culture and tourism. One of the early aims of the department was to update the ward's tourism strategy, which outlines a basically 'theme park' approach to tourism, with the idea of Shitamachi providing the central theme that runs through the document (Taitô Ward Government 2000). Shitamachi, it should be added, is the historical and cultural heartland of the city, and although the urban fabric – even more so than in the rest of the city – has been several times destroyed by disasters, the spirit and traditions of the old city are seen as living on in the area. The cultural products of Shitamachi have been commodified ever since they were first produced, and they are all the more so today. Taitô Ward, with Asakusa at its heart, stands in the centre of the old Shitamachi.

The theme-park approach is an echo of a much older policy that is nowhere better evidenced than on Ueno Hill, where the leaders of Meiji Japan established a park and a 'culture district' of museums modelled explicitly on South Kensington in London (Waley 2005a). Ueno Hill today is a strange mixture of cultural sites and blue tarpaulin tents of the homeless, a testimony both to the harsh exclusions of a closely patrolled society and to the same society's capacity for spatial accommodation of the socially excluded. The three contrasting (and architecturally notable) buildings of the Tokyo National Museum stand at the back of the hill, inconvenient to access and infrequently visited. On the hill between the railway station and the National Museum stand a number of other important sites, including museums and a concert hall. Also on the hill there is a famous old temple building and an equally old pagoda and shrine, built in memory of the first Tokugawa shogun. These latter buildings are designated as National Treasures, *kokuhô*, and yet despite this designation and despite their obvious beauty, they bear a rather haphazard appearance and appear unattended and poorly maintained.

As for Asakusa, a half-hour walk east from Ueno, the crowds have been present since the city's early days; only their composition has changed, with foreign tourists now making up a significant proportion of the visitors. Although very few indeed of any of today's structures are old, the temple grounds bear a sort of innocent timelessness. The temple itself owns its precincts and the surrounding land, but the TMG owns those of the buildings that it has not sold off. In recent years, one of the streets on the west side of the temple grounds has become popular with young Tokyoites and tourists. The owners of the drinking establishments on either side of the road are virtually all of Korean descent. They have become the beneficiaries of an urban nostalgia that manifests itself in street-level consumption of the sort of food and drink redolent of a period when life was 'cheaper and more cheerful'. After decades of obscuring any reference to their Korean past, the bar owners now advertise their premises and products in Korean, and Asakusa, like some other parts of Tokyo, now has its own retro and drinking quarter. Other streets in Asakusa have had retro-fits, streets and shop fronts re-clad in historical 'costume'. One parade of shops have had their frontage replaced with traditional, old Edo cladding, but sculpted ninja peering up from the eaves give this gesture a strong sense of spoof. Tourist-laden rickshaws ply the streets. Many other parts of Asakusa, however, have changed little over the last 30 or more years, and remain insistently down-at-heel.

Ueno and Asakusa with their various tourist attractions represent interesting cases of neglect. There is little evidence of gentrification, either in Ueno and Asakusa or anywhere else in Taitô Ward, with the possible exception of Yanaka, a district that we will examine below. Significant culture-led regeneration projects are absent. Some buildings are preserved under the legislative framework, but there is little sense of a concerted effort to incorporate these sites into the wider urban landscape. There are some clear reasons for this. A distinctive land ownership pattern – the metropolitan government in the case of Ueno Hill, the temple in the case of the Asakusa Kannon precincts and surroundings – has encouraged this sense of difference. There are also historical and cultural reasons. Temple precincts were associated in pre-modern times with pursuits of a moral ambivalence that later grew less and less acceptable; they were linked to outcaste groups, and those associations have never entirely disappeared. Ueno Hill and the area around Shinobazu Pond have long been preferred locations for the homeless, and while this has been and continues to be a hard fought struggle for space, there is likely to be some impact on numbers of domestic tourist visitors.

The emphasis in Taitô Ward's tourism strategy is principally on people. People figure prominently in publicity and policy, in terms in particular of preserving livelihoods. Thus the artisan as heritage is seen as important, and the ward has set up a system of designated ateliers (the neighbouring ward of Sumida established a more extensive model some years previously) (www.designers-village.com). Concern is evinced in the strategy for foreigners, the elderly and those with physical disabilities, in particular in terms of infrastructure such as toilets and street signs. The strategy is equally revealing for what it leaves out. No mention is made of the problems of homelessness, despite its enormous impact in social and urban terms. There is relatively little attention paid to aesthetic improvements (Taitô Ward Government 2000, 23). Preservation of the existing built environment – or parts of it – is not articulated as an aim of policy.

Yanaka: civil society and conservation without regulation

The neglected state of Asakusa and Ueno testify to the disinterested policy of the state towards the conservation of historical sites when they are located outside cultural enclaves such as Kyoto and Nara. This disinterest has opened a space into which civil society has gingerly entered. Such is the case, for example, in Yanaka, one of Tokyo's very few attractive, older neighbourhoods. Yanaka is located on the north side of Ueno (but still therefore no more than a 20 minute metro ride from the centre of the city). The area, lying on a west-facing hillside sloping down to a culverted stream that once flowed into Shinobazu Pond, was urbanised largely in the late seventeenth and early eighteenth centuries. A number of temples were moved out here from the city centre. Alongside them stood the houses of minor members of the military class, as well as the more cramped quarters of the townspeople. Yanaka retained this mixed social fabric in modern times, when academics and artists chose it as an amenable and convenient district in which to live. At the top of the hill, alongside the Tokyo National Museum, the Tokyo National University of Fine Arts and Music has its main campus. Nearby too is Yanaka cemetery, one of the two main public cemeteries in the central part of the city. The cemetery was long known for its cherry trees and for the Tennôji Pagoda, which was burnt down in a suicide pact on 6 July 1957 and never rebuilt.

Yanaka today is generally considered to retain the atmosphere of old Tokyo – whatever one might mean by old, and to whatever period one might be referring. The buildings are mostly still two storeys high. The roads remain narrow; there are two small-scale shopping streets largely free of chain stores; and there are few larger condominiums. This is an urban landscape that is virtually unique within Tokyo, and it culminates in something else that is very rare, a large open space (the cemetery) at the top of the hill. In most other cities of the size and wealth of Tokyo, one would expect some level of gentrification in a district such as Yanaka. The area is indeed home to a number of academics, and some of them have been instrumental in local campaigns, including the one examined below to save Shinobazu Pond. Artists too live in Yanaka, generally in less stable and well-appointed circumstances. But there is nothing to compare with the process of gentrification – however one defines the term – that has been underway for decades in roughly equivalent areas of European and North American cities. That is not to say that there has been no gentrification at all, but it consists almost entirely of movement into newly built apartments – and it is around this construction activity that controversy has gathered. Some landowners, using set-back space to adhere to planning regulations, have managed to build condominiums on the site of older housing, especially along the main streets.

Maintaining the present mixed urban ecology is difficult. It requires a spirit of negotiation and compromise, and also a high degree of community-level activity. In the case of Yanaka, much of this activity can be traced back to the founding of a local journal called *Yanesen* which carries stories on local history, local people, local products, local restaurants and the like. *Yanesen*, now approaching its 100th edition, started a vogue. It was one of the first such 'town sheets' and remains among the best, in terms both of design and content. It became known throughout the country, not least through the activities of one of its founders, Mori Mayumi, who is a well-known commentator on family and community affairs. Despite a creeping process of development and reconstruction, Yanaka – along with the neighbouring districts of Nezu and Sendagi (whence the name of the magazine *Ya-ne-sen*) – has become the focus of a considerable amount and variety of civil society activities. There are groups promoting street art, creating and tending urban oases, discovering nature in corners of Yanaka and involving children in a host of events. Many of these activities are run from Yanaka Gakkô (school), a building over 100 years old that was turned in 1989 into an office and meeting room for civil society groups in the Yanaka area.

There have in recent years been two civil society organisations active in conservation in Yanaka, working in different ways for the same ends. The first is the Taitô History Urban Research Group and the second Hitomachi CDC (CDC for Community Development Corporation, in English). The Taitô History Group, a registered NPO, is a sort of consultation agency in Yanaka and surrounding areas. It gives advice on conservation, on structure and on ways to rehabilitate buildings, encouraging and advising owners as to how best to conserve old buildings and use them in new ways. The group rents houses that are awaiting a decision on onward sale and then sub-rents them to students. The students pay a peppercorn rent, but in return, they maintain the buildings and make various improvements. The hope is that as a result the owner of the property will wish to retain what has become an improved building with a higher exchange value. Resourceful as this approach is, it can only ever operate at a limited level, and it reveals the considerable limitations imposed by a system that upholds the regulatory framework for conservation only for buildings of special historic and cultural significance.

Even more than the Taitô History Group, Hitomachi CDC is non-confrontational in its approach. Here too, consciousness-raising is a primary aim. Rather than challenge the owners of old houses, it argues the benefits of conservation, and if this fails it tries to ensure that new apartment buildings are constructed to a height and in a style that is in harmony with the surrounding urban landscape. It recognises that opposing property owners who are intent on rebuilding is fruitless, but there is mileage to be gained from talking to them and cajoling them into holding onto existing buildings. The emphasis with Hitomachi CDC is also therefore on support and advice, not only to property owners but also to the local community association.

In the case of both the Taitô History Group and Hitomachi CDC, the outside observer is struck by the limits within which it is considered necessary to work in order to be effective. In the context of Tokyo, no matter where in Tokyo, the chances of designating an Important Preservation District for Groups of Historic Buildings is non-existent. And this is not only because a discrete neighbourhood of such buildings no longer exists anywhere in the city. Yanaka's buildings are neither old enough, nor important enough, nor do they form a sufficiently coherent block. Conservation does not appear to be a priority for Taitô Ward Government. For Taitô Ward, as for the Tokyo Metropolitan Government, tourism has entered the policy consciousness, but this has not in itself led to a sense of the potential importance of conservation strategies. This lack of activity and lack of concern has left a space into which civil society has moved. Having moved there, however, its ability to act and its room for manoeuvre are severely circumscribed.

Shinobazu: car park or pond

Shinobazu Pond lies just to the south of Yanaka, in the north of inner city Tokyo, under Ueno Hill and a five minute walk from Ueno Station, one of Tokyo's biggest termini. Despite its status as a famous city landmark, a plan was announced in 1986 to build a large car park under the pond. It was only after an imaginative and long-drawn-out campaign that the plan was revoked. The campaign pitched an alliance of residents of the neighbouring district of Yanaka, professors at local universities, and a number of environmentalists against local business people and ward officials, who were drafting and promoting the plan. The case is a highly unusual one in the context of Tokyo in that the decision was taken not to build, a victory for the conservationists and environmentalists, but also perhaps a reflection of the economic conjuncture, coinciding with Japan's long period of economic slowdown.

Shinobazu Pond is a remnant of the sea, formed by water flowing down a stream whose course is today traced by the Chiyoda metro line. When an adviser to the first Tokugawa shogun started building a great temple on Ueno Hill, he had the pond enlarged so that it would mirror in miniature Lake Biwa near Kyoto. The pond, sitting as it did under a prominent temple complex, became one of the most celebrated sites of the city, depicted in woodblock prints by various artists including Hiroshige. Its waters, covered by lotus leaves, contained an island with a shrine on it linked to its banks by an earthen embankment and lined by tea-houses. In the 1880s, after the fall of the shogunate and the advent of imperial government, horse races were held for a while around the pond, with the emperor and empress in occasional attendance. Tokyo's zoo was built on its banks, later spilling out and taking over part of the pond as well. During the Pacific War, a section of the pond was filled in and turned into vegetable fields. Not long after the war, a proposal was made to convert the pond into a baseball stadium. This was turned down, on historical rather than environmental grounds.

Shinobazu Pond today is divided into three sections. The western area is a boating pond. The northeastern section forms part of the zoo and is inhabited largely by cormorants. The southeastern section is covered by lotus plants in summer and reeds in winter. In recent years, the pond, like much of the adjacent Ueno Park, became a favoured spot for the homeless, and its banks and central islands were punctuated by their neat blue tarpaulin tents, a sight at once both sad and striking.

The first plan to build a car park under the pond was drafted jointly by the Ueno Tourist Association (Ueno Kankô Renmei) and Ueno Shopkeepers Association (Ueno Shôtenkai) in 1986. It was announced to general surprise through an article in the mass-circulation *Yomiuri* newspaper as a plan drafted by the local government office, Taitô Ward (Shimizu 1998, 9). The plan envisaged a three-floor area with spaces for 2,000 cars and 62 buses (Ogawa 1990, 11). The facility was to have an elevator leading up a tower projecting out of the ground with a restaurant on top and a monorail encircling the site (Mori 2003). The pond was to have been drained, and the car park built through excavation. The plan was widely criticised. The following year, a second plan was drafted, under which the car park was to be limited to one-third of the expanse of the pond but built much deeper, to five floors. A number of subsequent plans issued from the ward government, along with reports confirming the need for a car park. Each iteration involved a design for fewer spaces and a smaller area. Finally, in 1997, the plan was abandoned altogether. A much smaller car park has since been built, not without considerable technical difficulties, alongside the Ginza metro line under the nearby Chûô Street.

The withdrawal of the plan represents a rare unequivocal victory for advocates of conservation. The announcement of the initial plan by the tourist and shopkeepers' associations was accompanied by longstanding claims that more needed to be done to attract a younger clientele to the shops of Ueno. The plan elicited a rapid response from a number of residents of Yanaka, among them several resident foreigners (Miyauchi 1990). They argued that for much of the time existing car parks in the area had empty spaces. As well as publishing a regular newsletter (from 1989 to 1997), they undertook surveys of the pond's ecosystem and natural life. With several well-placed supporters, including professors of nearby universities, they took their campaign to the television screens, and encouraged letters of protest to be written by foreign residents to the mayor of Taitô Ward. They held festivals on the banks of the pond in which they celebrated its history. They warned the ward's mayor that the project might very well cause structural damage to surrounding buildings (Shimizu 1998, 3).

The struggle for Shinobazu Pond provides an interesting case of conflict between what I have somewhat crudely labelled old and new civil society. That such classic examples of compliant, old civil society as the tourist and shopkeepers' associations struck a common chord with officials in the ward office is not really surprising. Theirs is a mainstream approach that encourages development in order to stimulate the local economy. One might call it IMBYP, or 'in my back yard please'. IMBYP movements in Japan, whether on the scale of the Aichi World Expo or campaigns to site railway stations, are generally successful. That this one failed is a testament to the historical resonance of the pond itself but also and more particularly to the skilful execution of the campaign to halt the construction of the car park.

Concluding thoughts: the past cannot be eliminated

This chapter started with an assertion about the different ways in which the past is referenced in contemporary cities. It is, so I argued, commemorated, preserved and broadcast, with the state generally playing a leading role in each of these activities. In the case of Tokyo, however, neither central nor metropolitan nor even local government have been more than peripherally interested or involved, leaving the space open therefore for civil society groups.

There is, first of all, an absence of state-sanctioned commemorative space – of places where the past is commemorated – in Tokyo. This can be attributed in part to Tokyo's celebrated empty centre, celebrated, that is, by Roland Barthes in his *Empire of Signs* (1983, 30). But a more significant and complex explanation lies in the country's failure to come to an agreed position on its role in the Second World War, of which this absence of official *lieu de mémoire* is such a poignant statement. If there is little agreement about who was responsible for Japan's war and the suffering experienced by people throughout the region, then it is hard to memorialise this moment of history. Similarly, if for somewhat different reasons, the state has been little interested in cherishing the physical reminders of the past. Conservation efforts are largely left to weakly positioned but generally enthusiastic civil society groups – and indeed to religious organisations, especially the powerful Buddhist sects who own the great temples of Kyoto and thousands of much smaller ones, as well the Asakusa temple. In Tokyo, the examples of Yanaka and Shinobazu Pond suggest that for the authorities history has a place somewhere else – in Kyoto, Nara or in historically oriented theme parks. This has led to rampant commodification of the past where this is profitable, for example, in mementos of old Edo. In the third sphere of activity too, the promotion or broadcasting of the past, the state has been notable by its absence. Only recently, prompted by a realisation of the kudos to be gained from large sporting events, has the state begun to spend money and initiate campaigns, although the extent of its commitment is unclear at this point.

I have explained this absence of the state in terms, at least in part, of a lack of agreement about how to write the past. But there are other explanations too. From within Japan, the tendency has been to advance a culturalist explanation, a cultural proclivity according to which memories are seen as being more important than monuments. This is a leitmotif of Japanese cultural theory which we can find advanced in various disciplinary arenas (see for example the work of Augustin Berque or of various architects such as Ashihara Yoshinobu). The classic refrain is that this is a culture of wood not stone. Wooden buildings are not made to last long, especially vernacular buildings for residential purposes. It is better therefore to conserve if one can the people, practices, traditions and memories, and let their physical manifestation in the built environment be knocked down and replaced.

In the more specific context of Tokyo, a different set of pressures exist which might help to explain the state's failure to find space for the city's past. Sensitive conservation of the built environment is expensive and time-consuming. For many decades in the twentieth century Japan was a country in a rush, and one that found it easier therefore to consign the physical manifestations of its history to clearly demarcated and themed historical zones. The rush to catch up with the West has been superseded by a period of greater uncertainty. This uncertainty has been marked by a reappraisal of the country's history (in all sorts of ways) and to some extent of its landscape, but lower economic growth rates combined with the ever closer prospect of a declining population have fuelled the pace of urban restructuring and made it harder to hold onto remnants of the past. Despite the pressures on everyday life-spaces exerted by the never-ending process of urban restructuring, civil society groups have been busily involved in place-based conservation and place-making activities. However, with the state largely absent in these areas, civil society groups face considerable difficulties, lacking an intellectual and regulatory framework within which to operate and sometimes finding themselves confronting each other.

Note

1 The author would like in particular to thank Professor Tejima Naoto of Tokyo Kasei University, Suzuki Takanori of Taitô Ward Government, Enbutsu Sumiko and Mizutani-san for their invaluable help on a number of occasions, especially during field visits in December 2003 and March 2005. The interpretations here are entirely those of the author, as is the responsibility for any errors.

References

Azaryahu, M. (2003). RePlacing memory: the reorientation of Buchenwald. *Cultural Geographies* (10), 1–20.

Barthes, R. (1983). *Empire of Signs*, translated by Richard Howard. London: Jonathan Cape.

Broudehoux, A.-M. (2004). *The making and selling of post-Mao Beijing*. London: Routledge.

Chang, T.-C. and B. Yeoh. (1999). New Asia – Singapore: communicating local cultures through global tourism.' *Geoforum* 30(2), 101–15.

Creighton, M. (1995). Japanese craft tourism: liberating the crane wife. *Annals of Tourism Research*, 22(2), 463–78.

Enders, S. and N. Gutschow, eds. (1998). *Hozon: architectural and urban conservation in Japan*. Stuttgart: Edition Axel Menges.

Fujii, S., J. Okata and A. Sorensen. (2007). Inner-city redevelopment in Tokyo: conflicts over urban places, planning governance, and neighborhoods. In: A. Sorensen and C. Funck, eds. *Local empowerment? Citizens' movements, machizukuri and living environments in Japan*. London: Routledge, pp. 375–84.

Hajdu, J. (2002). Nagasaki, Japan's window to the west: protecting its western heritage. In: D. Logan, ed. *The disappearing 'Asian' city: protecting Asia's urban heritage in a globalizing world*. New York: Oxford University Press, pp. 88–104.

Henrichsen, C. (1998). Historical outline of conservation legislation in Japan. In: S. Enders and N. Gutschow, eds. *Hozon: architectural and urban conservation in Japan*. Stuttgart: Edition Axel Menges, pp. 12–21.

Hohn, U. (1997). Townscape preservation in Japanese urban planning. *Town Planning Review* 68(2), 213–55.

Ishida Y. (1994). *City planning and city life (Toshi keikaku to toshi seikatsu)*. Tokyo: Jichitai Kenkyûsha.

Kong, L. (2007). Cultural icons and urban development in Asia: Economic imperative, national identity, and global city status. *Political Geography* 26(4), 383–404.

Kong, L. and B. Yeoh. (2003). *The politics of landscape in Singapore: constructions of 'nation'*. Syracuse, N.Y.: Syracuse University Press.

Kusno, A. (2004). Whither nationalist urbanism? Public life in Governor Sutiyoso's Jakarta. *Urban Studies* 41(12), 2377–94.

Light, D. (2001). 'Facing the future': tourism and identity-building in post-Socialist Romania. *Political Geography* 20(8), 1053–74.

Logan, D. (2002). Introduction: globalization, cultural identity, and heritage. In: D. Logan, ed. *The disappearing 'Asian' city: protecting Asia's urban heritage in a globalizing world*. New York: Oxford University Press, pp. xii–xxii.

Lowenthal, D. (1985). *The past is a foreign country*. Cambridge: Cambridge University Press.

Miyauchi, S. (1990). The direction and problems of the underground car park plan (*Chika chushajô keikaku no dôkô to mondaiten*). In: Shinobazu Ike Chika Chushajô Mondai o Kangaeru Tsudoi Jikkô Iinkai (Executive committee of the assembly to consider the problem of the Shinobazu Pond Underground Car Park), ed. *Shinobazu Pond: waterside space in the heart of the city (Shinobazu ike: toshin no mizube kûkan)*. Tokyo: Shinobazu Pond Executive Committee, pp. 14–17.

Mori M. (2003). *Tokyo's heritage: from conservation to resuscitation and use (Tôkyô isan: hozon kara saisei, katsuyô e)*. Tokyo: Iwanami Shoten.

OECD (Organization for Economic Co-operation and Development). (2002). *National tourism policy review of Japan*. Available at www.oecd.org/dataoecd/43/48/33649824. pdf. Accessed 7 July 2007.

Ogawa, K. (1990). The value of the Shinobazu Pond environment and the importance of its preservation (*Shinobazu ike no kankyô no kachi to hôzen no jûyôsei*). In Shinobazu Ike Chika Chushajô Mondai o Kangaeru Tsudoi Jikkô Iinkai (Executive committee of the assembly to consider the problem of the Shinobazu Pond Underground Car Park), ed. *Shinobazu Pond: waterside space in the heart of the city* (*Shinobazu ike: toshin no mizube kûkan*). Tokyo: Shinobazu Pond Executive Committee, pp. 2–13.

Pekkanen, R. (2006). *Japan's dual civil society: members without advocates*. Stanford, CA: Stanford University Press.

Purvis, M. and D. Atkinson. (2008 forthcoming). Contested memories of conflict: the Risiera di San Sabba, Trieste. *Social and Cultural Geography*.

Rimmer, P. (1992). Japan resort archipelago: creating regions of fun, pleasure, relaxation, and recreation. *Environment and Planning A*, 24(11), 1599–625.

Saaler, S. and W. Schwenter, eds. (2007). *The power of memory in modern Japan*. Folkestone: Global Oriental.

Sand, J. (2001). Monumentalizing the everyday: the Edo-Tokyo Museum. *Critical Asian Studies* 33(3), 351–78.

Shimizu, H. (1998). Ten years of the 'Love Shinobazu Pond Group' linking through to the 21st century' (*Nijû isseki e tsunagu 'Shinobazu ike o aisuru kai' no 10 nen*). In: Shinobazu Ike o Aisuru Kai (Love Shinobazu Pond Group), ed. The current state of the underground car park issue: looking back over the ten years of the Love Shinobazu Pond Group (*Chika chûshajô mondai no ima: Shinobazu ike o aisuru kai no 10 nen o furikaette*). Tokyo, pp. 2–3.

Sorensen, A. (2002). *The making of urban Japan: cities and planning from Edo to the twenty-first century*. London: Routledge.

Taitô Ward Government. (2000). Taitô Ward tourism vision: aiming for an international tourism city – Shitamachi theme park of colourful attractions (*Taitôku kankô bijon: kokusai kankô toshi Taitô o mezashite – tasai na miryoku no Shitamachi tēma pāku*) Tokyo: Taitô Ward Government.

Takahashi T. (2006). The national politics of the Yasukuni Shrine. In: N. Shimazu, ed. *Nationalisms in Japan*. London: Routledge, pp. 155–180.

Tan, H.-J., and P. Waley. (2006). Planning through procrastination: the preservation of Taipei's cultural heritage. *Town Planning Review* 77(2), pp. 531–55.

TMG (Tokyo Metropolitan Government). (2002). The Tokyo 2000 concept: aiming for a world city that welcomes all (*Tôkyô kôsô 2000: senkyaku manbiki no sekai toshi o mezashite*). Tokyo: TMG.

TMG (Tokyo Metropolitan Government). (2004a). www.tourism.metro.tokyo.jp; accessed 9 September. 2004.

TMG (Tokyo Metropolitan Government). (2004b). Basic guidelines for urban planning and tourism promotion in Tokyo (*Tôkyôto kankô machi-zukuri kihon shishin*). Tokyo: TMG.

TMG (Tokyo Metropolitan Government). (2005). General framework for the improvement of the attractiveness of waterside space (*Tôkyô no mizube kûkan no miryoku kôjô ni kansuru zentai kôsô*). Tokyo: TMG.

TMG (Tokyo Metropolitan Government). (2007). Tokyo tourism promotion plan: Tokyo, aiming to be a dynamic and stylish world city (*Tôkyôto kankô sangyô shinkô puran: katsuryoku to fûkaku aru sekai toshi Tôkyô o mezashite*). Tokyo: TMG.

Tsujinaka, Y. (2003). From developmentalism to maturity: Japan's civil society organizations in comparative perspective. In: F. Schwartz and S. Pharr, eds. *The state of civil society in Japan.* Cambridge: Cambridge University Press, pp. 83–115.

Vosse, W. (2000). The domestic environmental movement in contemporary Japan: structure, activities, problems, and its significance for the broadening of political participation. Ph.D. thesis, University of Hanover.

Waley, P. (2002). Moving the margins of Tokyo. *Urban Studies* 39(9), 1533–50.

Waley, P. (2005a). Parks and landmarks: planning the Eastern Capital along western lines. *Journal of Historical Geography* 31(1), 1–16.

Waley, P. (2005b). Ruining and restoring rivers: the state and civil society in Japan. *Pacific Affairs* 78(2), 195–215.

Waley, P. (2006). Re-scripting the city: Tokyo from ugly duckling to cool cat. *Japan Forum*, 18(3), 361–81.

Waley, P. (2007). Tokyo-as-world-city: reassessing the role of capital and the state in urban restructuring. *Urban Studies* 44(8), 1465–90.

Yamasaki, M. (2003). Kyoto and the preservation of urban landscapes. In: N. Fiévé and P. Waley, eds. *Japanese capitals in historical perspective: place, power and memory in Kyoto, Edo and Tokyo*, London: RoutledgeCurzon, pp. 347–67.

9 Gendered modes of appropriating public space

Ingrid Getreuer-Kargl

Summary

Space is gendered. It is a general assumption in feminist approaches to urban studies that gender relations – as, of course, other social relations – are inscribed in spatial arrangements (Becker 2004: 652). The initial consideration sparking my interest in research on gender and space was the search for an approach that would accommodate both the macro and the micro aspect of gender relations; that would allow me, in other words, to look both at hegemonic rules guiding gender performance and at individual enactment of gender.

How 'space' and spatial behaviour meet this requirement will constitute the point of departure in this chapter where I will first lay out my concept of space and its generally gendered character. Next, spatial behaviour will be defined as such nonverbal behaviour as determines the use and appropriation of space and as such is pivotal to the construction of both gender and space. Following this theoretical framework I will present the results of my empirical analysis of gendered nonverbal behaviour in public transportation facilities and at stations in Tokyo. I will conclude this chapter by discussing its relevance and attempt a synthesis of how men and women in Japan constitute public space and how they appropriate this space.

Space and gender

People moving in public places do so in very different ways. Among the various approaches to analysing the differences, such as looking into the age or class of people, my interest lies in gender differences. And on gender I will, for clarity's sake, focus on almost exclusively in the following argument – though being well aware that behaviour is never one-dimensionally determined by a single differentiating feature but is always the result of a combination of features, especially age or class. Before, however, considering the way men and women move in public places and thus considering the way gender and nonverbal behaviour interrelate, it is expedient to discuss the concept of public places and the underlying concept of space.

Space does not simply exist materially and is then filled and put to various uses, rather, it is the result of various social processes through history. The conception of space as static and bounded by fixed borders been long since been replaced by a conception in which time and social relations are integral elements in the constitution of space.

Social anthropologist Shirley Ardener postulated that 'space defines the people in it and people define space' (Ardener 1993: 2–3). In other words, space does not just exist for people to perform their actions in but is only constituted as a perceptible and describable space through the actions of people: a train station has to be designed as a space where trains stop on their route from one destination to another and where people may board these trains. Just as importantly, people cannot act independently of space and their actions cannot be interpreted independently of the space where they occur. This is evident when looking at the example of train stations. A person running through the building without looking right or left will be considered not a fugitive from law, for instance, or as training for the next city marathon, but as intent on reaching his train. The space 'train station' defines him as a passenger and his actions will be interpreted accordingly. However, a train station might on occasion be used as a temporary refuge by homeless people or as an exceptional site of a cultural event, in which case people have defined the space as different from its normal use.

The way in which space is defined and defines is elaborated in theoretical depth by sociologist Martina Löw. In *Raumsoziologie [Sociological Theory of Space]* (Löw 2001) she depicts a model of how space is socially constructed through human action in everyday routine by defining space as a relational order of social goods and human beings ('Raum ist eine relationale (An)Ordnung sozialer Güter und Menschen', Löw 2001: 224). Löw argues that space is constituted by a twofold human effort: by spacing – here she uses the English word – and by an act of synthesis (Syntheseleistung). Spacing refers to the act of placing (positioning) artefacts, social goods and beings, including selves, in particular arrangements to form a space. Spacing is inevitably tied to power, because the question of *who* may place *what* and *where* is a process of negotiation and therefore a question of power. Synthesis refers to the recognition of such arrangements-through-positioning as a particular space by individual persons who draw on their perception, imagination or memory. The perceptions, imaginations or memories of people are, in turn, pre-structured by class, gender or culture habitus. Therefore, while both men and women will recognise a train station for a train station they might well associate different feelings or different secondary purposes with the space 'train station'.

The emphasis on power as a constitutive element of space is a recurrent theme and echoes critical geographer Doreen Massey who postulated that the spatial relation may be seen as an 'ever-shifting social geometry of power and signification' (Massey 1994: 3). Indeed, if one agrees that social relations in itself are inevitably and everywhere imbued with power then it follows that any concept of space as socially constructed has to give consideration to power aspects (Massey 1994: 3–5).

Space is not only a manifestation of power relations, space is also gendered. Gender is equally pervasive in all social acts as power is. 'It has been variously proven that gender as a structuring principle permeates every action and thus the perception of spaces and cities as well as all placing in the cities. Every action is simultaneously an act of gendering and is interpreted against the background of the cultural construction of a binary gender modus' (Löw *et al.* 2008: 48). The gendering of spaces occurs through the way perceptions are organised, especially through the perceiving gaze – in Löw 2001, as mentioned above, gender habitus is explicitly named as an agent in connection with the act of synthesis. Perception, in modernity predominantly through gazing, is defined as the selective and constructive process of experiencing and interpreting social reality (Löw *et al.* 2008: 13). Perception is shaped by gender and so are the body technologies corresponding to them. Body technologies refer to a choice of place and to a praxis of placement ('spacing', in other words) that reproduce, in terms of somatising social order, structuring principles of society of which gender constitutes one. By such bodily practice the gender relation is inscribed in the production of spaces, in the reproduction of spatial differentiations and in the perception of cities (Löw *et al.* 2008: 50).

To sum up, space is conceptualised as gendered and as a manifestation of power relations. Such space lends itself ideally to probing into the structural gender relations (Geschlechterverhältnis) and the power relations or hierarchy at work within it. Using Löw's approach of spacing (the body praxis of placement) and synthesis (perception), gendered behaviour and the power relations between men and women in various spaces can be made observable. I will concentrate mainly on spacing, that is, on the body technology of placement, especially and more narrowly, on the placement of one's own body. To some extent I will also touch on atmosphere, which constitutes the emotional part of the act of synthesis.

Placement of oneself is done by positioning and moving one's body, in other words, by nonverbal behaviour. This paper will focus on everyday observable behaviour and interactions, namely on the appropriation – or even constitution – of public space through what is commonly, and in my opinion very appropriately, called 'body-language'. Nonverbal behaviour plays a pivotal role in constituting, affirming and transforming gender relations, even though I would contend that the importance of the embodiment of gender is not yet sufficiently mirrored in academic research. Appropriation of public space as understood in this chapter means to (temporarily) occupy a specific space with one's body and thereby imbue it with meaning. An analysis of the different ways men and women appropriate space through their bodies, that is, of the way men and women move and hold their bodies, may contribute towards a better understanding of the gendered character of public urban space.

While public space is often understood in terms of Habermas' public sphere, that is, as 'sites for political and theoretical dialogue', following Tamari Tomoko, I will use the term rather in the sense of 'public life' (Tamari 2006:107). Public space therefore shall refer to places that are basically accessible to everybody at any time, even though this male understanding ignores that women have been denied access to such public places time and again. Places that have been classically labelled public are streets, squares, parks, railway stations or market places (Schroer 2006: 232–234). Such public places are usually considered to be interactive and communicative, as well as to foster the mixing of social groups and to promote processes of opinion making (Löw *et al.* 2008: 22). To be in a public place always means to be potentially visible and audible for everybody (Schroer 2006: 235).

Analysing gender relations through space allows analysing simultaneously gender relations and power relations at a macro level. Urban planning scholar Gabriele Sturm postulates four components of a given space (Sturm 2000: 200), of which two may be read as a spatial manifestation of society as such. One component refers to the structuring regulations of space and in the space such as laws relating to public places, ownership rights or any rules relating to, for example, the use of train stations. The other takes into consideration the historical formation of space in the past and present, which would include, in the case of train stations, certain historical restraints for women travelling alone and possible traces of such restraints in present-day behaviour. Formation of space in the present is done through everyday behaviour, in other words, through body techniques. By drawing on Löw's concept of spacing, more narrowly on the act of people positioning themselves, the micro level may be established. Such positioning always implies individual nonverbal behaviour, which may be indicative of challenges to or assertions of hegemonic gender and power relations. Through spatial arrangements and spatial behaviour, therefore, structural as well as individual gender relations become observable.

I will next detail how nonverbal behaviour relates to gender and power relations.

Nonverbal behaviour, gender and status

Space, then, is not a given natural environment but rather a social construct dependent on the people's actions and perceptions. This holds true for gender as well. Gender can be defined 'as a routine, methodological, and recurring accomplishment' and is constituted through interaction, if following the ethnomethodological approach of Candace West and Don Zimmerman, (West and Zimmerman 1991: 13, 16). Being a social male or female requires permanent 'doing' in the interaction with other human beings. Since such interaction usually takes place in direct contact, the interaction partners are physically present. This means that 'doing' gender usually requires physical presence and being physically present is equivalent to behaving nonverbally by positioning or moving one's body. Nonverbal behaviour therefore is a major means of 'doing gender'. By proper male or female behaviour the 'weakly dimorphic species' of man (Birdwhistell 1970: 42) is transformed into easily recognisable male and female individuals. Proper gender-different bodily demeanour is not something in the manner of clothing, to be put on and taken off as the situation might demand. Rather, proper gender-different bodily demeanour is acquired behaviour of long duration, it is an internalised behaviour that people seldom become conscious of. As such, it corresponds exactly to Pierre Bourdieu's concept of bodily hexis.

Bodily hexis denotes the bodily realisation of a habitus, which is thus made observable. Bourdieu originally conceived habitus in terms of social class, but later extended his concept to gender. Habitus refers to the way persons belonging to the same segment of society perceive the world think and act. Though habitus does not determine individual behaviour, it effectively controls and restricts it. Bodily hexis as the embodiment of habitus consists in a 'permanent disposition, a durable manner of standing, speaking, and thereby of feeling and thinking' (Bourdieu 1977: 94). Attention should be paid to the last part of the sentence, 'and *thereby* of feeling and thinking'. Our usual perception is that feelings and thoughts are expressed through the body, in the causal chain 'feelings/ thoughts lead to body reactions'. Research in psychology and neurology has amassed impressive evidence that not only do the mind and emotions influence the body, but that the body through facial and/or body feedback has an important impact on the mind and emotions (cf. Storch 2006). Probands instructed to keep up a body posture indicative of pride, for example, showed greater pride in the same achievement than probands forced to remain in a bent position (Storch 2006: 47–48). Proper gender-different bodily demenanour, or, indeed, any differences in the bodily demeanour of men and women is not solely the expression of a sense of decorum as often believed, but, far more importantly, it is also an expression of a state of mind or of emotions while at the same time reinforcing this state of mind and these emotions. Gender is 'embodied' in that gender and is 'done' through proper shaping, positioning and moving of the body (= nonverbal behaviour) and this 'doing' contributes to a state of mind proper for each gender.

Bourdieu's concept of bodily hexis and the vast body of research in nonverbal behaviour help to understand the meaning of Löw's spacing processes that relate to the spacing of the self. People place themselves, that is, their bodies, through 'embodied' postures and movements, which Bourdieu calls bodily hexis. If bodily hexis is shaped by gender, then the way men and women place themselves in Löw's spacing processes ought to be different. And as spacing is tied to power, it is necessary to understand how power relations are expressed through deportment and body movements. Research in nonverbal behaviour ('body language') has established its role in establishing and demonstrating the hierarchical position of individuals.

Nonverbal behaviour, as has been convincingly argued in the pioneering work of Scheflen and Scheflen in 1972, is a major instrument for maintaining the existing social order and consequently of the existing binary gender system. Scheflen and Schlefen concluded that 'the usual purpose of kinesic and territorial systems is preservation of the existing order' (Scheflen and Schlefen 1972: 132). Through nonverbal behaviour interpersonal relations are expressed with the two main dimensions dominance–submission and affiliation–rejection. Dominance correlates with greater degree of relaxation, submissiveness with tension (cf. e.g. Mehrabian 1972: 10–11, 30). Status is expressed by size of territory: high status with bigger, low status with smaller territories (cf. e.g. Argyle 1996:

289). In my work I make no further distinction between 'territory' and 'personal space'.

As we are concerned with spatial dimensions, 'self' in this context of spacing first of all means the solid body of a person. However, the skin is but the ultimate border of one's body and people are wrapped in an 'invisible, portable, adjustable bubble of space surrounding an individual that is actively maintained to protect the person from physical and emotional threats'. This invisible bubble with changeable boundaries is called personal space. Intrusions on one's personal space are likely to create discomfort and may provoke flight or avoidance; intrusions on one's territory rather provoke aggression (Burgoon *et al.* 1996: 76).

To determine power relations in self-spacing processes, it is therefore necessary to pay attention to two aspects: (1) to signals of status and dominance sent through bodily hexis/nonverbal behaviour and (2) to intrusions on the personal space of men and women.

Nonverbal behaviour in public transportation facilities in Japan

Urban planning revolves around public transportation, as does individual planning of everyday chores and amusements. For these reasons, gender relations in an urban environment may well be reflected in its public transportation facilities. For my observation I have chosen a local station and local trains of Tokyo's Chûô Line at daytime. The empirical data have been collected during a one-year field study in Kunitachi, Tokyo in 1997/98 through participant observation and interviews. Wherever possible and socially acceptable, photographs and later on video-tapings have been taken. A detailed analysis is given in my habilitation thesis (Getreuer-Kargl 2003).

When observing an underground station or any other station, one may distinguish three distinctive areas: the station entrance with the ticket vending machines, the platforms and the interior of trains. Approaching a station, one usually encounters a familiar bustling of people entering or leaving at different speeds, from running to ambling. Collisions are rare even in heavy traffic, which raises the question of who makes way for whom, who goes out of his or her way to make room for another? For two reasons this question is extremely difficult to answer. One is the methodological banality that videotaping or photographing in crowded places is ineffective (photos show only one massive block of backs) or altogether impossible (for lack of space to hold the camera steady). The other reason lies in innate or socialised reaction to possible collisions. People subconsciously anticipate obstacles in their way and adjust their route accordingly some metres ahead. It is therefore little more than a surmise who went out of their way for whom, with one exception: groups of both genders usually continue their direct route while single walkers make room for them. Hurrying to catch a train or reach one's destination minimizes gender-typical female walking behaviour as does moving in groups.

What does characterise male and female nonverbal behaviour? I have previously (Getreuer-Kargl 2003) distinguished between 'neutral', 'gender-typical' and 'gender-specific' behaviour. 'Gender-typical' postures and body movements are such that are frequently seen in one gender and only occasionally in the other, 'gender-specific' postures and movements are exclusively observed either in men or women. Actually there is little nonverbal behaviour that is specific for one gender. One might consider nonverbal behaviour a continuum with specifically masculine behaviour at one and specifically feminine behaviour at the other, while a broad middle range is occupied by gender-neutral behaviour. Gender-neutral postures and movements might also be called 'natural' behaviour in that they are the most effortless postures and movements for the purpose, that is, they demand the least muscle tension.

Typical for women is a visible/notable body tension in moving, standing or sitting that gives an upright appearance. Shoulders are drawn back, the body is kept erect and the head is carried high. Arms, especially elbows, are held close to the body; and feet, especially knees, are held as close together as possible. Typical for men is no special manipulation of posture or movements and therefore a relaxed or, as the situation may require, purposeful attitude. For female walking behaviour these general characteristics result in shortened steps with footprints in a narrow line, arms that are not allowed to swing freely and an immobile upper body so that movement appears restricted to the hip-downward part of the body. Men in contrast typically walk with all their body, arms and shoulders swinging loosely in rhythm, the length of their steps in accordance with their speed and feet coming down to the right and left of an invisible ribbon roughly the width of a big fist. Female walking behaviour becomes gender specific if all typical characteristics are observed, specifically male walking behaviour is characterised by extreme slouching or pronouncedly big steps and corresponding big arm movements (Figures 9.1 and 9.2).

To resume, the entrance area of the station is mostly an area to be passed through on the way to the platforms with a necessary halt to buy tickets. Apart from mitigated gender-typical walking movements little difference is to be seen. This picture changes when people wait for someone, for then women adhere more closely to gender-typical postures. Altogether, it seems more common for women to wait for someone than for men or at least women are more demonstratively waiting while men seem to pass their waiting time by scrutinizing the newspaper paper-stand or similar activities.

Once at the platform waiting for the train to pull in, either ambling along or standing in line, gender-typical behaviour becomes more pronounced. Women stand with their elbows to their sides, one or both arms either hanging down or bent in front of them. Feet are kept close together, heels touching or only a little apart; knees straight. When feet are apart, one frequent posture is the 'supporting leg – non-supporting leg' one with the weight on one leg, the other being stretched out sideways, usually with in-turned knee or toes. Men like to stand with their weight on both legs, feet about a foot apart, elbows kept near the body. This posture is gender-neutral, that means, it may not only be commonly

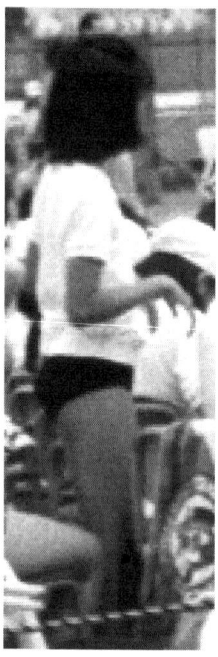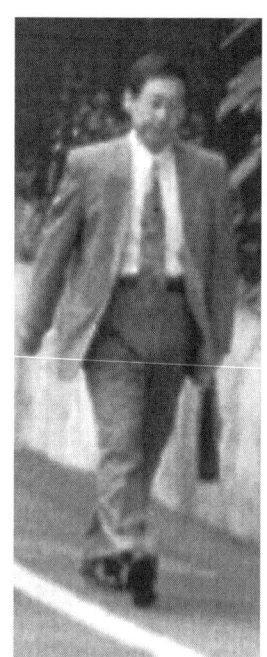

Figure 9.1 Walking.

Figure 9.2 Walking.

observed in women, too, but also costs the least muscle effort and thus might be considered the 'natural' posture. Deviating from this common posture, men almost invariably pose their feet farther apart and elbows further from the body. Underarms are held in a variety of positions. Men's relaxed attitude contrasts with the controlled one of women (Figures 9.3 and 9.4).

Gendered behaviour becomes even more pronounced once people mount the train. Of the three basic deportments, sitting is generally the most gender-differentiated one. Women almost invariably sit with their knees touching, elbows usually slightly in front of their body. Feet may be set apart with toes pointing inwards to keep knees together. Even if dozing, only the heads are allowed to drop forward, hair often obscuring the face, while some tension is retained in shoulders and back. Women seldom take up more room than necessary, holding (smaller) bags on their laps. Gender-typical or gender-specific behaviour is most pronounced with women in their twenties and thirties. Younger girls display a broader variety of postures, from extremely feminine to quite masculine ones. Older women, too, may relax their body control unless they have fully internalised it. No such differences by age are seen in men. Note: social class would be a valid factor but was too difficult to establish properly in this context. Men hardly ever sit with closed legs, though feet may be kept close to each other. Knees are allowed to fall apart at least as far as a relaxed attitude demands, often they are intentionally set apart. Equally popular is sitting with crossed legs, either both legs stretched out and crossed at the ankles, or legs crossed at the knees with one foot sticking out. When women cross their legs, they take care to keep the crossed leg close to the supporting one. Men never keep their elbows in front of the body, but at the most to the side of the body, even on crowded trains, and often further out, as when reading a newspaper. The back, with the head as extension, is slightly rounded, no effort being made to keep the upper body straight. Dozing men let their heads fall to the side, allowing them to rest on their neighbour's shoulder – if at all available, it is always a female shoulder. Just as when standing, men take a relaxed attitude when seated (Figures 9.5, 9.6 and 9.7).

One very interesting phenomenon is the gendered group-behaviour of men and women. All-female groups orient their bodies towards each other. They form a circle or a segment of a circle: knees and/or toes are aligned along the inside curve of the circle, as is the torso. By this orientation towards each other they express affiliation and signal a positive attitude towards each other while excluding non-members. Men form more loosely knit groups with less body orientation towards other group members. Often they seem to form a straight line rather than a circle (segment) and the orientation towards the other members of the group rather follows the necessities of verbal behaviour. By their nonverbal behaviour men express more distance and send fewer signals of affirmation. This nonverbal group formation is a pattern I observed repeatedly. For women, the nonverbal signs of affiliation and sympathy (the German word *Zu-neigung*, 'toward-inclination', in fact, expresses exactly this attitude) would appear to be more important than the accompanying verbal exchanges, or possibly a necessary step

Figure 9.3 Standing.

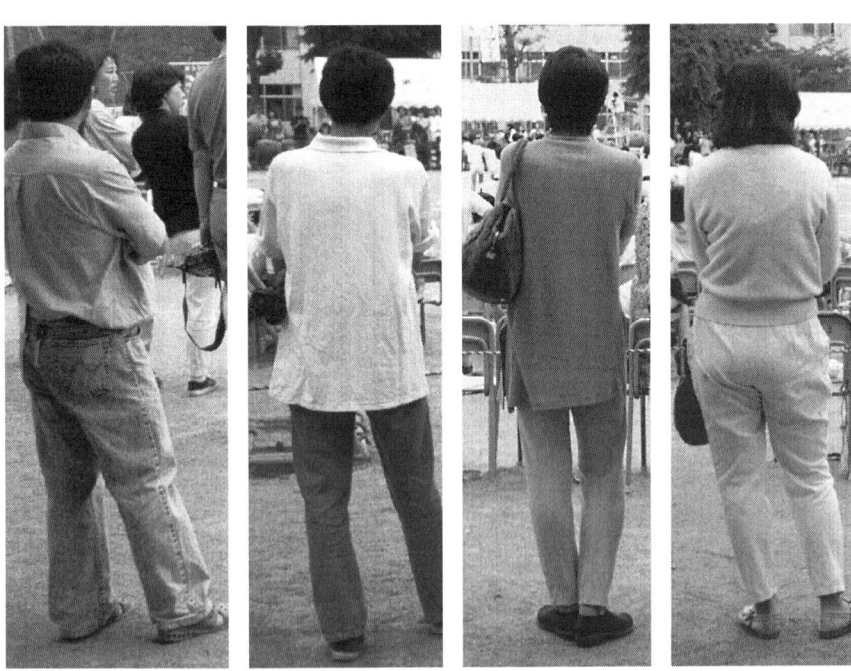

Figure 9.4 Standing.

Figure 9.5 Sitting.

 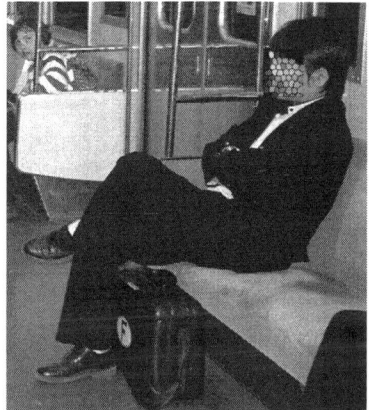

Figure 9.6 Sitting.

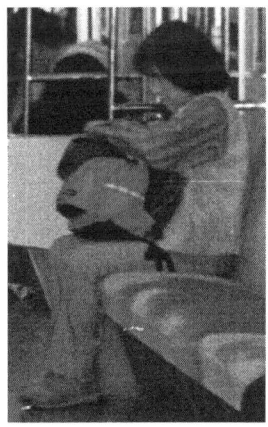 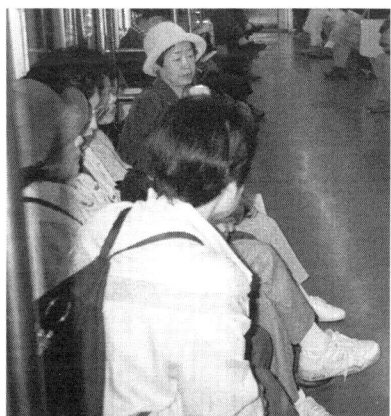

Figure 9.7 Sitting.

before entering intensive verbal interaction. If this is indeed so, it would demonstrate women's greater sensibility to atmosphere.

The process of placing one's self as one aspect of spacing is an act of nonverbal behaviour. This behaviour is no random behaviour and rarely intentional, but is the bodily manifestation of habitus, hexis. When speaking of male and female hexis it is important to keep in mind that although there are very important typical and sometimes specific ways of moving, standing and sitting for men and women, there also exists a large overlapping area of gender-neutral, postures and movements that might be called 'natural' in that they do not require more effort (muscle tension) than necessary.

The gender habitus enacted through this hexis is acquired during the process of socialisation by internalising different concepts. From my interviews and various writings, three major concepts can be made out for women in Japan. One is the concept of 'good manners'. This comprises being considerate towards other people, for example by not taking up more space than necessary or by giving way to others. Good manners are a desirable socialisation goal for boys, too, but are far more rigorously enforced in girls. Another concept is 'body control'. Accountable full members of society (adults) are expected to control their drives, especially their sexual drive. Body tension signals control, which is of utmost importance for women when seated. Women sitting with their legs apart are seen as sexually inviting, that is, as giving way to their sexual drive in public. Of course, this concept also applies to men, with the important difference that most people are resigned to the seeming fact that the male sexual drive may at times be too strong to be controlled even with the greatest effort. The third important concept is appearance (good looks, attractiveness). Most girls grow up with exhortations to walk graciously, sit properly and to care for their outward appearance.

The concepts applying for men are less easily established. One surmise is that they are raised to be competitive and achievement-oriented. Good manners and body control apply to boys as well, but there seems to be an open agreement that boys are less easily manageable and success therefore indifferent. One certain concept is strength. Boys have to be strong or they run the risk of being despised.

Essentially, male bodily hexis can be characterised as spatially extensive and relaxed or vigorously goal-oriented. Female bodily hexis can be characterised as spatially confined, controlled (tense) and other-oriented. Drawing on well-founded results of research into nonverbal behaviour, power relations can be made out. Female hexis shows the characteristics of submission: 'a constricted closed position and range of movement, hunched body (reducing one's size), downward-turned head, or tense, rigid posture, or a forward lean, all convey submission.' Male hexis shows the characteristics of dominance, which is generally 'conveyed with behaviors implying strength, comfort-relaxation, and fearlessness. ... As such, postural relaxation is seen as an indicator of dominance. An expanded range of movement (e.g. arms akimbo) or increased freedom of movement (rocking while seated) also conveys dominance' (Mehrabian 1981, as cited in Harper 1985:34). In this context, it is also remarkable that the group behaviour described on trains correlates to this finding. Women in groups try to face each other, whereas men do not. A 'direct body orientation is a sign of deference and respect, whereas an indirect positioning or even showing one's back is a sign of dominance, presumably reflecting a lack of fear'.

When women place themselves in a more controlled (tense) way they decrease their freedom of movement and thereby take up less room (territory). The private space of women, the 'bubble' surrounding them, is smaller because they make their physical bodies more compact. Even though women's personal space is smaller, it is still more easily violated as the example of dozing men resting their heads on female shoulders demonstrates. Conversely, men place themselves in a relaxed manner and make generous use of their freedom of movement. They thereby create a bigger personal space and better manage to keep it inviolate.

Finally, I will take a short look at the second aspect of constituting space, at synthesis. Synthesis, the second aspect of Löw's constitution of space, consists in the recognition of a particular arrangement as space. This is a cognitive, culturally determined, objective process. Atmosphere means the effects an arrangement of social goods and people has on a person recognising this space. Repeated or institutionalised arrangements objectify atmosphere. In general, it is not the arrangement that is perceived but rather the atmosphere, that is, the interaction between the perceiving individual and the symbolic-material effect of the perceived.

The effects of enacted placing and habitualised synthesis spell comfort or rejection, belonging or distance on the emotional level. The subjective sensation caused by the atmosphere hides the very real power relations behind the arrangements. Real or imagined threats to women in urban spaces affect female placings of self (Löw 2001: 215–217).

Women, especially when on their own, generally make sure by their behaviour that they may not be mistaken for a 'loose' woman, that is, one who does not attempt to control her sexual drive. Being in groups makes one much less assailable, so one's behaviour need not be monitored as closely. This also means that they yield room to men. When a man sitting next to a woman inadvertently touches the woman's leg with his, usually the woman draws back: '*yokeru, yappari yokeru*', as the group of women I discussed this phenomenon with, all agreed. And they went on,

> as for the men, they do not care at all. I don't think they touch deliberately, that would be *chikan*. They just sit down with their legs wide and then, when they touch … some apologise, but others do nothing at all. Why it is so unpleasant to be touched? Well … it is just unpleasant to be touched by a totally unknown man. If it is somebody like one's son, then that is alright, but a stranger? Of course, one moves over a bit, even if it is a child, I think. … Well, if it is the behind, there is nothing to be done, but if it is the legs, then one dodges. Women never do that, they always sit sideways, so they do not touch even if the train is full.

The sexualisation of the female body probably is the reason why women dislike being touched so much. As potential objects of male sexual desire they have to be on their guard. In one interview, a woman told me about a very unpleasant experience with a *chikan* when she commuted to school. As the man evidently attempted to follow her, she overrode her station for the *juku* on purpose and got into trouble. Yet another complained about *chikans*, especially late at night. Many women have actual experience with sexual harassment on trains. Even if there is no danger of sexual harassment, women are very much aware of the gaze of others. For them, it is important to present a proper appearance.

Constituting the space of public transportation facilities

Industrialisation has brought in its wake a spatial segregation of productive and reproductive labour, of workplace and home. The place of women is inside, in the home, going outside is the business of men who want to return to a home made comfortable by a woman. Doreen Massey still perceives remnants of this normative 'historical formation of space' (cf. Sturm) when she argues that women's mobility tend to be seen as threatening the fixed patriarchal order, as running counter 'the masculine desire to fix the woman in a stable and stabilizing identity' (Massey 1994: 11). It was therefore of interest to look at a space exclusively serving the purpose of mobility. Generally speaking, public transport facilities in Japan may be considered to make little formal distinctions between genders with the notable exception of 'ladies-only' carriages in rush hours. Gabriele Sturm's second component of any given space that relates to structuring regulations reveals no discrimination of women on the macro level.

Also, superficial observations show little gender-relevant peculiarities when looking at a local railway station and its trains during the day. Night-time is different, and so are, from my limited experience, long-distance trains as the Shinkansen. There, the majority of passengers tend to be male, at night-time as likely as not heavily inebriated. Both observations, unsystematic as they are at present, endorse the above said in that there seem to exist spatial and temporal restrictions on female mobility. Local day-time traffic is different because women stay closer to their homes and will be home at night-time to care for the children and to prepare for the return of their husbands. As likely as not, they are using local trains and train station for purposes relating to their conventionally allotted reproductive function.

As we have seen, three distinctive patterns of spacing may be observed. In the busy entrance area with most people intent on their purpose and often in a hurry perceiving gazes are not obviously directed at others. Hastening to catch the next train, looking up fares and buying tickets or passing through the ticket barriers, leaving the station leaves little attention for observing others. Here, women ease monitoring their nonverbal behaviour and fall into more natural (anatomically adequate), gender-neutral movements such as characterise men in this area. Where women are more likely to draw gazes as is the case when they are waiting for somebody and therefore remain in the same place for a longer period of time, they assume more gender-typical behaviour. Still, on the whole the spacing pattern in the entrance area is fairly gender-neutral for both men and women, perceiving gazes are seldom directly bent on others or felt to be so.

Platforms present another pattern. Here, people have more time to spare and are less preoccupied with an immediate task at hand. There is more opportunity to watch each other while waiting for the train, which means that perceiving gazes frequently fall on others. Consequently, women monitor their nonverbal behaviour more closely and assume more gender-typical behaviour which may even become gender-specific when seated. Men, on the other hand, retain their 'natural', gender-neutral posture when standing while also assuming gender-typical to gender-specific behaviour when seated. Apparently, more stationary behaviour increases the possibility of being observed and this acts as a spur to fall into conventional and therefore approved behaviour. Conventional gendered behaviour also means that men demonstrate dominant, and women subservient behaviour, thus creating a clear gender hierarchy.

This holds true even more for the inside of trains where people find themselves in a closed common destiny community for a short period of time. Due to the usual arrangement of seats alongside the train, it is almost impossible not to observe the persons opposite unless the train is full, in which case the persons seated may be observed by those standing in front of them. Close body contact is possible and at times inescapable. Women, especially between ages 20 and 40 and when alone, appear to be especially vulnerable to the gaze of others. They monitor their postures closely, all the more so when sitting, while men see little need to deviate from their comfortable gender-specific sitting poses regardless of age. When the analytic category of age is included, little additional information is gained for men. It is otherwise for women: young girls show a broad spectrum of behaviour, from gender-specific female to almost gender-typical male, and old women often are quite relaxed and apparently indifferent to the perceiving gaze of others.

Through these subtle strategies, the social order of a hierarchical gender-system is maintained. The different manner of placing themselves shows that men subconsciously assume that they have the 'right of place'. They expect others to make room for them and they themselves take all the room they need. Women are careful not to inconvenience others and not to expose themselves to sexual molestation. They tend to shrink and make themselves smaller than they actually are. By their nonverbal behaviour, men and women constitute public transportation facilities to different degrees as a gendered space where men do not doubt their right of way and so demonstrate power, and women are careful to demonstrate good manners and not to render themselves liable to being identified as sexual objects. The degree to which this takes place depends on the actual or potential intensity of the perceiving gaze of others. Public gaze, in other words, is a monitoring factor for female self-placing and therefore constituent for public space.

The above depicted gender-hierarchical arrangements that result from the different ways of spacing of men and women are not usually recognisable as such.

What is recognisable, or rather perceptible, is atmosphere. Western research in the past few years confirmed that many women develop sensations of fear in public places which often leads to a voluntarily restriction of their radius of movement such as avoiding certain urban places or streets at night (Löw *et al.* 2008: 152). While this probably applies for women in Japan as well, what may be definitely stated is that women restrict the radius of their movements in almost all everyday ordinary spatial behaviour in the public.

The act of synthesis in the constitution of the space 'public transportation facilities' elicits different emotional and cognitive response in men and in women. Women sense a latent threat of sexual harassment in the atmosphere of the space to which evidently no similar misgiving on the side of men corresponds. Female mobility, it seems, is still not accepted as being as normal as male mobility. Women who leave the shelter of their reproductive sphere to penetrate into the outer world of men are at least relegated to a smaller, inferior place. They accept male dominance of space by the manner they place themselves and this manner probably arises at least to some extent from the atmosphere of latent intimidation emanating from male passengers. In public space, individuals style themselves by behaviour that is meant to simultaneously fulfil two purposes: to veil what ought to be withhold from an only partially calculable social environment, and it needs to display sufficiently clearly that which is necessary for successful interactions (Löw *et al.* 2008: 22). Interactions in public transportation facilities are successful, one might conclude, if men display dominant and women chaste and mannerly behaviour.

Conclusion

I have drawn what might look an exaggerated picture of the constitution of space by men and women. It certainly is exaggerated when looking at individual men and women. However, the picture is accurate on the macro level of structural gender relations on which I have focused. Observations of the micro level of individuals will show a much more sophisticated reality. Deviations from the behaviour depicted above will shed light on changes in gender relations as well as on the degree to which an individual reinforces or challenges these relations.

References

Ardener, Shirley (1993) *Women and Space: Ground Rules and Social Maps.* Oxford: Berg (Cross-Cultural Perspectives on Women; 5).

Argyle, Michael (1996) *Körpersprache und Kommunikation.* Paderborn: Junfermann (Innovative Psychotherapie und Humanwissenschaften; 5).

Becker, Ruth (2004) 'Raum: Feministische Kritik an Stadt und Raum', Ruth Becker and Beate Kortendiek (eds): *Handbuch der Frauen- und Geschlechterforschung. Theorie, Methoden, Empirie.* Wiesbaden: VS Verlag für Sozialwissenschaften (Geschlecht und Gesellschaft; 35), pp. 652–664.

Birdwhistell, Ray L. (1970) *Kinesics and Context: Essays on Body Motion Communication.* Philadelphia: University of Pennsylvania Press (Conduct and Communication; 2).

Bourdieu, Pierre (1977) *Outline of a Theory of Practice*. Cambridge: Cambridge University Press.

Burgoon, Judee K., David B. Buller and W. Gill Woodall (1996) *Nonverbal Communication: The Unspoken Dialogue*. 2nd ed. New York *et al.*: McGraw Hill [11989].

Getreuer-Kargl, Ingrid (2003) *Geschlecht und Raum. Eine Untersuchung zur Hierarchie des Geschlechterverhältnisses in Japan*. Unpublished habilitation thesis, University of Vienna.

Harper, R.G. (1985) 'Power, dominance, and nonverbal behavior: Basic concepts and issues' S.L. Ellyson and J.F. Dovidio (eds): *Power, Dominance, and Nonverbal Behavior*. New York: Springer, pp. 29–48.

Löw, Martina (2001) *Raumsoziologie*. Frankfurt/M.: Suhrkamp.

Löw, Martina, Silke Steets and Sergej Stoetzer (2008) *Einführung in die Stadt- und Raumsoziologie*. 2. akt. Aufl. Opladen & Farmington Hills: Barbara Budrich (= UTB 8348).

Massey, Doreen (1994) 'General Introduction', *Space, Place and Gender*. Minneapolis: University of Minnesota Press, pp. 1–16.

Mehrabian, Albert (1972) *Nonverbal Communication*. Chicago and New York: Aldine-Atherton.

Scheflen, Albert E. and Alice Scheflen (1972) *Body Language and Social Order. Communication as Behavioral Control*. Englewood Cliffs, NJ: Prentice-Hall.

Schroer, Markus (2006) *Räume, Orte, Grenzen. Auf dem Weg zu einer Soziologie des Raums*. Frankfurt/M.: Suhrkamp.

Storch, Maja (2006) 'Wie Embodiment in der Psychologie erforscht wurde', in: Maya Storch et al.: *Embodiment. Die Wechselwirkung von Körper und Psyche verstehen und nutzen*. Bern: Hans Huber, pp. 37–72.

Sturm, Gabriele (2000) *Wege zum Raum. Methodologische Annäherungen an ein Basiskonzept raumbezogener Wissenschaften*. Opladen: Leske+Budrich.

Tamari Tomoko (2006) 'Rise of the department store and the aestheticization of everyday life in early 20th century Japan', *International Journal of Japanese Sociology* 15 (2006), pp. 99–118.

West, Candace and Don H. Zimmerman (1991) 'Doing gender', Judith Lorber and Susan A. Farrell (eds): *The Social Construction of Gender*. Newbury Park, Ca.: Sage, pp. 13–37.

10 Walking the city

Spatial and temporal configurations of the urban spectator in writings on Tokyo

Evelyn Schulz

Introduction: city walker and *flâneur*

In the history of western literature a connection between intellectual activity and walking can frequently be discovered. Numerous writers walked to write, thus taking their place in the ancient tradition of so-called peripatetic writers. The word 'peripatetic' derives from Greek and refers to the teaching method of Aristotle. To clear his thinking Aristotle lectured while he and his students were walking in circles through the Lyceum. Famous examples of peripatetic writers are Robert Walser (1878–1956), Henry David Thoreau (1817–1862) and Jean-Jacques Rousseau (1712–1778). Particularly Rousseau's *Reveries of the Solitary Walker* (*Les rêveries du promeneur solitaire*, 1782) reveal such a connection between observation, reflexion, and imagination that lays the basis of the modern literature of walking.

In the history of walking a drastic shift occurred in modern times from roaming in the wild nature to promenading in the urban street. In contrast to the walkers of the Romantic age who explored rural areas in order to find writing inspiration, it was the city that became more and more dominant as a setting for walkers during the nineteenth century.[1] The circumstances of the genesis of the *flâneur*, the city walker or urban stroller, were characterised by rapid industrialisation, the rise of capitalism and dramatic rates of urban growth. The figure of the *flâneur* mainly derived from the works of the French poet Charles Baudelaire (1821–1867) and the German-Jewish writer and philosopher Walter Benjamin (1892–1940). For Baudelaire and, in his wake Benjamin, the *flâneur* was the archetypal modern subject of the city. The *flâneur* strolled the boulevards of Paris to observe the city life and to put himself on display. He did not only survey the city's present state but also acted as an amateur archeologist of the recently vanished past.

Benjamin in particular became the great interpreter of the *flâneur*. In works such as *The Arcades Project* (*Das Passagen-Werk*), an immense unfinished study of nineteenth-century Paris and *Charles Baudelaire: A Lyric Poet in The Era of High Capitalism* (*Charles Baudelaire: Ein Lyriker im Zeitalter des Hochkapitalismus*) the *flâneur* is portrayed as a solitary wanderer and idle passerby, who strolls contemplatively through Paris, seemingly without any destination.[2]

It is not surprising then that the *flâneur* has become the 'hero of modernity',[3] a key trope in understanding the modern urban experience and the modern city in general. Aimless walking is a means of spatial freedom, the concept of the *flâneur* also includes resistance or criticism of modernity respectively. Benjamin's *flâneur* has become an important reference in the field of urban, cultural as well as literary studies. Benjamin's major works have been translated not only into English but also into Japanese.[4] The last 20 years have seen a flood of scholarship centred on the *flâneur*. Drawing on Benjamin, historians, urban sociologists and literary critics have used the *flâneur* as 'an emblematic representative of modernity and personification of contemporary urbanity'.[5] His meanderings through Paris 'served to focus critical theory on the many different kinds of relationships within the city and within modern society'.[6] Scholars draw on the *flâneur* to explain the tumult of metropolitan life, to represent alienation and the detached relationship between the individual and modernity, and even to trace class tensions and gender divisions in the city.[7]

The word *flâneur* is translated into Japanese *toshi yûhôsha* (literally meaning: 'somebody who walks for pleasure in the city').[8] The Japanese equivalents for 'purposeless walking' or 'walking for pleasure' are *sansaku* and *sanpo*. The urban stroller has become a steady element of urban writing in Japan. In recent years, dozens of publications have been pushed onto the market, all of them guiding the reader on walking tours through Tokyo. Titles such as *Tôkyô nijikan wôkingu: Aruku, kanjiru, egaku* (*Walking in Tokyo for 2 Hours: Walking, Feeling, Drawing*) or *Watashi dake no Tôkyô sanpo* (*Tokyo Walks by Myself*) indicate that the focus is on leisurely walks through both the city's past as well as its present.[9]

Due to the ambiguity and vagueness of the concept various interpretations of the *flâneur* have come into being. There are indeed so many interpretations that one might get the impression that '*flânerie* has become so common a term to describe urban spectatorship that it has begun to seem hollow.'[10] However, despite its popularisation, the *flâneur* can be a very useful instrument for analysing both the perception as well as the appropriation of urban space from the point of view of the individual.

Benjamin's concept of the *flâneur* and the appropriation of urban space in Japan through narrative

For this purpose, Benjamin's memoirs of his childhood in Berlin are of particular interest. These memoirs exist in various versions and were written during the 1930s, when Benjamin mostly lived in exile in Paris. They are preserved under the titles of *The Berlin Chronicle* (*Berliner Chronik*) and *Berlin Childhood Around 1900* (*Berliner Kindheit um Neunzehnhundert*).[11] In these works, Benjamin introduced the type of the diachronic *flâneur*.[12] This type of *flâneur* shows himself sensitive to the traces that not only he himself but also earlier residents have left in the city. These works can be seen as Benjamin's attempts to reconstruct his own life, as well as the life of an epoch, as they were both shaped by the city. Benjamin's Berlin is a city of memory in a double sense: not only the past, but also the traces of that past which was preserved in the present, were, at the time of writing, accessible to Benjamin only as memories.

Compared to Paris and Berlin, both cities being the focal point of Benjamin's writings, Tokyo seems to be a city that is probably even better suited for investigating the relationship between the built environment, history and textual and visual representations of both personal and collective memory as it is stressed by Benjamin.

This is due to the fact, that, as Paul Waley described it,

> great Japanese cities like Kyoto and Edo-Tokyo have stories where other cities have monuments. This is a narrative urbanism, and an urbanism of narrative. Japanese cities are fast reinvented and redefined. At one level this is reflected in a shaping and moulding of collective memories. At another, it simply means that buildings are frequently torn down and replaced by something more profitable.[13]

Indeed, the history of Tokyo can be described as an ongoing cycle of destruction and rebuilding. Events such as the modernization of Tokyo in the course of the Meiji Restoration of 1868, the Great Kantô Earthquake of 1923 and the city's subsequent rebuilding, Tokyo's destruction during the war years of 1944 and 1945 and its rebuilding and forced industrialisation in the post-war period, the modernisation projects in the run-up to the Olympic games of 1964, Tokyo's formation as a global city and the building boom of the 1980s have become an important point of reference in the historiography of Tokyo. These events initiated large-scale city planning projects and brought about a redefinition of Tokyo's topography, of its social segregation and of its systems of representation. They laid the basis for extensive rebuilding and for both the disappearance and the creation of urban spaces and mnemonic sites. They thus constituted Tokyo as an object of philosophical, cultural, economic and political speculation.

Benjamin suggested that many cultural innovations of the nineteenth century can be seen as an attempt to come to grips with the new urban *milieux*: the instances he cites include, besides the well-known examples of Baudelaire's poetry, the detective story, panoramic literature, the lithograph, new forms of painting and photography.[14] This situation resembles that in Tokyo from the end of the nineteenth century onwards. The growth of the population, industrialisation, the introduction of public transport and city planning projects fostered a market for new media that offered information about the city. New mass media such as cinema, radio, newspapers, etc., as well as new leisure activities and sports emerged. Popular literature was serialised in both newspapers and magazines, the 'New Theatre' (*Shinpa*) made the breakthrough, and the gramophone started to become an everyday commodity for the emerging middle class. These developments came along with Tokyo's growing role in the process of Japan's becoming a nation.

As the capital of two different historical Japans – premodern and modern Japan – Tokyo represents the unstable identity of the nation, for it is the city where, more than in any other city, Japanese nationalism and modernity have been staged and restaged, presented and contested. Until today, there has been a thirst for knowledge, representation and definition of urban space. A large and diverse body of texts about Tokyo have come into being, covering a wide range of genres – illustrated guidebooks, gazettes, social and economic analyses, topographical descriptions, philosophical and political treatises, reportages and literary texts. A lot of them have reached a wide circulation.[15]

Particularly interesting for the subject discussed here is the overwhelming number of guidebooks and topographical descriptions about Tokyo. Many of them are structured as strolls through Tokyo or even beyond. The city, its present as well as its past, are explored on foot.

Walking and writing in Japan

Nagai Kafū as the chronicler of Tokyo

In this context, the writings of Nagai Kafū (1879–1959) can be seen as a starting point for the emergence of the *flâneur* in Japan. Kafū has been called the chronicler of Tokyo, and he is indeed an urban writer par excellence. As many artists and writers of his time, Kafū was very much attracted to France and in particular to Paris, the so-called capital of the nineteenth century. Kafū had spent the year of 1908 in Lyon and in Paris and could read French fluently. He was inspired by the poems of Charles Baudelaire whom he admired very much and whose works he had read intensely.[16] Kafū was very fond of the popular culture of the Quartier Latin and its demimonde, both being for him an equivalent to Edo's pleasure quarters. The world of the theatres and redlight districts became a major topic of his writings. After his return to Japan in 1908, Kafū translated some of Baudelaire's poems into Japanese.[17]

Kafū, who named himself '*Kafū sanjin*', literally meaning 'Kafū, the gentleman of leisure' or 'Kafū, the man about town', has become famous for his lifelong habit to undertake daily walks through Tokyo and to write about his experiences. He often added photographs and sketches to his reports.[18] In most of his works Tokyo is the stage where all of the action takes place. Issues of spatial dynamics in general and the Edo-Tokyo transformation in particular form the underlying context of most of his writings.

At this point, it is important to have a look at particular strategies of spatial mapping in Japan. In general, the so-called *meisho* and *sakariba* constitute the underlying structure of spatial representations in Japanese culture. *Meisho* means 'famous place' and is used to mark topographically or historically important landmarks. *Sakariba* refers to thriving places of gathering and leisure such as market streets, theatres and entertainment districts. The Japanese reading for *meisho* is *nadokoro*, literally meaning 'places with a name,' although the word for 'name' also implies 'reputation,' and so the word *meisho* is translated as 'famous place,' 'celebrated location' or 'place of interest.'

Meisho and *sakariba* could both be described as social practices that are given concrete form in particular places, thus also representing an instrument for a shaping and moulding of collective memories. They constitute a system for the representation of landscapes and cities that changes along with their transformation. With W.J.T. Mitchell, one could say that *meisho* are 'both a represented and presented space, both a signifier and a signified, both a frame and what a frame contains, both a real place and its simulacrum, both a package and the commodity inside the package.'[19] This means that behind each representation of *meisho* lies a different set of assumptions about both the social and historical functions of a particular place.

Representations of *meisho* depend on the intentions of the interest groups that create them and the historical junctures at which they come into being. The *meisho* not only contribute to the creation of particular memories but also to the construction of a territorial identity. This is obvious when analysing representations of *meisho* in Tokyo. For example, Meiji period representations of famous places in Tokyo often support the interpretation that this period marks a break with the past. In fact, due to the transformation of Tokyo into a modern capital, the matrix of Edo's *meisho*, which mainly consisted of natural landmarks such as hills and rivers where seasonal events and shrine festivals took place, was overlaid with a system of 'new famous places' (*shin meisho*) such as European-style monuments, government institutions, museums and parks. Such a binary opposition of old and new 'famous places' is also characteristic for Kafū's works. In many of his works the narrator strolls through Tokyo, acting as a critical spectator of modernity while lamenting the passage of time and with it the loss of the past. In this respect, Kafū can be regarded as the prototype of the diachronic *flâneur*. Kafū depicted a Tokyo that was very different from the new Tokyo as it was outlined by the government's modernisation policy and represented in official guidebooks of the time. His focus was on spaces that were located outside the realm of the *bunmei kaika* policy, i.e. the civilization and enlightenment paradigm that was associated with rational thinking, public hygiene, progress in technical and cultural terms, mass transport and the construction of wide roads, the so-called *omotedôri*.

The binary opposition of Edo and Tokyo forms a counter-discourse to the modern Meiji state. Early novels such as *Fukagawa no uta* (*Songs from Fukagawa*, 1909) are constructed as symbolic journeys taken through Tokyo's two competing transport systems, the crowded and squeaking trams of the modern age are set against the quiet waterways of old Edo. The chapters of his masterpiece *Bokutô kidan* (*A Strange Tale from East of the River*, 1937) are arranged like a walk through Tokyo. In this and other works of fiction Kafū elevates the artists and geishas, who are living and working in the pleasure quarters, to the last remaining guardians of Japan's premodern, indigenous culture. He thus suggests that hope for an 'authentic' Japanese modernisation lies only in the margins of the despised, the remains of Edo, the non-new, in the space that is non-central to the city of Tokyo.[20]

Kafû's Hiyorigeta (1914) as a model for walking guidebooks of Tokyo

An important example of Kafû's writings about Tokyo is *Hiyorigeta* (*Fair-weather Clogs* or *Wooden Clogs for Good Weather*), a collection of essays about strolls through Tokyo, published in 1914.[21] *Hiyorigeta* is regarded as a classic of topographical writing as well as a guidebook of Tokyo. It is famous for its elegant, refined essayistic style. This style is typical for the Japanese tradition of essays, the so-called *zuihitsu*. Its associative character seems to be particular suited for representing the activity of walking in a text. In writing *Hiyorigeta*, Kafû was probably inspired by *En flânant à travers la France: Autour de Paris* (*Walking across France: Around Paris*), a travelogue by the journalist André Hallays (1859–1930), published in 1911.[22]

Similar to a guidebook, *Hiyorigeta* offers a simultaneous approach to both the spatial as well as the temporal aspects of urban space. This work convincingly shows that Kafû's Tokyo is a discursive structure based on the binary opposition of Edo and Tokyo. *Hiyorigeta* leads the reader to the cultural and spatial margins of the city. The title itself refers to Kafû's intention to report about the 'other', the non-modernized, the authentic Tokyo. In the Edo period *hiyorigeta* were wooden clogs worn by men strolling through the pleasure quarters and by prostitutes.

Hiyorigeta is far away from simply being a record of walks through places of scenic and historic interest. It is much more an exploration of Tokyo's multilayered, historical topographies, thereby focusing on the transformation of the urban landscape and with it of people's life-style. The transformation is made comprehensible by Kafû's reflections on the passage of time and anecdotes of encounters with people on the one hand, and quotations from well-known Edo period guidebooks and references to visual representations of Edo such as woodblock prints by the famous Andô Hiroshige (1797–1858) on the other. Such a web of intertextual references to Edo period representations forms the basic layer of the Tokyo in *Hiyorigeta*.

For his exploration of the Edo in Tokyo, Kafû did not rely on the new maps that were inspired by Western geographical knowledge but on the so-called *Edo kiriezu*, i.e. portable patchwork maps made by woodblock printers. These *Edo kiriezu* perfectly served Kafû's ends, since they were made for walkers. He used them for his discovery of both traces left by people living in the margins of modernity as well as mementoes of a premodern and in his view more authentic Japan. Edo had previously been called a 'city on water.' Its infrastructure and transport system were based on an extensive network of moats, canals and rivers. People traversed the city using a boat or on foot. This type of map was not based on accurate geographical data and was therefore often misleading due to deformation or deletion of detail. Such maps mainly indicated the locations of residential mansions for *daimyô* and warriors, temples and so on.

Similar to Edo period guidebooks such as *Murasaki no hitomoto* (*A Sprig of Purple*) by Toda Mosui (1629–1706), in *Hiyorigeta*, too, urban space is segmented into natural and cultural elements that all have all been there long before

Tokyo has become the centre of the nation, and which still form the basic layer of the city and the foundations of its everyday life.[23] *Hiyorigeta* consists of eleven chapters. Three of them discuss the importance of topographical features and natural elements such as trees (*ki*, chapter 3), water (*mizu*, chapter 6) and slopes (*saka*, chapter 10) for Edo becoming a functioning city.[24] Another category of chapters deals with institutions and spaces essential for premodern urban life such as 'shrines of evil deity' (*inshi*, chapter 2), temples (*tera*, chapter 5) and alleyways (*roji*, chapter 7).[25] In a chapter about maps (*chizu*, chapter 4) Kafû discusses the difference between Edo period maps and modern maps in their potential for acquiring knowledge about the city.[26] Symbols of modern Tokyo such as the Western-style parliament, the imperial palace or train stations are only mentioned. The counter-discourse to official representations of Tokyo as revealed in *Hiyorigeta* becomes obvious when looking at popular guidebooks about Tokyo of that time. For example, *Tôkyô annai* (*Guide to Tokyo*) published in 1907, is a comprehensive two volume introduction to Tokyo's geography and history. *Tôkyô annai* starts with information about the symbolic centre of modern Japan, namely the imperial palace.[27] In contrast, *Hiyorigeta* starts with reflections on the advantage of exploring the city on foot and to have a look at those places where people actually live.

The streets conduct Benjamin's *flâneur* into a vanished time. The city constitutes for him an epic book through and through, a process of memorising while strolling around.[28] Indeed, in *Hiyorigeta* Tokyo is presented as an archeological deposit in whose vertical cuts scenes come to light where, in a certain way, lives and events are either already extinguished but somehow still survive or are in danger of being removed soon. In this context, the chapter about *roji* is very revealing. *Roji* are narrow alleyways, often located beyond the *omotedôri*, the newly constructed wide main roads. Usually *roji* can only be accessed on foot or by bicycle. According to Kafû, the vitality of the city in the Edo period was to an important part located in the teeming back alleys, which were lined with shops, small houses, restaurants and brothels.[29] People lived next to one another with very little space and even less privacy. Life inevitably spilled out into the little streets, the *roji*. At the time of writing *Hiyorigeta*, the *roji* still were spaces of major importance for everyday life, but were in danger of being replaced by more modern houses.

In later years, the *roji* and the respective lifestyle of its inhabitants have become more and more the focus of Kafû's approach to the city. He perceived the *roji* as enclosed spaces, which were separated from Tokyo's modernity in both geographical and cultural terms.

Following Kafû's footsteps: Kimura Shôhachi's writings on Tokyo

Kafû's reflections on Tokyo take the reader on a personalized tour of Tokyo. Most of the chosen routes are the cracks that run through modern Tokyo. Nagai Kafû was the prototype of the diachronic *flâneur* who considered it indispensable to study the persistence of traces from the past in the city of the present. In the following years, *Hiyorigeta* has become a canonical text of walking literature and a starting point for similar accounts of Tokyo. Many writers followed in Kafû's footsteps.

An important author of such writings is Kimura Shôhachi. Kimura wrote numerous essays on Tokyo in which urban space is explored at street level and city history, personal memory and reflections on the passage of time as embodied in the transformation of *meisho* are neatly tied together. Kimura was born in 1893 in Ryôgoku, a central part of Edo's Shitamachi (low city) located by the Sumidagawa. When he died in 1958 this area had been completely rebuilt several times. Kimura's writings cover a period of more than 30 years. Focusing on the transformation of Tokyo since the Meiji Restoration, Kimura devoted his work to the investigation of spaces of everyday life of the past and their remnants in modern Tokyo and their respective lifestyle and customs. Some of his works contain illustrations he has painted himself. Kimura knew Kafû personally as he made the illustrations for Kafû's masterpiece *Bokutô kidan* (*A Strange Tale from East of the River*, 1937). Taken all together, his works can be read as a chronicle of Tokyo.

Several of his essays about Tokyo are based on strolls through the city. His conception of Tokyo is reminiscent of that of Kafû. Both authors were looking for the old in the new. Kimura, too, acted like a diachronic *flâneur*. Kimura's best-known essay about Tokyo is *Tôkyô hanjôki* (*Report on the Prosperity of Tokyo*), published in 1958. Since it is a highly personal account of a tour around Tokyo in the 1950s and appeared soon after his death, it is regarded as his legacy.[30] In the 1950s, Tokyo as a whole was going to be redesigned along a system of roads and railways and most of the city's waterways had already been buried or bridged in the name of public sanitation, economic efficiency and flood control. In particular the first chapter of *Tôkyô hanjôki* reveals something of Kimura's conception of Tokyo and his view of modern Japan's history.[31] Kimura entitled this chapter *Sumidagawa ryôgan ichiran*, meaning *A View of Both Banks of the Sumidagawa*. This title is an allusion to the *Ehon Sumidagawa ryôgan ichiran*, an *Illustrated View of Both Banks of the Sumidagawa*, a famous series of woodblock prints by Katsushika Hokusai (1760–1849), printed around 1800. With the aim to depict famous landmarks and scenes from everyday life along the Sumidagawa, Hokusai had set sail in a boat near the small island of Tsukudajima in the bay of Edo and travelled upstream to Ryôgoku and further on to Yanagibashi.

More than 150 years after Hokusai, in June 1955, Kimura took a boat and travelled on the Sumidagawa. Over centuries the Sumidagawa has represented 'the city on water.' To this day the river connects people with a network of canals providing access to the innermost parts of the city. Kimura divided his trip into two parts: starting from Ryôgoku he first went upstream to the bridge of Nishi-Araibashi, and then travelled downstream to Tsukudajima.

At first glance, *Tôkyô hanjôki* appears to be a report onTokyo in the 1950s, but in fact it can be read as a reconstruction of Edo in the midst of Tokyo. Kimura's concept of Tokyo is closely associated with Kafû's Tokyo both in geographical and in cultural terms. *Tôkyô hanjôki* consists of ten chapters. The chapters are ordered like a journey on foot or on boat through areas where 'modern Tokyo' and 'Edo' meet and through areas that still seemed to be untouched by modernisation.

Kimura's Tokyo mainly consists of areas such as Nihonbashi, Shiba, Asakusa, Fukagawa, Mukôjima and Tsukudajima, which all have been very famous *meisho* of Edo and are even today often depicted in the literature on Tokyo. Kimura looks very closely at the numerous *roji*, the alleyways, where elements of the material culture and lifestyle of Edo still seem to have been preserved, but which are at risk of falling prey to the impact of the industrialisation of the respective area.

Kimura ends his trip on the Sumida River at the small island Tsukudajima in Tokyo bay. Until today, Tsukudajima is famous for its carefully restored *roji* areas. According to Kimura, Tsukudajima was famous for its festivals during the summer, in particular for the dances during the O-Bon festival. But pollution has put an end to old customs. The water is so dirty that the *mikoshi*, the portable shrine, cannot be carried out into the river anymore, Kimura closes this chapter with the remark that in former times Tsukudajima had been famous for its whitebait, a local variety of fish and a *meibutsu* (famous thing, specialty), which was often mentioned in premodern literature.[32] Together with a hunting and fishing settlement in Fukagawa, Tsukudajima had given rise to the great fish market at Nihonbashi and had sustained the kitchens of Edo.[33]

Kimura states that until recently the inhabitants of Tsukudajima had mainly made a living by fishing and had thus been able to lead a life that was completely different from that of the people of modern Tokyo, but as pollution was causing the fish population to diminish, an essential element of the specific culture of this island would disappear. In the near future the people of Tsukudajima would have to give up their long-established life as fishermen and adopt a lifestyle similar to that of the typical modern Tokyo resident. Tsukudajima would thus lose its status of a counter world to modern Tokyo, as an area where elements of the city of water could be preserved.[34]

Kimura leaves the reader with the impression, that with Tokyo losing its waterways, the people who actually live and work the city's waters lose their basis of life. Due to the fact that Kimura wrote this report on Tokyo at the end of his life, he looked back on more than 50 years of Tokyo's history. In contrast to Kafû's Tokyo, which to a large extent consists of a web of intertextual references to Edo period representations of the city, Kimura's Tokyo is much more based on his own experiences and childhood memories.

Writing one's own city: Kobayashi Nobuhiko's 'Tokyo trilogy'

In recent years, the term autotopography has been coined in order to think more generally about the interweaving of autobiography and place.[35] Such texts are centred on an intense relationship between the built environment, personal and collective memory, and history. In present-day Japan, spatial autobiographies constitute a major genre in the writing about Tokyo. Such texts are often arranged as walking tours through Tokyo. A representative example of such writing is the so-called Tokyo trilogy (*Tôkyô sanbusaku*) by Kobayashi Nobuhiko (born in Tokyo in 1932). Taken together, these works cover a period of nearly 70 years. In Japan, Kobayashi's works about Tokyo are characterised as 'autobiographical treatises about Tokyo' (*jidenteki Tôkyôron*) and an 'extreme personal account of Tokyo's history' (*kyokushiteki Tôkyôshi*).[36]

Kobayashi's earliest autobiographical text about Tokyo is *Shisetsu Tôkyô hanjôki* (*My Interpretation of the Account of Tokyo's Prosperity*) published in 1984.[37] This work focuses on the economic high growth period of the 1960s and 1970s. During these years, existing city fabrics that had acted as containers of historically and socially bound values and cultures were systematically removed or destroyed. Countless old quarters, the *roji* in Kafû's and Kimura's terms, were torn down and replaced by apartment buildings. Kobayashi's second work about Tokyo is entitled *Shisetsu Tokyo hôrôki* (*My Interpretation of the Account of Loitering in Tokyo*) published in 1992.[38] The title is an allusion to the famous *Hôrôki* (*Journal of Wandering*, 1928) by Hayashi Fumiko (1903–1951). Kobayashi's *Tôkyô hôrôki* focuses on the period of the burst of the 'bubble' economy in the early 1990s. However, the underlying context of Kobayashi's depiction of Tokyo is determined by the extensive urban development projects in the decades before. In particular the 1980s are remembered as an era in which an unparalleled construction boom extended from central Tokyo to its hinterlands. The construction frenzy testifies to the fragmentation and commercialisation of Tokyo's urban space resulting from the globalisation of the Japanese economy. Tokyo was becoming a global financial centre and attracted a huge influx both of Japanese and foreign corporate headquarters, financial institutions, etc. The keen shortage of office space created a collective urge to meet the demands and make profits by re-developing Tokyo's urban structure.[39] The third part of Kobayashi's trilogy, *Shôwa no Tôkyô, Heisei no Tôkyô* (*Tokyo in the Shôwa Period, Tokyo in the Heisei Period*), was published in 2002. This work is a collection of essays about various aspects of life in Tokyo.[40]

All these works have in common that they are based on strolls through central Tokyo's main areas such as Asakusa, Nihonbashi, Shinjuku, Roppongi, etc. Similar to Kafû and Kimura, Kobayashi's texts, too, constitute an attempt to reclaim the urban territory for the individual. Kobayashi also acts like a diachronic *flâneur*. He maps Tokyo with the memory of his childhood and youth before its metamorphosis into a metropolis. Walking through the alleyways, Kobayashi categorises negatively the increasing commercialisation of the city that encroaches upon the urban space previously available for the private domestic sphere. For example, he regretfully observes on several occasions that houses are soon to be replaced by new office blocks.

Similar to Kimura, who added illustrations, Kobayashi draws not only on textual but also on visual representations of the city. *Tôkyô hôrôki* contains some illustrations by his brother Kobayashi Yasuhiko. *Shisetsu Tôkyô hanjôki* (*My Interpretation of the Account of Tokyo's Prosperity*) is particularly interesting as, in this case, Kobayashi not only draws on his memories to document the transformation of Tokyo, but also on photographs taken by the well-known contemporary photographer Araki Nobuyoshi (born in 1940).[41]

Many of Araki's series of photos and photographic volumes such as *Tokyo* (1973), *Tokyo Blues* (1977), *Tokyo Autumn* (1984), *Diary Tokyo* (1987), *Tokyo Story* and *Tokyo Nude* (1989), *Love You Tokyo* (1993) or *Tokyo Novella* (1995) bear the name Tokyo in their titles. His entire oeuvre appears to be a homage to this city.[42] His photographs document his intimate relationship to Tokyo on the one hand and the complex and contradictory spatial realities of Tokyo on the other. His pictures are characterised by the confrontation with life and death, reality and fantasy, sexuality and Eros. They include shots of cityscapes, flowers, nudes, girls, exotic fruits and animals. Many of them, like those that have been included in *Shisetsu Tôkyô hanjôki*, depict the everyday life in the alleyways of Tokyo's Shitamachi neighbourhood.

Walking the *roji*: the rediscovery of the back alleys in present-day writings on Tokyo

There is little doubt that the practice of walking and the reflection on urban walks contribute to a counter-discourse of the urban. This discourse derives its power from relational oppositions to modernist conceptions of city form and its changing structure that have been motivated by the master narrative of capitalist urbanisation. Walter Benjamin, followed by Ronald Barthes and Michel de Certeau among others have drawn upon this counterpoint in their representations of the urban.[43] For example, Roland Barthes stated in his famous *Empire of Signs* (*L'empire des signes*, 1970):

> This city can be known only by an activity of an ethnographic kind: you must orient yourself in it not by book, by address, but by walking, by sight, by habit, by experience; here every discovery is intense and fragile, it can be repeated or recovered only by memory of the trace it has left you.[44]

Walking is a kind of ethnographic activity to reshape urban knowledge and to experience the city's multilayered time. Expressions such as *machiaruki* (city walking) and *sanponian* (stroller) are part of the vocabulary of the contemporary discourse on Tokyo. Not only literary works but also numerous films address the politics of walking from different points of view.[45] Writers such as Kobayashi Nobuhiko and Kawamoto Saburô explore the narrow alleyways in order to discover 'their' Tokyo. The film and literary critic Kawamoto Saburô wrote numerous essays about Tokyo. For example, Kawamoto's *Watashi no Tôkyô machi aruki* (*My Walking of Tokyo's machi*, 1990) is an account of his exploration of Tokyo's remaining *roji*.[46]

Another way of exploring Tokyo's history is to go out for 'literary strolls' (*bungaku sanpo*) and to visit both the areas where famous writers actually lived and major scenes of their works. Numerous canonical works of modern Japanese literature such as Higuchi Ichiyô's and Nagai Kafû's novels were staged in *roji* areas.[47] In recent years, stimulated by a renewed interest in Kafû's relationship with Tokyo and in particular in *Hiyorigeta*, it has become popular walking practice to draw on *Edo kiriezu* in order to explore Tokyo's *roji* areas.[48] Publications such as *Ô-Edo burari kiriezu sanpo* (*Leisure kiriezu Walks through Greater Edo*) and *Kiriezu – gendaizu de aruku Edo Tôkyô sanpo* (*Walking Edo Tokyo Using kiriezu and Present-day Maps*) have in common that they guide the reader to spaces of everyday life, in particular those small-scale areas and alleyways that are still untouched by urban development projects.[49] In this respect, value is placed on the discarded, seemingly unimportant spaces that are rarely seen to hold significance in conventional urban discourses.

Japanese urban discourse is characterised by a keen interest in spatial concepts that are located outside Western modernist discourse of the urban. For example, in the 1960s the architect Maki Fumihiko drew on indigenous spatial thinking and evolved the loosely defined concept of *oku*, meaning 'depth'. In this context, *oku* refers to spatial arrangements that are not structured by the (Western) idea of a centre but by the idea of depth.[50]

In the current urban discourse in Japan the specific urbanity of the *roji* and its small housing structures is being rediscovered and reassessed. *Roji* seems to become a central concept of spatial arrangements that point to an urbanity that cannot be grasped with terms grounded in Western ideas of modern city planning. According to Kurokawa Kishô, one of the leading representatives in the field of Japanese architecture, *roji* represent high-density communities in which different generations and classes lived together in symbiosis. They were intermediary spaces where a clear-cut division between private and public life did not exist. Kurokawa Kishô goes as far as to claim in his publication *Toshi no kakumei* (*The Revolution of City*, 2006) that the revitalization of the *roji* is the key to the future of Japan's cities.[51]

The notion of the *roji* not only fills an epistemological but also a phenomenological gap. In recent years, the idea of what a *roji* could be or should be has been diversified. For example, in publications such as *Shôwa rojiura dai hakurankai* (*Grand Exhibition of the Backstreets of the Shôwa Period*) and *Rojiura no minzokugaku. Anata mo shiranai Shôwa 30 nendai* (*Ethnology of the Backstreets. The Third Decade of the Shôwa Period that Even You Don't Know*) the *roji* function as spaces where the innovations of the everyday life of the Shôwa period can be located.[52] Publications such as *Nihon no rojiura 100* (*Hundred Backstreets of Japan*) and *Roji: Wandering Back Alleys* show that *roji* are not limited to Tokyo.[53] Both books contain numerous photographs of *roji* from all over Japan. Furthermore, Satô Hideaki depicted not only well restored and tidy backstreet *roji* but also *roji* that are empty and often cluttered spaces between two buildings. In this case, *roji* can even be a wasteland.[54]

The activities of organisations such as the *Zenkoku roji no machi renraku kyôgikai* (*National roji Communication Convention*) and the local organisation of Kagurazaka contribute to the revitalisation of those urban structures that seem to have been overcome by modernist patterns of city planning.[55] Such ongoing revitalisation of *roji* areas is part of the livable city discourse and can also be regarded as another facet of *machizukuri*.[56] In these discourses, both, *roji* as well as *machi* can be understood as 'glocalised' spaces in the globalising urban world.

To sum up, the discourse on everyday life as located in the *roji* points to an aesthetisation of a local, indigenous urbanity. The *roji* is insofar a very democratic spatial concept as everybody can explore it on his own terms. To stroll through *roji* areas means to experience the city from below. The *roji* seem to be particular urban spaces where both particular images of the past and visions of the future find their place. They function as alternative spaces to the globalised zones of Japan's big cities and shed light on their dual structure that is formed and maintained by means of hierarchical street patterns, i.e. the two dramatically contrasting elements of a modern city, namely the global and the local element.

Conclusion and outlook: walking, streetlife and *roji*-like spaces in East Asia

Rapid urbanisation, particularly in the East Asian region, has necessitated the physical extension of cities along strategies based on modernist planning theories. At the same time, conservation of historical areas has gained increasing acceptance, over the last decades. Tokyo, as many other cities in the East Asian region, has become a global city. Much of Tokyo's space was rendered to capital accumulation on the one hand, but on the other hand this gain also signifies loss, because this process requires the inhabitants to identify with the drastically different city at the cost of losing more and more of their concrete space of everyday life.[57]

The current popularity of the *roji* and their ongoing revitalisation and preservation have to be seen in this light. However, not only in contemporary Japan but also in China and in East Asia in general, the improvement of the urban environment has become an urgent issue. In particular in Shanghai and Beijing, both cities being epitomes of Chinese urban modernity, similar discourses are going on. As the other side of large-scale modernisation projects, a revival and nostalgia for indigenous life-styles and their respective urban space can be observed: the *roji* in Japan, the so-called *lilong* in Shanghai, the *hutong* in Beijing and the *golmok* in Korea. Such terms imply a search for alternative East Asian perspectives to Eurocentric modernity and US-style globalisation. All these spaces have in common that they are associated with the notion of the old, the traditional, the indigenous and the backward, as well as the marginalised. In a vast and fast globalising world, the urban dweller is searching for personal space of retreat, the 'come home effect' and a place to slow down. In this respect, spaces such as *roji*, *lilong*, *hutong* or *golmok* contribute to the formation of an inverse urban tissue of the global city.

They point to glocalised everyday life-styles, and to patterns of community that are at risk of going to be lost in the race for becoming global. Cities such as Tokyo, Shanghai and Beijing are caught between forces of global capitalism and national interests. The literature of walking reveals the temporal and topographical complexity of such cities. Such texts address aspects of their past, present and future through 'pathways' which lead the reader through the city's history as well as its contemporary culture and concerns. Wandering through the small and narrow streets is one way of mapping these things out and to make these cities home – not only for the native population but also for those people who have migrated into these cities.

Although much has changed since Baudelaire's and Benjamin's meditations, I assume that the *flâneur* as a theoretical instrument to explore the relationship between the urbanites and the urban environment where they live and work will probably have a brilliant career in historical and literary scholarship in Japan, even if his career is just in the beginning. The urban strollers mentioned above practice city walks in order to explore the specific geographical, cultural as well as historical peculiarities of urban sites, which in turn have to be read in the light of both literary and historical narratives as well as the memories of the inhabitants that actually live there. This clearly reveals a strong connection to Benjamin's *flânerie*, although in a totally different cultural and temporal context. There are different, even divergent politics of strolling but they all presuppose a person that walks and strolls around in search of the symbolic meaning of certain urban spaces and sites. Regardless of the tremendous changes of the modern metropolis due to certain events such as the modernisation of means of transport, industrialisation and migration as well as the rapid evolution of its media representations in literature, photographs and movies, it seems that at least in Japan the *flâneur*'s relationship to the city hasn't been loosened at all. Until today the *flâneur* is closely associated with the *roji*, the particular urban space that has to be explored on foot.

Notes

1 For an overview of the walkers of the Romantic age cf. Jarvis 1997, pp. 1–28, and Solnit 2000, pp. 81–102.
2 *The Arcades Project* was drafted between 1927 and 1940. However, only over four decades after its author's death, the German publication appeared in 1982, the English version in 1999. For the German edition cf. Benjamin 1982, for the English edition cf. Benjamin 1999.
3 Cf. Tester 1994, p. 6.
4 For Benjamin's reception in Japan cf. Mitsugi 1999.
5 Cf. Tester 1994, p. 1.
6 Cf. Parkhurst Ferguson 1994, p. 22.
7 For general analyses of the *flâneur* cf. for example Buck-Morss 1986 and 1989, Charney and Schwartz 1995, Featherstone 1998, Tester 1994, Wolff 1985.
8 Cf. Benjamin 1994.
9 *Tôkyô nijikan wôkingu. Aruku, kanjiru, egaku* is a series of illustrated walking guidebooks through Tokyo's central areas; cf. Yabuno 2002. *Watashi dake no Tôkyô sanpo* is a two-volume edition (Yamanote and Shitamachi-Toshin area) of texts by well-known present-day writers and artists, each of them visiting the area of Tokyo where she/he has been brought up or has lived for a while. Each chapter contains photographs of the respective area made by famous photographers such as Araki Nobuyoshi and Takanashi Yutaka; cf. *Watashi dake no Tôkyô sanpo* 1995.

10 Cf. Shaya 2005.
11 After leaving Germany in 1932, Walter Benjamin wrote *Berliner Kindheit um Neunzehnhundert*, a collection of 42 texts that functions as a childhood memoir, distilling the poignancy of a lost childhood from vividly remembered places, things and experiences. Cf. Benjamin 1987.
12 For the term 'diachronic *flâneur*' cf. Muñoz Millanes 2000.
13 Cf. Waley 2003, p. 385.
14 Cf. Savage 2000, p. 43.
15 An important source for the study of the literature about Tokyo (published until 1945) is Tsuchida Mitsufumi, *Tôkyô kiroku bungaku jiten: Meiji gannen–Shôwa 20 nen* (*Encyclopaedia of Documentary Literature about Tokyo: The First Year of Meiji— The Twentieth Year of Shôwa*), cf. Tsuchida 1994.
16 For a depiction of Kafû's stay in France, cf. Imahashi 1993, pp. 199–222.
17 Kafû published translations of poems by Charles Baudelaires, Arthur Rimbaud, Paul Verlaine etc. under the title *Sangoshû* (*Collection of Corals*, 1913). Until today these translations are classics of this genre.
18 Most of these photographs were lost in the turmoil of the air raids of Tokyo in 1944/45.
19 Cf. Mitchell 1994, p. 5.
20 Cf. Hutchinson 2001 and Schulz 1998.
21 *Hiyorigeta* was first published in eleven installments in the monthly literary magazine *Mita bungaku* (*Mita Literature*) from the summer of 1914 on. In 1915 *Hiyorigeta* was subtitled *Ichimei Tôkyô sansaku ki* (*Report of Walks through Tokyo*) and published as a monograph. For a reference edition of *Hiyorigeta* cf. Nagai 1992–95, Vol. 11, pp. 109–189.
22 Hallay's work is also mentioned in *Hiyorigeta*, cf. Nagai 1992–95, Vol. 11, p. 114. For an analysis of the impact of Hallay's travelogue on *Hiyorigeta* cf. Takehara 1990.
23 *Murasaki no hitomoto* had been completed by 1683 but was not published for another two centuries. Cf. Elisonas 1994, p. 285.
24 Cf. Nagai 1992–1995, Vol. 11, pp. 122–127 (chapter 3), pp. 140–151 (chapter 6), and pp. 179–183 (chapter 10).
25 Cf. Nagai 1992–1995, Vol. 11, pp. 120–121 (chapter 2), pp. 132–139 (chapter 5), and pp. 152–155 (chapter 7).
26 Cf. Nagai 1992–1995, Vol. 11, pp. 152–155.
27 Cf. Tôkyô toshi hensan 1974, p. 1.
28 Benjamin refers here to his review of *Spazieren in Berlin* by Franz Hessel (1880–1940); cf. Benjamin 1991.
29 Cf. Nagai 1992–1995, Vol. 11, pp. 122–127 (chapter 3).
30 *Tôkyô hanjôki* was first published in 77 instalments in the newspaper *Yomiuri shinbun* in 1955, and thus enjoyed a wide circulation. Three years later, the instalments were published as a book. *Tôkyô hanjôki* has been published several times. Two different versions of the text exist. The first edition consists of ten chapters and an introduction by the author (cf. Kimura 1958 and 1959). A nine-chapter version has been published in *Tôkyô fûzokujô* (*Book about Customs and Traditions in Tokyo*, 1975), a collection of essays (cf. Kimura 1975), and the Iwanami paperback edition of 1993 (cf. Kimura 1993). In both editions the final chapter, *Sengo jûnen Tôkyô fûzoku* (*Customs and Traditions in Tokyo – Ten Years after the War*), has been removed. This chapter was originally published in four instalments in the newspaper *Yomiuri shinbun* from 11 to 14 August 1955. The ten-chapter version of the text is only included in Kimura's collected works, cf. Kimura 1982–83a.
31 Cf. Kimura 1982–1983b, pp. 191–218.
32 Cf. Kimura 1982–1983b, p. 202.
33 Cf. Jinnai 1995, p. 103.
34 Cf. Kimura 1982–1983b, p. 222, 257.

35 Representative of this trend is Bal 2002.
36 Cf. the description of Kobayashi's *Shôwa no Tôkyô, Heisei no Tôkyô* (2002) at Amazon Japan (www.amazon.co.jp/gp/product/4480421335/503–0009053–2220779? v=glance&n=465392) [viewed 23 February 2007].
37 Eight years later, in 1992, a second, revised edition was published (Kobayashi and Araki 1992). This edition contains an additional chapter entitled *Hachi nen nochi* (*Eight Years Later*). In this chapter Kobayashi reflects on the changes and transformations of Tokyo since its first edition in 1984. The second edition is of particular interest because Araki added new photographs in order to document these changes and transformations. For the newest edition cf. Kobayashi and Araki 2002.
38 Cf. Kobayashi 1992.
39 For a rough depiction of Tokyo's growth and development since the 1960s cf. Huang 2004, pp. 68–69, for a detailed account cf. Sorensen 2002, pp. 288–332.
40 Cf. Kobayashi 2002.
41 Cf. Kobayashi and Araki 1994.
42 Araki himself has published more than 300 books of photographs. For a comprehensive introduction to his work cf. Araki 2003.
43 Cf. Rossiter and Gibson 2000, p. 439.
44 Barthes 1982, pp. 35–36.
45 Famous examples are the works of Ozu Yasujirô and Naruse Mikio. Both film directors depicted Tokyo's Shitamachi and in particular *roji* areas. For Ozu's depiction of Shitamachi cf. Satô Tadao 2002, pp. 17–34, for Naruse cf. Satô Tadao 2002, pp. 47–72.
46 Cf. Kawamoto 1998. This publication contains numerous photographs by Takeda Hana.
47 The poet and literary critic Noda Utarô (1909–1984) published early examples of this pattern of writing about Tokyo, cf. Noda 1951. For a recent example cf. Sakazaki 2004. This publication introduces to major *roji* scenes of Japan's modern literature.
48 For an early example of the rediscovery of *Hiyorigeta* as a guidebook for the remains of Edo's topography, architecture, and lifestyles in the present cf. Tomita 1979. For Kafû's relationship with Tokyo cf. the detailed study Kawamoto 1996. Ishizaka 1994 is a study of the role of *kirezu* as a tool for understanding Tokyo's topography in Kafû's works, in particular *Hiyorigeta*. Iwagaki 2007 is a walking guide of Tokyo based on *Hiyorigeta*.
49 Cf. Nawata 1995 and Jinbunsha henshûbu 2002.
50 Cf. Maki 1979.
51 Cf. Kurokawa 1991, in particular the chapter on 'The philosophy of the street and intermediary space' (pp. 99–109), and Kurokawa 2006, p. 86.
52 Cf. Ichihashi 2001 and Rekishi minzokugaku kenkyûkai 2005.
53 Cf. Satô Hideaki 2005 and Nakazato 2004.
54 Cf. Satô Hideaki 2005, pp. 110–111.
55 The *Zenkoku roji no machi renraku kyôgikai* published a *Roji Manifest* (*Roji sengen*, August 28, 2005) in order to explain its activities and objectives, cf. www.mmjp.or.jp/ jsurp/roji/rojisenngen.htm. Since April 2003 the publishing house Keyakisha publishes the quarterly *Kagurazaka machi no techô* that reports about the history and culture of the *roji* of Kagurazaka in Tokyo.
56 Cf. Shin-toshi haujingu kyôkai – Toshi kyojû kankyô kenkyûkai 2006 and Aoki 2007.
57 Cf. Huang 2004, p. 9.

References

Aoki Hitoshi (2007) *Nihongata machizukuri no tenkan. Mini kodate saigairo no fukken.* Kyoto: Gakugei shuppansha.

Araki Nobuyoshi (2003). *Araki by Araki. The Photographer's Personal Selection 1963–2002.* Tokyo: Kôdansha.

Bal, Mieke (2002). Autotopography. Louise Bourgeois as Builder, in: *Biography*, Vol. 25, No. 1, Winter, pp. 180–202.

Barthes, Roland (1982). *Empire of Signs.* New York, NY: Hill and Wang.

Benjamin, Walter (1982). *Das Passagen-Werk.* Edited by Rolf Tiedemann. Frankfurt am Main: Suhrkamp Verlag.

Benjamin, Walter (1987). *Berliner Kindheit um neunzehnhundert.* Frankfurt am Main: Suhrkamp Verlag.

Benjamin, Walter (1991). Die Wiederkehr des Flaneurs, in *Kritiken und Rezensionen.* Ed. Hella Tiedemann-Bartels. Vol. 3 of *Gesammelte Schriften.* Frankfurt am Main: Suhrkamp, pp. 194–199.

Benjamin, Walter (1994). *Toshi no yûhosha.* Tokyo: Iwanami shoten.

Benjamin, Walter (1999). *The Arcades Project.* Translated by Howard Eiland and Kevin McLaughlin. Cambridge, MA: Harvard University Press.

Buck-Morss, Susan (1986). The *Flâneur*, the Sandwichman and the Whore. The Politics of Loitering, in: *New German Critique*, No. 39, pp. 99–140.

Buck-Morss, Susan (1989). *The Dialectics of Seeing. Walter Benjamin and the Arcades Project.* Cambridge, MA: The MIT Press.

Charney, Leo and Vanessa Schwartz (eds) (1995). *Cinema and the Invention of Modern Life.* Berkeley, CA: University of California Press.

Elisonas, Jurgis (1994). Notorious Places. A Brief Excursion into the Narrative Topography of Early Edo, in: McClain, James, John M. Merriman and Ugawa Kaoru (eds). *Edo and Paris. Urban Life and the State in the Early Modern Era.* London *et al.*: Cornell University Press, pp. 253–291.

Featherstone, Mike (1998). The *Flâneur*, the City and Virtual Public Life, in: *Urban Studies*, No. 35, pp. 909–925.

Huang, Michelle Tsung-Yi (2004). *Walking Between Slums and Skyscrapers. Illusions of Open Space in Hong Kong, Tokyo and Shanghai.* Hong Kong: Hong Kong University Press.

Hutchinson, Rachael (2001). Occidentalism and Critique of Meiji. The West in the Returnee Stories of Nagai Kafû, in: *Japan Forum*, Vol. 13, No. 2, pp. 195–214.

Ichihashi Yoshinori (2001). *Shôwa rojiura dai hakurankai.* Tokyo: Kawade shobô shinsha.

Imahashi Eiko (1993). *Ito shôkei. Nihonjin no Pari.* Tokyo: Kashiwa shobô.

Ishizaka Mikimasa (1994). *Toshi no meiro. Chizu no naka no Kafû.* Tokyo: Hakuchisha.

Iwagaki Araki (2007). *Kafû Hiyorigeta yomiaruki.* Tokyo: Machi to kurashi sha.

Jarvis, Robin (1997). *Romantic Writing and Pedestrian Travel.* New York, NY: St. Martin's Press.

Jinbunsha henshûbu (2002). *Kiriezu – gendaizu de aruku Edo Tôkyô sanpo.* Tokyo: Jinbunsha.

Jinnai Hidenobu (1995). *Tokyo. A Spatial Anthropology.* Berkeley: University of California Press.

Kawamoto Saburô (1996). *Kafû to Tôkyô. Danchôtei nichijô. Shichû.* Tokyo: Toshi shuppan.

Kawamoto Saburô (1998). *Watashi no Tôkyô machi aruki.* With photographs by Takeda Hana. Tokyo: Chikuma shobô, (1990).

Kimura Shôhachi (1958). *Tôkyô hanjôki.* Tokyo: Engeki shuppan sha.

Kimura Shôhachi (1959). *Tôkyô hanjôki.* Tokyo: Engeki shuppan sha.

Kimura Shôhachi (1975). Tôkyô hanjôki, in: *Tôkyô fûzoku jô*. Tokyo: Seiabô, pp. 179–311.

Kimura Shôhachi (1982–1983a). *Kimura Shôhachi zenshû*. Tokyo: Kôdansha.

Kimura Shôhachi (1982–1983b). Tôkyô hanjôki, in: *Kimura Shôhachi zenshû*, Vol. 4. Tokyo: Kôdansha, pp. 183–346.

Kimura Shôhachi (1993). *Shinpen Tôkyô hanjôki*. Ozaki Hotsuki (ed.). Tokyo: Iwanami shoten.

Kobayashi Nobuhiko (1992). *Shisetsu Tôkyô hôrôki*. Tokyo: Chikuma shobô.

Kobayashi Nobuhiko (2002). *Shôwa no Tôkyô, Heisei no Tôkyô*. Tokyo: Chikuma shobô.

Kobayashi Nobuhiko and Araki Nobuyoshi (1984). *Shisetsu Tôkyô hanjôki*. Tokyo: Chûô kôron sha.

Kobayashi Nobuhiko and Araki Nobuyoshi (1992). *Shisetsu Tôkyô hanjôki*. Tokyo: Chikuma shobô.

Kobayashi Nobuhiko and Araki Nobuyoshi (2002). *Shisetsu Tôkyô hanjôki*. Tokyo: Chikuma shobô.

Kurokawa Kishô (1991). *Intercultural Architecture. The Philosophy of Symbiosis*. Washington, DC: American Inst. of Architects Press.

Kurokawa Kishô (2006). *Toshi kakumei. Kôyû kara kyôyû e*. Tokyo: Chûô kôron shinsha.

Maki Fumihiko (1979). The City and Inner Space, in: *Japan Echo*, Vol. 6, No. 1, pp. 91–103.

Mitchell, W.J.T. (1994). Imperial Landscape, in: Mitchell, W.J.T. (ed.). *Landscape and Power*. Chicago *et al.*: University of Chicago Press, pp. 5–34.

Mitsugi Michio (1999). Zur Benjamin-Rezeption in Japan. Eine Skizze, in: Garber, Klaus and Ludger Rehm (eds). *Global Benjamin – Internationaler Walter Benjamin Kongreß 1992*. München: Wilhelm Fink Verlag, Vol. 3.VII (Rezeption und Regulation), pp. 1410–1423.

Muñoz Millanes, José (2000). *The City as Palimpsest*. Lehmann College & Graduate Center, CUNY, www.lehman.cuny.edu/ciberletras/v03/Munoz.html [Viewed: 8 January 2010].

Nagai Kafû (1992–1995). *Kafû zenshû*. Tokyo: Iwanami shoten.

Nagai Kafû (1999). *Hiyori geta. Ichi mei Tôkyô sansaku ki*. Tokyo: Kôdansha.

Nakazato Katsuhito (2004). *Roji. Wandering Back Alleys*. Tokyo: Seiryû shuppan.

Nawata Kazuo (1995). *Ô-Edo burari kiriezu sanpo. Jidai shôsetsu o aruku*. Tokyo: PHP kenkyûjo.

Noda Utarô (1951). *Shin Tôkyô bungaku sanpo*. Tokyo: Nihon dokusho shinbun.

Parkhurst Ferguson, Priscilla (1994). *Paris as Revolution: Writing the Nineteenth-Century City*. Berkeley *et al.*: University of California Press.

Rekishi minzokugaku kenkyûkai (2005). *Rojiura no minzokugaku. Anata mo shiranai Shôwa 30 nendai*. Tokyo: Hihyôsha (*Rekishi minzokugaku*, Vol. 24).

Rossiter, Benjamin and Katherine Gibson (2000). Walking and Performing 'the City'. A Melbourne Chronicle, in: Gary Bridge and Sophie Watson (eds). *A Companion to the City*. Malden, MA: Blackwell Publishing, pp. 437–447.

Sakazaki Shigemori (2004). *Ichiyô kara hajimeru Tôkyô machiaruki*. Tokyo: Jitsugyô no Nihon sha.

Satô Hideaki (2005). *Nihon no rojiura 100 [hyaku]*. Tokyo: Pie Books.

Satô Tadao (2002). *Eiga no naka no Tôkyô*. Tokyo: Heibonsha.

Savage, Mike (2000). Walter Benjamin's Urban Thought. A Critical Analysis, in: Crang, Mike, and Nigel Thrift (eds). *Thinking Space*. London and New York: Routledge, pp. 33–53.

Schulz, Evelyn (1998). Die Stadt in der Literatur am Beispiel von Nagai Kafûs *Fukagawa no uta* (Lied von Fukagawa; 1909), in: *Asiatische Studien = Études Asiatiques. Zeitschrift der Schweizerischen Asiengesellschaft = Revue de la Societé Suisse-Asie*, Vol. 52, No. 4, pp. 1151–1158.

Shaya, Gregory (2005). *The Flâneur, the Badaud, and the Making of a Mass Public in France, circa 1860–1910*, www.historycooperative.org/journals/ahr/109.1/shaya.html [Viewed January 7, 2010].

Shin-toshi haujingu kyôkai – Toshi kyojû kankyô kenkyûkai (2006). *Arukitakunaru machizukuri. Machi no miryoku no saihakken.* Tokyo: Kajima shuppankai.

Solnit, Rebecca (2000). *Wanderlust. A History of Walking.* New York: Penguin Putnam.

Sorensen, André (2002). *The Making of Urban Japan. Cities and Planning from Edo to the Twenty-First Century.* London and New York: Routledge.

Takehara Makoto (1990). Toshi yûhosha Kafû 'Hiyori-geta', 'En flânant' ni okeru toshi. Tôkyô, Pari, Riyon, in: *Hikaku bungaku kenkyû*, Vol. 59, pp. 175–188.

Tester, Keith (1994). 'Introduction', in: Tester, Keith (ed.). *The Flâneur.* London: Routledge, pp. 1–21.

Tôkyô toshi hensan (1974). *Tôkyô annai.* Tokyo: Meiji bunken, (1907).

Tomita Hitoshi (1979). *Tôkyô haikai. Nagai Kafû 'Hiyori geta' no gojittan.* Tokyo: Shô-nensha.

Tsuchida Mitsufumi (1994). *Tôkyô kiroku bungaku jiten. Meiji gannen – Shôwa 20 nen.* Tokyo: Kashiwa shobô.

Waley, Paul (2003). Conclusion. Power, Memory, and Place, in: Nicolas Fiévé and Paul Waley (Hg.). *Japanese Capitals in Historical Perspective. Power, Memory and Place in Kyoto, Edo and Tokyo.* London: RoutledgeCurzon, pp. 385–91.

Watashi dake no Tôkyô sanpo (1995). Tokyo: Sakuhinsha.

Wolff, Janet (1985). The Invisible *Flâneuse.* Women and the Literature of Modernity, in: *Theory, Culture and Society*, No. 2, pp. 37–48.

Yabuno Ken (2002). *Tôkyô nijikan wôkingu. Aruku, kanjiru, egaku. Yamanote-hen.* Tokyo: Chûô kôron shinsha.

11 Shrinking cities and liveability in Japan

Emerging relationships and challenges

André Sorensen

Introduction

Japan faces an imminent population decline sharper than any yet seen in a developed country. This is certain to have profound impacts on land and housing markets, and will change both the meaning of urban space and the urban policy context. This chapter examines the hypothesis that one impact will be a profound re-orientation of urban politics, and that a new primary driver of urban policy will be the imperative to retain and attract population, in attempts to prevent spirals of population and economic decline. If such pressures result in a shift to a prioritisation of urban liveability and quality of life, it would represent a major break with the past, as even more than in most developed countries, urban policy in Japan has been focused on economic development and profitability, rather than social infrastructure and quality of place.

As argued elsewhere, a major factor behind that orientation has been the fact that central government during the twentieth century kept a tight grip on most policy levers, including urban policy and planning, and allowed municipal governments few powers to achieve their own governance priorities (Sorensen 2002). Whereas municipal politicians have significant incentives to prioritise policies favourable to local residents, central government is much more effectively insulated from such pressures, and consistently used its power to ensure that economic development was prioritised above other issues such as local quality of life (Broadbent 1998; Tsuru 1999). During the 1990s that began to change, as more powers were devolved to local governments, that now have more autonomy than before (Ishida 2006). At question is how those new powers will be deployed, whether they will be sufficient to allow significantly new approaches to local governance, and how they will respond to pressures of population shrinkage.

During the last decade there has been a renewed concern about the importance of cities for economic competitiveness, population health and wellbeing and global environmental security. In large part this stems from the accelerated globalisation of the world economy, with increasing flows of goods, information, people and investment between countries. In the process of globalisation, cities are widely seen both as the primary nodes through which such flows are channelled (Castells 1996), and as aggregations of fixed capital, local institutions and governance structures that serve to mediate between global forces and flows and local places and spaces (Eade 1997; Goetz and Clarke 1993; Knox and Taylor 1995).

The dominant interpretation is that globalisation has created an imperative to greater competition among and between world cities. This competition is deployed by both urban administrations and national governments as a key rationale for urban policies to improve the competitive position of their cities (e.g. London First, Tokyo 4th National Capital Region Plan). Property development corporations exploit the resulting sense of insecurity to demand regulatory policies favourable to the profitable production of urban floorspace (Fainstein 1994; Sorensen 2003). Critical urban theorists also see increased inter-city competition as a key issue, with a decidedly pessimistic and dystopian interpretation of the main outcomes (Brenner and Theodore 2002; Marcuse and van Kempen 2000; Swyngedouw and Kaika 2003).

A considerably more optimistic interpretation of the imperative to create globally competitive locations for investment suggests that a key ingredient in the competitiveness of cities is urban quality of life and amenity. Perhaps most famously argued by Richard Florida (Florida 2002, 2005), the idea is that in advanced postindustrial economies an increasing share of the economy, and the most lucrative growth industries are in high technology, communications, culture, pharmaceuticals and producer services such as legal, finance and marketing (Sassen 1991). All these industries require highly skilled workers, who have multiple employment options, and tend to value quality of life and quality of urban environment highly. This means that local planning and urban management for high amenity, high quality urban spaces can be considered an economic competition strategy.

The concept of a global division of urban strategies is a similar idea in which the global city system is divided into manufacturing bases, extraction centres, global financial and headquarters cities, research and development centres, and high amenity resort and retirement locations (Lo and Marcotullio 2000). The problems of urban competition identified above are thus not eliminated, but are experienced unevenly, with some places gaining in environmental amenity and quality of life as part of their competitive strategy, and others permitting low environmental standards to lower costs in the competitive urban marketplace. Of course, even in cities that successfully position themselves as high amenity places, those amenities may be shared unevenly, or will benefit only a minority if they are private amenities that make few contributions to the public realm (Brenner and Theodore 2002; Kunstler 1993; McKenzie 1994). These two interpretations of the implications of globalisation-induced competition among world cities are often blurred. For example, Tokyo Governor Ishihara has often insisted on the need for Tokyo to provide a more attractive environment in order to be competitive in the international marketplace, but it is not clear whether the environment he speaks of is the physical environment or the investment environment.

Another emerging concern is for the impact of cities on population health and wellbeing. One manifestation of this has been the growth of research on the human health impacts of cities, urban form and urban policies (Aicher 1998; Davies and Kelly 1993; Frank *et al.* 2003; Takano 2003). In countries with universally available publicly funded health care systems, (that is, all the developed countries including Japan but not the United States) the enormous fiscal implications of marginal improvements or deteriorations of population health creates a huge incentive to make cities more healthy, liveable places. The more detailed policy implications of that realisation are just beginning to be worked out.

It is clear that there are diverse pressures and incentives on urban actors in their engagement in processes that change urban places. While it is certainly the case that some processes may lead to greater urban vitality, sustainability, liveability and quality of life, other processes lead in the opposite direction, toward socio-economic polarisation, environmental decline, individual and collective hardship and rising social and health costs. The question is how those pressures play out in particular places, when and to what extent they are amenable to deliberate intervention, and by which actors. The hypothesis presented here is that population decline may present a major new incentive in favour of policies that promote liveability, and that Japan will be an important test case in this regard.

This chapter explores these issues of urban governance and the project of building liveable cities in the Japanese context, and asks: How are population ageing and decline affecting municipal governance strategies in Japan, and is there any evidence that population pressures are changing the priorities of municipal governments? The first section briefly introduces the idea of liveability as an emerging policy priority for local governments around the world, and notes the special challenges for Japanese municipal governments in addressing those issues. The second section outlines two key vectors of urban change in Japan: the ageing and declining population, and the large-scale population movements of the second half of the twentieth century that will continue to influence and structure urban change well into the future. Those processes have combined to create a structured set of liveability challenges for different kinds of places in Japan. The third section examines the legacies of those population movements in different parts of the Japanese urban system, while the fourth section looks at some initial responses of municipalities to pressures created by population shinkage, that demonstrate significant efforts to attract population, albeit with modest results so far. A concluding section brings the discussion back to the question of building liveable cities, and asks whether conditions in Japanese cities seem likely to support the project, or work against it.

Two key vectors of urban transformation

Cities are fantastically complex phenomena, so predictions of future changes are highly risky, but there are some things that we know with relative confidence. First, the Japanese population will certainly decline significantly over the next

50 years and the percentage of elderly will continue to increase. Second, the migration patterns and trends of Japanese cities during the last half-century have left a legacy of accelerated decline in some places and growth in others. These two vectors of urban change – population decline and population migration – interact in complex ways, and combine to produce quite different outcomes in different places.

Population ageing and decline

The Japanese population grew from 44 million in 1900 to a peak of almost 128 million in 2004. Because of a rapid decline in fertility over the last 40 years, to the point where Japan has one of the lowest fertility rates in the world, population is expected to decline to 117 million in 2030, and to 100 million in 2050 in the absence of major changes in fertility or migration patterns. Although the Japanese population continued to grow until recently, declining fertility has already contributed dramatically to the demographic ageing of Japanese society that was already being driven by increased longevity, as the share of the population over 65 has increased from 4.9 per cent in 1950 to 19.5 per cent in 2004, and is expected to rise to 29.6 per cent by 2030 (Japan Ministry of Internal Affairs and Communications 2005; Smil 2007).

While most other developed countries are experiencing similar fertility declines and demographic ageing, many have promoted large-scale immigration to counteract these trends. Immigrants counteract both trends because they tend to be young adults, and in most countries also have higher fertility rates than host populations, at least among the first generation. It seems unlikely that Japan will allow immigration into Japan at a scale large enough to counteract these trends, as maintaining a stable population until 2030 would require some 11 million immigrants, or about 500,000 per year. Even for traditional immigrant-receptor countries like Canada and the US that is a very large number, and Japan has particular difficulties with immigration, as discussed thoughtfully by Sakanaka (2005). Instead, the Japanese government is encouraging women to have more babies, and is attempting to make it easier for women to balance careers with families, such as with improved policies for daycare provision and family-related work-leave (Peng 2003). Those policies have not yet, however, had a discernable impact on fertility rates.

Population decline on the scale projected for Japan during the next century has never been seen in a developed country. By rejecting the option of large-scale immigration Japan is, in effect, carrying out a grand socio-economic experiment, and is venturing into truly unknown territory. It is therefore impossible to predict with any confidence all the ramifications of these changes. The economic impacts, in particular, are hard to predict. Household formation is an important economic stimulus in countries whose economy is based primarily on domestic demand, as is Japan's. Younger people, and especially young families, tend to buy more than the elderly, so a declining population and the slowing of household formation will certainly depress economic growth. It may be possible to

solve the shortage of workers by increased investment in technology, outsourcing to other countries or by temporary work permits, and each of these solutions
have different economic and social implications. For the purposes of this paper I
assume that moderate economic growth will continue, based on Japan's high
levels of accumulated social, intellectual and money capital. It is not impossible
that economic collapse will accompany a rapidly declining population, but that
is not a possibility considered here.

One of the most profound impacts of population ageing and decline will be
on housing demand, which can be expected to decline in future, as a shrinking
population produces a growing surplus of housing units over population. Two
factors will serve to mitigate or delay the impacts of those processes. First, in
Japan, as elsewhere in the world, the average size of households is steadily
decreasing. In 1950 the average household had about five members. That had
dropped to 3.41 by 1970, 2.67 in 2000, and is projected to decrease to 2.37 by
2025 (Japan Ministry of Internal Affairs and Communications 2005). More
people are living alone, and fewer people live in multiple-generation households,
so for a given population, more housing units are needed. During the first phase
of population decline the number of households will continue to increase,
although at a slowing rate. The total number of households is expected to peak
in 2015. During the second phase of population decline after 2015, the increasingly rapid decrease of population will mean that the absolute number of households also will start to decline, suggesting a rapid increase in the number of
vacant units.

Also influencing housing demand is the fact that with increasing affluence
many Japanese have increasing expectations for housing size and quality, so
small older units are less attractive. As a result there is still significant pent-up
demand for better housing. Even today, many Japanese families are seriously
under-housed compared to people with similar incomes in other developed countries. High land prices and a complete lack of minimum housing standards combined to encourage the production and continued use of vast quantities of very
poor quality housing in the inner cities and inner suburbs. Not only are there
many very tiny units, but also large numbers of poorly and cheaply constructed
houses built too close together with flammable materials and inadequate mois-
ture or heat barriers. The risks of such dwellings became clear in the Kobe earthquake, where over 80 per cent of fatalities from collapses and fires occurred in
older areas with such tightly packed wooden housing. Disaster risk issues lend a
sense of urgency to housing issues in major urban areas, and contribute to
demand for new and better housing units. Such pent-up demand means that there
is still considerable need for – and profit to be found in – the development of
new housing. That demand has been manifested in the boom in housing construction of the last 10 years as land prices declined and it again became possible
to develop housing at a price many households could afford (Shimizu 2004).

Here, it is worth considering the situation as population decline accelerates,
and shifts to a net loss of households. Even if today's pent-up demand for better
housing produces a sustained wave of investment and construction in Japanese

cities in the medium term, that boom seems unlikely to continue when the number of households also starts to shrink on an annual basis after 2015. Some housing investment and construction will certainly continue, but it is likely to be at a much-reduced scale. Many individuals will inherit multiple properties from parents and relatives, and there will be fewer young households entering the housing market. Although it is possible that the demand for higher quality will continue to drive some construction, there will be an ever-increasing number of vacant units. Continued investment in new housing either in high-rise forms or in previously undeveloped urban fringe locations will only exacerbate the increasing number of vacant dwellings.

It seems certain that while some attractive cities that are still creating jobs, and/or provide a high amenity environment and good housing will continue to gain in population and will retain a degree of vitality, those cities with declining employment bases, that have environmental problems and/or poor quality housing will tend to see an accelerated population decline over the next decades, and will need different policy approaches if national population decline is not to result in disastrous spirals of urban decay. The continued development of land on the urban fringe seems likely to promote the spread of pockets of decline in both large and medium sized cities, as there is already an oversupply of new urban lots. Already, the problem of vacant stores, vacant housing and declining neighbourhoods is evident in many urban areas, particularly in regions that have stagnant or declining populations.

Legacies of inter-regional migration and urban deconcentration

While the demographic projections described above clearly provide the over-arching vector of urban change, their local impacts will be quite diverse as a result of two cross-cutting patterns of urban population movement during the post-war period: inter-regional migration which was primarily from remote regions to the metropolitan core areas; and deconcentration from urban core areas to suburban fringe areas in cities throughout the country. These have left a diverse pattern of spatial settlement and age profiles that can be expected to structure the patterns of population ageing and decline in significant ways. A major factor is that most internal migrants in Japan were young, so their departure served to increase average ages in the area of origin, and decrease them in their area of destination. Their migration also tended to reduce the rate of natural population increase and household formation where they left, and increase it where they settled.

From the 1950s to the 1970s there was a vast migration of millions of young people from rural and remote regions of the country to the metropolitan belt from Tokyo to Osaka (Tsuya and Kuroda 1989). Although there was some return migration from the metropolitan areas to regional cities and towns (J-turn and U-turn migrants) post-war migrations created a legacy of declining and ageing population in most prefectures outside the metropolitan areas (Kuroda 1990). During the 1980s and 1990s that trend continued, but with population growth only in the Tokyo-centred region. As a result, there are four main types of demographic structure in Japan: The remote rural towns that have experienced absolute population decline and demographic ageing continuously during the last 40 years; the medium and larger regional cities – whose decline was somewhat mitigated by in-migration from more remote areas and some return from the metropolitan regions – that experienced population stability and absolute population ageing; the metropolitan regions apart from Tokyo, which gained population rapidly until the 1970s and then stopped seeing net in-migration after 1980 have lower average ages than in either the remote rural areas or regional cities, but stagnant or declining populations during the last 20 years has given rise to serious problems of decline, particularly in inner-city and environmentally compromised locations. And the Tokyo region, which has seen continued in-migration until the present, resulting in the youngest population profile in the country, and continued population increase (Kurasawa 1986). These varied demographic profiles will clearly give rise to quite different experiences in different places, as population has already been long declining in some remote rural areas, is just starting to decline in regional towns and metropolitan areas apart from Tokyo, and will be somewhat delayed in Tokyo compared to the rest of the country.

The other major process of migration that has been seen in urban regions throughout the country is that of decentralisation from the high-density areas of the old inner cities to lower-density suburban areas on the urban fringe. There has been a massive flow of population from formerly very high density inner urban areas to the suburbs over a period of 40 years from the 1960s almost until the present (Shimizu 2004; Sorensen 2001). As a result inner urban areas in cities of all sizes have seen continuous decreases of population. This movement is primarily of younger families moving to the suburban fringe in search of housing, both pushed from the centre by overcrowding, redevelopment to business uses and rising land prices, and pulled to the suburbs by the promise of cheaper, newer and less crowded residential areas. Because such families were young, their departure again tended to increase average ages in their areas of origin, and decrease them at their destinations, meaning that the suburbs often have a younger age profile than the central cities.

The flow of young families to suburban areas transformed the inner city areas from which they left. Inner city areas now have among the oldest populations in the metropolitan areas, many older shopping areas have declined with the outflow of population, with many vacant stores and diminished prospects. Many of the stores that remain are small-scale establishments run by elderly proprietors. It is common for such stores to remain vacant for long periods when they finally close, if no successors are interested in taking on the family business. Many such families are reluctant to sell the property, even if unable to continue the enterprise, so the stores stay vacant and contribute to the decline of the district. Another secondary impact has been the closing of schools in inner city areas, or most recently their conversion into facilities for the aged. At the same time, in the suburbs the vast and sustained growth of population has required the building of schools, hospitals and other facilities to cater for young families moving in. The process of urban deconcentration and suburbanisation has thus added another layer of diversity to the urban demographic patterns resulting from inter-regional migration described above.

Diverse urban issues in different places

Declining metropolitan inner city areas

The spectre of large-scale decline and abandonment of urban housing and shops may seem remote for those familiar primarily with the cores of the major metropolitan areas, or vibrant subcentres such as Shibuya or Shinjuku, but in many older industrial inner areas, such as east-central Tokyo and northern Osaka, where the outflow of younger population has been longstanding, the problem is very visible. The old shopping streets (*shôtengai*) of such districts have faced challenges of decline for decades, with a reduced customer base, empty shops and ageing shop owners without successors. The political response to the decline of such shopping districts has focused primarily on protection from competition by new, large-scale retailers (Otake 1993; Upham 1993), but it is more fundamentally a problem of an ageing society and urban deconcentration. Population is declining primarily in older areas of cities, where narrow roads, tiny plots and old wooden housing make redevelopment difficult, and earthquake risks are highest. These issues will be intensified as population ageing is combined with an absolute decrease in population nationally.

There has been considerable concern in Japan that this might lead to an 'innaa shitii mondai' (inner city problem) comparable to that of the United States (the literature is reviewed in Alden *et al.* 1994). It seems clear that the experience of complete abandonment of inner-city areas seen in many US cities (Bright 2000) is unlikely to be repeated in Japan, for a number of reasons. Racial discrimination is not such a driver of flight from the inner city in Japan, mostly because there is much less socio-spatial polarisation in Japanese cities than in the US (Fujita and Hill 1997) and much smaller minority populations. Although discrimination against both foreigners and the traditional Japanese outcast class is still widespread in Japan, it is less of a driver of settlement patterns.

There is no doubt, however, that the issues of urban deconcentration and urban decline are linked. It is not necessary to believe that Japan will follow the path of the US to be concerned about the decline of inner city areas, and the rising number of vacant and decrepit properties in the inner suburbs. Large numbers of dwellings in inner city areas are rental units, and there are increasing vacancy rates in the lower quality units. Adding to this problem is that many small houses in inner city areas are owner-occupied by elderly residents whose children, if any, live elsewhere. Such owners have little incentive to invest to upgrade their property, and many are too poor to do so. As they die, or move to old age homes or hospitals, their homes and shops often stay empty, as there is little demand for older inner city shops and housing. Rebuilding such properties is often expensive, because of lack of direct access for trucks delivering materials. In many cases the plots do not conform to the building code because they lack road frontage, and cannot legally be rebuilt, providing another powerful disincentive to reinvestment.

On the other hand, in many older Japanese inner city neighbourhoods that have remained attractive, with good environmental qualities, redevelopment and reinvestment has continued. Unfortunately, because until recently there was no legal restriction on the division of urban plots into smaller pieces, or minimum plot size regulations, a gradual process of redevelopment and intensification on a small scale has led to the demolition of older spacious structures, replacement with several smaller ones, and the disappearance of valued environmental qualities. Although some of the newly built buildings contribute to local environmental quality and amenity, many others do not, either because they are ugly, are overcrowding small sites or occupying the last vestiges of open space in the district.

The recent boom in condominium development in inner areas has often resulted in very large buildings being built into old low-rise neighbourhoods. In some cases this is welcomed by local shopkeepers for bringing new customers into their shopping streets. In other cases it causes huge opposition by local residents because the buildings are felt to be out of scale for the neighbourhood, and destroy the traditional scale of the urban environment (Brumann 2006; Fujii, *et al.* 2007). In each of these three types of inner city area, those experiencing declining populations and decay, those seeing gradual small scale reinvestment and intensification, and those experiencing massive change through the building of large-scale high-rise apartments or office blocks, the question is how to ensure that new investments protect and improve the environment, rather than do harm.

Unfortunately, planning and development control systems in Japan allow very little leverage over the design or form of private building projects. Building permits are as-of-right if they conform to the building code and zoning, which is very permissive in most areas, especially in the inner city. The main restriction is usually a result of the width of the street the property fronts on, rather than the zoning or building code. This means that a lot of interesting and unusual buildings get built in Japan, which would probably never be approved in the other developed countries. It also means that it is virtually impossible to restrict the building of inappropriate buildings, or to bargain planning gain from private investment to create a better urban environment.

Another problem is that it has long been against government policy to provide support for renovation or rehabilitation of private property. This is in great contrast to many European and North American countries, where in designated areas the support for private investment in rehabilitation can be quite significant, up to a level of around 75 per cent of the costs in some cases. As a result, even where neighbourhoods work hard to improve their areas, lack of resources often limits the results. Such community-based efforts to revitalise and improve such areas (often described as *machizukuri undô* or community building movements) are widespread, and demonstrate the enthusiasm and willingness of Japanese people to work together to improve the liveability of their neighbourhoods (Sorensen and Funck 2007). Unfortunately, the weaknesses of the planning system, lack of design control and severe financial constraints of local governments have meant that only very gradual progress is being made in most such areas (Hein 2001).

With careful planning, many Japanese inner city neighbourhoods could be among the most liveable urban areas anywhere in the world. Their small-scale streets, local shopping districts, tight-knit communities and easy access to the larger city by excellent public transit networks could make them highly desirable places to live. That so many of these areas are being allowed to either decay with vacant shops and houses, or be overwhelmed by high-rise construction seems a waste. An alternative would be to promote and assist the small-scale renovation and replacement of structures, using some vacant properties to create new public spaces, some to provide more spacious new housing for in-migrants and others to combine some tiny plots into larger ones. Programmes could assist the transfer of vacant stores to new operators to prevent blight of still viable shopping streets. None of these ideas are new, and many are being pursued by local governments and *machizukuri* groups, but progress is so slow that the coming wave of depopulation seems likely to overtake such efforts where they have not already made significant improvements.

Suburban fringe areas

An important feature of deconcentration and suburbanisation in Japan is the characteristically unplanned, scattered pattern of development of most Japanese suburbs. Because land subdivision into smaller pieces is virtually unrestricted, and the planning system exempted very small-scale developments of less than $1,000\,\mathrm{m}^2$ (about 10 houses) from any requirement to provide contributions to local infrastructure or public goods such as sewers, roads and parks, most suburban development proceeds as a scattering of houses among farm fields (Hanayama 1986; Sorensen 2002: 236). As extensive areas build up rapidly, without significant infrastructure contributions by land developers, local governments struggle to provide even basic infrastructure. Improvements to roads and sewers come later, if at all. Parks, sidewalks and other discretionary public goods are scarce. Local governments have huge and expensive backlogs of unbuilt infrastructure (Hebbert 1994; Sorensen 2001).

Also, as land use change that does not include new buildings is not defined as 'development' in Japanese planning law, the location of car wrecking yards, truck terminals, aggregate crushers, industrial waste incinerators, used car lots and materials recycling facilities etc. is almost completely unregulated, resulting in serious environmental and aesthetic problems in many fringe areas. Everywhere in the suburbs, parking lots are replacing fields and forests, as they are often the most lucrative temporary land use, and car ownership and use per capita continues to increase.

The assumption was always that future development would gradually complete these half-built suburban areas, bringing rising taxes and the resources to complete infrastructure systems. In the context of a rising economy and a growing and increasingly affluent population, environmental problems could be resolved later. As population begins to decline, however, the calculus will inevitably begin to change. With fewer new young households seeking housing more of them will inherit multiple properties. In future it seems increasingly likely that only the most attractive suburban residential areas will see significant growth of population. Others have already begun the process of population decline. Many will remain half built out, irregular mixtures of housing, industrial and commercial buildings, set against a background of agricultural land. Such areas are enormous, and surround most Japanese cities.

The opportunity clearly exists to create really beautiful suburban districts in such areas. A number of real challenges exist, however. The fact that landowners cannot legally be prevented from converting farm or forest land to parking lots and waste management facilities, and cannot be restrained from subdividing their land into smaller plots, is an enormous obstacle to effective planning. Given the imminent end to population growth, it certainly makes sense to tightly constrain the conversion of more farm or forest land to urban use, as there may already be too much urban land in Japan. Although that would be unpopular among the owners of undeveloped urban fringe land, it would help to focus future urban investment on improvements to existing urban and suburban areas. Unfortunately, premature subdivision and servicing of rural land is still allowed (and even subsidised through land readjustment projects) to add to the huge stocks of vacant development land that already exist.

Although much land in fringe areas remains undeveloped, and often is still in farm uses, there are serious problems of lack of park space, road networks and public paths in such areas. Important environmental features such as streams and rivers are still routinely channelled into concrete culverts. Here the lack of public space is actually solvable. More and more farmland is lying fallow, as farming in many areas is no longer viable, and farm families face a growing lack of successors as the older generation passes away. Some of that land could be put to good use creating networks of greenways and paths as buffers along watercourses, restoring small ponds and wetlands and planting native trees and plants. Such green corridors would create valuable recreation space and walking and bicycling routes, at the same time as renewing natural stream and storm-water management functions.

For more badly contaminated sites such as solid waste dumps, car wrecking facilities and incinerators an active programme of restoration and remediation will also be needed. In other places simply placing restrictions on conversions of farm and forest land to gravel pits and parking lots etc. would go along way to stabilising landscapes and allowing the work of conservation groups to succeed. Both the will and the energy to achieve such local environmental improvement exist (Ishikawa 2004; Okata 1999). In many outer urban areas broad-based local movements dedicated to landscape preservation, greenspace management and ecological regeneration are active (Sorensen and Funck 2007). The main obstacle is the idea that land has future urban development value, and landowners feel obligated to maintain those potential values for their descendants. It seems that only when the profit potential in the conversion of rural to urban land is diminished will it be possible to do effective long range planning and environmental improvement of Japan's half-developed, half-degraded suburban landscapes. It seems possible that the rapid approach of a declining population may accomplish the destruction of future land development potential faster than any land policy could, but whether the social capacity to improve these areas can be created remains an important question.

Declining regional towns

Perhaps the most threatened places will be former industrial towns like Kitakyushu, Osaka or Muroran in Hokkaido, where the combination of industrial decline, loss of employment and contaminated brownfields lands may prove disastrous. These places are already suffering accelerated ageing compared to the rest of the country, many are still seeing outmigration of younger cohorts to jobs in the Tokyo area, and the likelihood of developing tourism or amenity based housing offerings seems remote. The resources required to clean up abandoned industrial lands and develop new industries are simply too large for local actors, and the era of large amounts of footloose investment seeking places in Japan to land seems to be over (Gilman 2001).

Many other regional towns and small cities that have steadily lost population face advanced ageing and loss of vitality as well. How will they stem continued population loss as national population starts to shrink ever more rapidly? Is it simply inevitable that they will shrink to a remnant population of the very old, some service providers, and those who have no resources to leave and nowhere to go? For local people, the loss of economic vitality will come as a double or triple blow of declining land values and declining opportunities with growing liabilities. Existing local businesses and services will face continually shrinking markets, and the ageing remainder will consume less apart from medical care and personal services. Equally, the legacies of former industries will impose large social and remediation liabilities, and the fixed costs and debts of the formerly larger local government still must be serviced. Without assistance from elsewhere those costs are likely to prove overwhelming. For example, according to a recent newspaper item, the city of Yubari, once a vibrant coal-mining centre in central Hokkaido recently filed for financial reconstruction, with debts of 36 billion yen compared to an annual municipal budget of 4.5 billion. The city is cutting half the municipal staff, consolidating seven elementary and four high schools into two facilities, and doubling user fees such as for water and sewer service and raising residential taxes. The current population of 13,000 was already expected to decline by half within 25 years, but now the exodus has accelerated (*Asahi Shimbun*, 16 November, 2006). A growing number of ghost towns seems one real possibility for Japan in the coming decades.

These will be the extreme cases, certainly, and the most desperate. Most places are unlikely to see such severe problems. The description of a spiral of collapse above may be overstated. There is no doubt, however, that the combination of economic decline and population decline with environmental problems will produce severe problems for many localities in Japan, and that for those living there the consequences will be severe. It is worth asking what efforts are being made now to prevent such outcomes.

The new place-making environment in Japan

In a context of population ageing and decline, preventing irreversible spirals of decline will mean that settlements will have to attract inward migrants. One important strategy for place success – though certainly not the only possibility – is thus to work towards creating places that are highly desirable to live in, to attract people who have choices about where to live. Local environmental conditions, including beautiful natural landscapes, good local amenities, clean air and water, etc. will all be conditions that serve as attractors, while places with degraded and polluted environments will be less attractive to such migrants. The places that are currently most active in trying to attract new residents are those with the longest history of population decline: rural communities and small regional towns.

Such settlements increasingly promote themselves in terms of 'nature', 'green', 'fresh air', 'clean water' and 'good local services', as suggested by recent attempts by localities to attract new residents. Among many examples: the 'Silver Arcadia' project of Nishinoshima of Shimane prefecture, that attracted 30 new households totaling 61 people by advertising the beautiful unspoiled landscapes of the islands, and ensuring that good quality housing and medical services were available for newcomers (www.ujiturn.net/intern/symposium2004/sym2004_04.pdf).

Several ministries have been encouraging such efforts, for example, the Ministry of Land Infrastructure and Transport (MLIT) has sponsored an annual conference since the mid 1990s called the National UJI Turn Settlement Symposium, which attempts to foster local strategies to attract newcomers to declining regional towns (see www.ujiturn.net), to discuss strategies for local revitalisation that have been successful (and not). They also publish testimonials of people now living in remote regions around the country who have enjoyed the migration from metropolitan areas to peripheral regions (www.ujiturn.net/uji/taiken2006/index2006.html). The MLIT is also promoting internship programmes for university students and others to take part in projects in remote parts of the country and experience life there. The keywords are 'fresh air', 'clean water', 'work experience', countryside lifestyle'.

Several central government ministries provide support for 'multi-habitation' (second-home ownership, or *kôryû-kyôjû* in Japanese), including the portal created by the Ministry of Internal Affairs and Communications (*Sômushô*) that provides information on a range of five different multi-habitation experiences ranging from short-term stays of one to three days per year, to longer stays of several weeks or months each year for potential migrants to learn more about an area, to opportunities for second home ownership (see http://kouryu-kyoju.net/index.php). The hope is that people will explore, develop contacts and consider moving permanently to rural areas. Sômusho also established a competition for projects that would help to produce attractive localities 'Locality Support Program' (*Sômushô 'Ganbaru Chihô Enjo Program*) (www.soumu.go.jp/ganbaru/pdf/ganbaru_070201_02.pdf). Although many such projects sponsored by national ministries focus primarily on the small towns and rural areas that are most at risk of depopulation, other larger settlements are framing their future success as based on livability and environmentally friendly policy approaches. A notable example is Sendai City's 'City of Trees Environment Plan' that advocates the creation of a 'city that learns from trees and lives with trees' (see www.city.sendai.jp/kankyou/kanri/plan/mori/index.html).

Other towns, including some in metropolitan areas, have focused on trying to attract young people and artists to their communities by arranging for them to live at reasonable rents in vacant houses (*akiya*). A growing number of NPOs are engaged in matching up people who want to leave the metropolitan areas with places that are looking for new residents: for example the Satochi Network (http://satochi.net/) promotes links between metropolitan area residents and villages throughout the country, and helps to encourage movement of people from the former to the latter.

The intention here is not to evaluate the success of such efforts but to note the wide agreement that to be successful settlements must attract new residents and that quality of environment and quality of local services are key to such efforts. It seems fair to suggest that the livability agenda is becoming more firmly established as a key ingredient in place making. This in itself is a major change.

Conclusions

Three main sets of issues and ideas suggested here are worth considering. First, the situation in Japan appears to present a rather different basis and context for projects of urban liveability, and Japan's grand social experiment in population decline may yield some insight into other possible motivations for the creation of liveable cities. Second, a major change in the understanding of place management, home ownership and local governance is needed, and may well be an important product of current trends. Third, the construction state apparatus, now employed to build public works on a large scale, is perhaps currently the greatest threat to such projects, but is conceivably also an instrument of salvation, if only its goals could be transformed.

Liveable cities in Japan?

Rather than based in global economic competition, or notions of a creative class, the incentive for Japanese communities to pursue projects of building more liveable places seems much more likely to be based on the need to attract new residents and prevent catastrophic localised population decline. The urge to create liveable cities, neighbourhoods and suburbs in Japan thus has a rather different base than that indicated in the global cities literature: it will be driven primarily by the imperative of attracting and retaining population. It seems possible that Japan will present a case where the imperative to promote healthy cities and desirable living environments, not just for the wealthy but for the whole population, could become a significant driver of public policy. At least, that is the optimistic scenario; a pessimist might foresee widespread distress and multiple spirals of decline. Most likely will be something in the middle: continuation of the current policy gridlock, with occasional rescue efforts but little significant change of direction.

Changing space, place and local governance in Japan

It seems clear that impacts of population ageing and economic slowing will be geographically uneven in Japan, with some places hit by decline sooner and harder than others. One factor that will be important will be the degree of success of localities in promoting a high quality of local environmental amenity, a good quality of life, beautiful local landscapes and good governance. Such places are likely to be more successful at retaining population than others that do not achieve such qualities. A key reason is that places that are polluted, indebted, ugly or declining will find it much harder to attract new residents from the declining pool of inter-city migrants. Japanese citizens are likely to have more choices in future about where to live, and where to buy land or housing, and are likely to become ever more selective as population decline become more pronounced.

After generations of housing being a seller's market, this new buyer's market will require a significant change in psychology for Japanese people. It is quite likely that some places will adapt more quickly to the new reality than others. Certainly places that have already been working to make themselves more liveable will have a head start. Many of the existing machizukuri processes dedicated to local environmental management and improvement are thus extremely valuable in generating new models of governance, civil society participation and social capital, as well as envisioning new priorities and goals. Governments at all levels should be working hard to ensure that these processes succeed. It is clear that more resources are needed, as are more effective ways of restraining unsuitable land development projects.

Transforming the construction state?

The fundamental importance of land development, redevelopment, infrastructure building and construction of all sorts in the political economy of Japan, particularly during the last 30 years, can similarly be seen both as a major problem and a great opportunity. There was a huge waste of money on projects that were both unnecessary and environmentally damaging, such as river channelisation and dams, concrete shorelines and mountainsides, unnecessary bridges and highways, in a privately profitable and publicly bankrupting process of perpetual topographic deformation of the Japanese archipelago.

This spending has created a vast dependent network of contractors, subcontractors, workers, equipment and materials suppliers and kickback receivers that has a vested interest in preventing a reduction of spending, or in fact any change to business-as-usual (McCormack 1996; Woodall 1996). This spending has also been a major cause of the disastrous and deepening indebtedness of virtually all governments in Japan, from village to city to prefecture to nation (Schebath 2006; Shirai 2005). Huge debts have greatly reduced the ability of Japanese governments to implement new and innovative policies to improve local environments or create more liveable and beautiful communities. Worse, corrupt bidding and tendering practices for such projects have distorted the Japanese political system, so that it has been very difficult for policymakers to change policy directions, or to rein in agencies that are used to spending vast amounts of public money.

It is not impossible, however, to imagine this system turning into a force for positive change in Japan. The habit of spending a huge portion of national income on construction and infrastructure may be hard to kick, but what if the project were different? What if the project was to create a beautiful, environmentally sustainable, liveable and healthy Japanese archipelago? Instead of levelling more mountainsides and encasing the last rivers in concrete troughs, why not embark on the project of restoring diverse forest ecosystems of native trees and plants, and renaturalisation of Japanese rivers and streams, so that they are self-sustaining and self-maintaining natural systems? Such a redirection has already begun in a small way (see Waley 2000).

The collateral benefit of such a transformed national project is that it would simultaneously prevent the huge shock to the economy and political system of simply shutting down the construction state, and provide needed resources to otherwise potentially terminally declining places. In many cases those places will not be able to do it themselves. Japanese urban engineers, designers and architects are rightly celebrated around the world. Japanese construction workmanship is skilled and disciplined. It is just that the project has been wrong.

If the new project were to create really attractive and lasting urban environments, with great public and private spaces, healthy ecosystems and excellent housing and public services, Japan could derive some real benefits from even reduced spending on public works. It is possible, of course, that existing beneficiaries of the construction state system are so entrenched that it will be impossible to change directions. It seems not impossible, however, that the shock of population decline might be enough to arouse the Japanese to their next great national project.

Triage

One final issue is the fact that any success by settlements in attracting new population will result in equivalent loss of population elsewhere, without major changes in immigration or birthrates. To a great extent, creating more liveable places to attract population will be a zero-sum game nationally, even if some collateral benefits in terms of urban quality of life are successfully achieved as a by-product. Considerable shrinkage of the urban system will be necessary, whether in terms of schools and other public facilities, or in terms of housing. Whether those processes will contribute overall to greater liveability by building more spacious and beautiful settlements, or to greater distress, socio-spatial polarisation, and spirals of decline, will be one of the great challenges for Japanese society during the coming century.

Acknowledgement

The author would like to acknowledge financial support from the Social Sciences and Humanities Research Council of Canada, and valuable comments by Professor Paul Waley of the School of Geography University of Leeds, and Professor Mark Selden, of the East Asia Program, Cornell University. An early version of the paper was presented at the Annual Conference of the German Association for Social Science Research on Japan in Königswinter, Germany November 2005, and was published in the journal *International Planning Studies* [2006] vol. 11 nos. 3–4. The material in the section 'The new place-making environment in Japan' was published in the online journal *Japan Focus* in 2007 as 'Towards Livable Communities in Japan? Population decline and the changing context of place-making'.

References

Aicher, J. (1998). *Designing healthy cities: prescriptions, principles, and practice*. Malabar, Fla.: Krieger Pub. Co.

Alden, J.D., Hirohara, M. and Abe, H. (1994). The impact of recent urbanisation on inner city development in Japan. In P. Shapira, I. Masser and D.W. Edgington (eds), *Planning for cities and regions in Japan*. 33–58. Liverpool: Liverpool University Press.

Asahi Shimbun. 16 November, 2006. Leaving behind a broke, aging city. *Asahi Shimbun, English Edition* (16928): 24.

Brenner, N. and Theodore, N. 2002. Cities and the geographies of 'actually existing neoliberalism.' *Antipode*. 34(3): 349–378.

Bright, E.M. (2000). *Reviving America's forgotten neighborhoods: an investigation of inner city revitalization efforts*. New York: Garland Pub.

Broadbent, J. (1998). *Environmental politics in Japan*. Cambridge, UK: Cambridge University Press.

Brumman, C. (2006). Whose Kyoto? Competing models of local autonomy and townscape in the old imperial capital. In C. Hein and P. Pelletier (eds), *Decentralization and the tension between global and local urban Japan*. London: Routledge.

Castells, M. (1996). *The rise of the network society*. Cambridge, MA: Blackwell Publishers.

Davies, J.K. and Kelly, M.P. (1993). *Healthy cities: research and practice*. London; New York: Routledge.

Eade, J. (1997). *Living in the global city: globalization as local process*. London: Routledge.

Fainstein, S.S. (1994). *The city builders: property, politics, and planning in London and New York*. Oxford, UK; Cambridge, MA: Blackwell.

Florida, R.L. (2002). *The rise of the creative class: and how it's transforming work, leisure, community and everyday life*. New York, NY: Basic Books.

Florida, R.L. (2005). *Cities and the creative class*. New York, NY: Routledge.

Frank, L., Engelke, P. and Schmid, T. (2003). *Health and community design: the impact of the built environment on physical activity*. Washington, DC: Island Press.

Fujii, S., Okata, J. and Sorensen, A. (2007). Inner-city redevelopment in Tokyo: conflicts over urban place, planning governance, and neighborhoods. In A. Sorensen and C. Funck (eds), *Living cities in Japan: citizens' movements, machizukuri and local environments*. London: Routledge.

Fujita, K. and Hill, R.C. (1997). Together and equal: place stratification in Osaka. In P.P. Karan and K. Stapleton (eds), *The Japanese city*. 106–133. Lexington, KY: The University Press of Kentucky.

Gilman, T.J. (2001). *No miracles here: fighting urban decline in Japan and the United States*. Albany, NY: State University of New York Press.

Goetz, E.G. and Clarke, S.E. (eds). (1993). *The new localism: comparative urban politics in a global era*. Newbury Park: Sage.

Hanayama, Y. (1986). *Land markets and land policy in a metropolitan area: a case study of Tokyo*. Boston: Oelgeschlager, Gunn and Hain.

Hebbert, M. (1994). Sen-biki amidst Desakota: urban sprawl and urban planning in Japan. In Philip Shapira, Ian Masser and David W. Edgington (eds), *Planning for cities and regions in Japan*. 70–91. Liverpool: Liverpool University Press.

Hein, C. 2001. Toshikeikaku and Machizukuri in Japanese urban planning: the reconstruction of inner city neighborhoods in Kobe. *Japanstudien: Jahrbuch des Deutschen Instituts fur Japanstudien der Philippp Franz von Siebold Stiftung*. 13: 221–252.

Ishida, Y. (2006). Local initiatives and decentralisation of planning power in Japan. In C. Hein and P. Pelletier (eds), *Cities, autonomy, and decentralization in Japan*. 25–54. London: Routledge.

Ishikawa, M. (2004). Green structure plan for sustainable urban-regional relationship in Japan. In A. Sorensen, P.J. Marcotullio and J. Grant (eds), *Towards sustainable cities: East Asian, North American and European Perspectives on managing urban regions*. 228–238. Aldershot: Ashgate.

Japan Ministry of Internal Affairs and Communications. (2005). *Statistical handbook of Japan*. Chapter 2, Population. Vol. 2005. Tokyo: Ministry of Internal Affairs and Communications.

Knox, P. and Taylor, P.J. (eds). (1995). *World cities in a world system*. New York, NY: Cambridge University Press.

Kunstler, J.H. (1993). *The geography of nowhere: the rise and decline of America's manmade landscape*. New York, NY: Simon and Schuster.

Kurasawa, S. (1986). *Social atlas of Tokyo*. Tokyo: University of Tokyo.

Kuroda, T. (1990). Urbanisation and population distribution policies in Japan. *Regional Development Dialogue*. 11(1): 112–129.

Lo, F.-C. and Marcotullio, P.J. 2000. Globalisation and urban transformation in the Asia-Pacific region: a review. *Urban Studies*. 37(1): 77–111.

Marcuse, P. and van Kempen, R. (eds). (2000). *Globalizing cities: a new spatial order?* London and Cambridge: Blackwell Publishers Ltd.

McCormack, G. (1996). *The emptiness of Japanese affluence*. Armonk, NY and London, England: M.E. Sharpe.

McKenzie, E. (1994). *Privatopia: homeowner associations and the rise of residential private government*. New Haven, CT: Yale University Press.

Ministry of Land Infrastructure and Transport. (2006). Interim report by Planning Section,

National Land Council, November 2006. Tokyo: Ministry of Land Infrastructure and Transport, Japan.

Okata, J. (1999). Land use control type machizukuri ordinances (Tochi Ryou Chosei Kei Machizukuri Jourei). In S. Kobayashi (ed.), *Local Community Building Ordinances in the Era of Local Rights (Chihou Bunken Jidai no Machizukuri Jorei)*. 111–149. Kyoto: Gakugei Shuppansha.

Otake, H. (1993). The rise and retreat of a neoliberal reform: controversies over land use policy. In G. Allinson and Y. Sone (eds), *Political dynamics in contemporary Japan*. 242–263. Ithaca, NY: Cornell University Press.

Peng, I. 2003. Social care in crisis: gender, demography and welfare state restructuring in Japan. *Social Politics*. 9(3): 411–443.

Sakanaka, H. 2005. The future of Japan's immigration policy: a battle diary. *Japan Focus*. www.japanfocus.org/-Sakanaka-Hidenori/2396.

Sassen, S. (1991). *The global city: New York, London, Tokyo* Princeton, NJ: Princeton University Press.

Schebath, A. (2006). Fiscal stress of Japanese local public sector in the 1990s: situation, structural reasons, solutions. In C. Hein and P. Pelletier (eds), *Cities, autonomy, and decentralization in Japan*. 81–100. London: Routledge.

Shimizu, M. 2004. An analysis of recent migration trends in the Tokyo city core 3 wards. *The Japanese Journal of Population*. 2(1): 1–16.

Shirai, S. 2005. Growing problems in the local public finance system of Japan. *Social Science Japan*. 8(2): 213–238.

Smil, V. (2007). The unprecedented shift in Japan's population: numbers, age, and prospects *Japan Focus*.

Sorensen, A. 2001. Building suburbs in Japan: continuous unplanned change on the urban fringe. *Town Planning Review*. 72(3): 247–273.

Sorensen, A. 2001. Subcentres and satellite cities: Tokyo's 20th century experience of planned polycentrism. *International Journal of Planning Studies*. 6(1): 9–32.

Sorensen, A. (2002). *The making of urban Japan: cities and planning from Edo to the 21st Century*. London: Routledge.

Sorensen, A. 2003. Building world city Tokyo: globalization and conflict over urban space. *Annals of Regional Science*. 37(3): 519–531.

Sorensen, A. and Funck, C. (eds). (2007). *Living cities in Japan: citizens' movements, machizukuri and local environments*. London: Routledge.

Swyngedouw, E. and Kaika, M. 2003. The making of 'glocal' urban modernities: exploring the cracks in the mirror. *City*. 7(1): 5–21.

Takano, T. (2003). *Healthy cities and urban policy research*. London; New York: Spon Press.

Tsuru, S. (1999). *The political economy of the environment: the case of Japan*. London: The Athlone Press.

Tsuya, N. and Kuroda, T. (1989). Japan: the slowing of urbanization and metropolitan concentration. In A.G. Champion (ed.), *Counterurbanization*. 207–229. London: Edward Arnold.

Upham, F. (1993). Privatizing regulation: the implementation of the large scale retail stores law. In G. Allinson, and Y. Sone (eds), *Political dynamics in contemporary Japan*. 264–294. Ithaca, NY: Cornell University Press.

Waley, P. 2000. Following the flow of Japan's river culture. *Japan Forum*. 12(2): 199–217.

Woodall, B. (1996). *Japan under construction: corruption, politics and public works* Berkeley, CA: University of California Press.

Index

Page numbers in **bold** denote figures.